Switching to a Mac® For Dummies®

KT-379-491

Cheat Sheet

Keyboard Shortcuts

Most Windows shortcut-key combinations, where you press Ctrl and a letter, work on a Mac if you press the command key (⌘) on the Mac instead. Thus, ⌘+C is copy, ⌘+X is cut, ⌘+V is paste, ⌘+Z is undo, and so on. Some shortcuts that are unique to the Mac include the following:

Key Combination	Command It Performs
⌘+Q	Quit the current application
⌘+.	Stop the current activity
⌘+I	Get info
⌘+Tab	Switch applications
⌘+`	Switch windows in the current application
⌘+D	Duplicate a file or folder
⌘+L	Make an alias for a file or folder
⌘+Shift+?	Get help
⌘+Option+W	Close all windows of the current application
⌘+Shift+3	Take a screen shot (or use the Grab utility)
⌘+Shift+4	Take a screen shot of a selected area

Special Key Symbols

Keyboard shortcuts, when they are available, are shown on Mac menus using the following standard symbols for special keys:

Key	Name
⌘	Command
⌃	Control
⎋	Escape
⌥	Option
⇧	Shift
⏏	Eject

Function Keys

Key	Command It Performs
fn+F8	Activate Spaces. Hold down Control and press an arrow key or number to switch among your spaces. (Note that Spaces need to be set up in System Preferences. See Chapter 12 for details.)
F3	Show all windows. Click to select one.
Ctrl+F3	Show all windows for the current application.
⌘+F3	Show the Finder.
F4	Show the Dashboard.

For Dummies: Bestselling Book Series for Beginners

Switching to a Mac® For Dummies®

Cheat Sheet

Top Mac Hints for Windows Users

Windows users can follow these tips when working on a Mac:

- ✔ To right-click when using a single-button mouse, hold down Control and then click.
- ✔ To right-click on a laptop, follow the previous instruction or click with two fingers on the trackpad.
- ✔ Closing an application's last window usually doesn't close the application.
- ✔ You can adjust window sizes by clicking and dragging the lower-right corner of the window.
- ✔ Click a filename once and then press Return to rename the file.

Boot Option Keys

When your Mac powers up, it normally uses the system on its internal hard drive, unless you change this by choosing Startup Disk in System Preferences. You can also change what your Mac does by holding down the following keys or key combinations during startup. See Chapter 18 for more on using these options in troubleshooting.

Key or Key Combination	Command It Performs
C	Start up from a CD or DVD.
D	Start hardware diagnostics. Install disc 1 must be in optical drive.
T	Start up in FireWire disk mode.
Spacebar	Boot in safe mode to repair the hard drive.
Option	Boot in Startup Manager. Use to switch startup disks or to switch between OS X and Windows in Boot Camp.
⌘+Option+P+R	Reset parameter RAM (PRAM).
⌘+S	Start up in single-user Unix command-line mode.
⌘+V	Boot in verbose mode. Shows all messages during startup.
Eject key, F12 or mouse button	Eject any disc (CD or DVD).

For Dummies: Bestselling Book Series for Beginners

by Arnold Reinhold

Wiley Publishing, Inc.

Switching to a Mac® For Dummies®

Published by
Wiley Publishing, Inc.
111 River Street
Hoboken, NJ 07030-5774

www.wiley.com

WILEY

About the Author

Arnold Reinhold has over three decades experience in the software industry. His first Apple product was a Mac 512. Arnold helped found Automatix, Inc., a pioneer in robotics and machine vision, and is coauthor of *The Internet for Dummies Quick Reference, E-mail For Dummies* and *Mac mini Hacks & Mods For Dummies*. He developed and maintains `diceware.com`, widely regarded as the "gold standard" in password security, and `mathinthemovies.com`.

Arnold studied mathematics at City College of New York and MIT, and management at Harvard Business School. You can check out his home page at `hayom.com/reinhold.html`.

Dedication

To Max and Grete who put me here, and Josh who keeps me going. B"H.

Author's Acknowledgments

Thanks to Barbara Model, Carol Baroudi, Barbara Lapinskas, and Erica Rome for their help and suggestions. And thanks to the folks at Apple computer and their loyal customers who keep alive a dream that personal computers are not just utilitarian machines but can be tools that empower and inspire us.

Publisher's Acknowledgments

We're proud of this book; please send us your comments through our online registration form located at www.dummies.com/register/.

Some of the people who helped bring this book to market include the following:

Acquisitions, Editorial, and Media Development

Project Editor: Rebecca Huehls

Sr. Acquisitions Editor: Bob Woerner

Copy Editor: John Edwards

Technical Editor: Dennis Cohen

Editorial Manager: Leah P. Cameron

Media Development and Quality Assurance: Angela Denny, Kate Jenkins, Steven Kudirka, Kit Malone

Media Development Coordinator: Jenny Swisher

Media Project Supervisor: Laura Moss-Hollister

Editorial Assistant: Amanda Foxworth

Sr. Editorial Assistant: Cherie Case

Cartoons: Rich Tennant (www.the5thwave.com)

Composition Services

Project Coordinators: Heather Kolter, Lynsey Osborn

Layout and Graphics: Stacie Brooks, Carl Byers, Barbara Moore

Proofreaders: Laura Bowman, Jessica Kramer

Indexer: Sharon Shock

Anniversary Logo Design: Richard Pacifico

Special Help: Virginia Sanders

Publishing and Editorial for Technology Dummies

    Richard Swadley, Vice President and Executive Group Publisher

    Andy Cummings, Vice President and Publisher

    Mary Bednarek, Executive Acquisitions Director

    Mary C. Corder, Editorial Director

Publishing for Consumer Dummies

    Diane Graves Steele, Vice President and Publisher

    Joyce Pepple, Acquisitions Director

Composition Services

    Gerry Fahey, Vice President of Production Services

    Debbie Stailey, Director of Composition Services

Contents at a Glance

Table of Contents

Introduction

• •

Maybe you love your iPod or iPhone and are curious about other Apple products. Maybe you've had one virus scare too many and are fed up with Windows. Maybe the daunting prospect of upgrading to Vista has made you open to other possibilities. Maybe you are a Mac fan who wants to show some friend how easy and productive Macs can be. Wherever you are coming from, I hope you find this book meets your needs.

Apple Incorporated of Cupertino, California, is over 30 years old, and few brands in the history of business generate such fierce customer loyalty as Apple and its Macintosh line of personal computers. That loyalty runs both ways. Apple knows that the people who decide to buy its products, for the most part, are the ones who actually have to use them. Offering systems that satisfy and even delight its users is a matter of survival for Apple.

Many of the virtues of the Macintosh are a matter of taste: the easy-to-use graphical interface, the elegant industrial design, and the integrated suite of software. But one virtue is a simple matter of fact: In recent years, when Windows users endured wave after wave of computer viruses, worms, spyware, and other evil software, Mac users were completely immune. 'Nuff said.

About This Book

Macintosh computers and the OS X operating system have more in common with Windows than all the hoopla would suggest. Still there are differences, big and little, that can cause problems for the unaware.

In this book, you find helpful guides for every aspect of your switch, from deciding that you do in fact want to switch to Macs, to making buying decisions, to setting everything up. You even find suggestions for what to do with your old PC.

Much of this book looks at switching to a Mac from a Windows user's perspective, but most any new Mac user can find help. You find out the best way to transfer your things from Windows to a Mac, as well as tips on how to do common Windows tasks the Mac way. But users of Linux and older Mac operating systems who want some perspective on switching to OS X can also find assistance in this book, especially in Chapter 16, which was written especially with these users in mind. Similarly, I address the needs of both home and business users who are making or considering a switch.

If you have already decided to buy a Mac, you can skip the first chapter. If you have already bought one, start with the second part of the book.

Of course, you may read this book from cover to cover, if you're that kind of person, but I try to keep chapters self-contained so that you can go straight to the topics that interest you most. Wherever you start, I wish you and your new Mac well.

Foolish Assumptions

Try as I may to be all things to all people, when it comes to writing a book, I had to pick who I thought would be most interested in *Switching to a Mac For Dummies*. Here's who I think you are:

- ✔ **You're smart.** You're no dummy. Yet the prospect of switching to a new computer platform gives you an uneasy feeling (which *proves* you're smart).

- ✔ **You own a personal computer based on an operating system different than Apple's OS X.** This book is mostly aimed at Windows XP users, but I think it will be helpful to users of Windows Vista, older Windows editions, DOS, and Linux, and even owners of older Macs.

- ✔ **You are considering buying or have bought an Apple Macintosh computer.** You want to transition to your new computer expeditiously. I suggest straightforward methods and don't attempt to cover every possible approach.

- ✔ **Alternatively, you're a Mac user who knows OS X well but wants a resource to give (okay, even lend) to friends who are considering abandoning the dark side. What a good friend you are.**

- ✔ **You have used the Internet and know about browsers, such as Internet Explorer, and search engines, such as Google.** (If not, I recommend picking up a current edition of *The Internet For Dummies,* by John R. Levine, Margaret Levine Young, and Carol Baroudi.) I do cover getting your own Internet connection in case you are not hooked up at the moment or it's time to update your service.

- ✔ **You are looking to buy a new Macintosh** (one based on microprocessors from Intel Corp.) rather than the older PowerPC or 68K models. While I briefly discuss the used market, this book primarily addresses the Intel Macs, which are all that Apple sells these days.

Whoever you are, welcome aboard. I think this book can help you.

How This Book Is Organized

I divide this book into the following highly logical (to me) parts. Each is self-contained for the most part. Feel free to skip about.

Part I: Informed Switching Starts Here: In this part, I explain why the Apple Macintosh is such a big deal and why you should consider getting one. I also introduce you to the Apple product line and present a few different approaches to conversion (no dunking in water involved).

Part II: Making the Switch: I help you decide what to buy and what you can reuse from your old setup. Then, I hold your hand as you make the big leap, moving your computing life to a Mac. OS X is a little different from Windows. I tell you what you most need to know to get started.

Part III: Connecting Hither and Yon: Macs are to networking what ducks are to swimming. It comes naturally, but there are a few tricks. We cover what you need to do to get your Mac online and talking to any other computers you have, including that old PC.

Part IV: More Software, More Choices: Your Mac comes with a ton of pre-loaded software (0.907 metric tons). And you can buy — or even download for free — a lot more. Windows advocates complain that little software is available for the Mac, but so much is out there that I could write several books. And, yes, lots of cool games are available.

Part V: Specialty Switching Scenarios: Kids, seniors, and businesses all have a lot to gain from the Mac way of doing things. I also talk about converting from other operating systems and dive a bit deeper into OS X.

Part VI: The Part of Tens: If you've read other *For Dummies* books, you're no doubt familiar with The Part of Tens, entertaining lists containing ten (more or less) elucidating elements. They're fun to write; I hope they're fun to read.

And more!: In addition to all this, I've included a glossary in the back of this book and a Cheat Sheet in the front. The Mac world talks with a vocabulary all its own, and you may encounter other technical terms on your switching journey (everything is a journey these days). I think you'll be happy to have this glossary of words and definitions on your bookshelf.

Typographic Conventions

For the most part, stuff you need to do on a Mac is graphical, but from time to time, I may ask you to type something. If it's short, it appears in boldface, like this: type **elm**. When I want you to type something longer, it appears like this:

```
terribly important text command
```

Be sure to type it just as it appears. Then press the Enter or Return key. Capitalization usually doesn't matter on a Mac. But OS X is based on UNIX (as I discuss in Chapter 17), and UNIX considers the uppercase and lowercase versions of the same letter to be totally different beasts.

In the text, Web addresses are shown in this typeface: www.ditchmypc.com. I leave out the geeky http:// part, which Mac browsers don't need you to type in anyway.

Apple keyboards have a special key with an Apple logo () and a fan-shaped squiggle that looks like this: ⌘. It has various nicknames — Apple key, fan key, propeller key — but I use its formal name, the *Command key,* in the text.

Icons Used in This Book

A little tidbit that can save you time or money, or make life a little easier. "Avoid jackrabbit starts to save gas."

Pay attention. Trouble lurks here. "Never open the radiator cap on a hot engine."

These are words of wisdom to keep in mind that could save your derriere in the future. "Have your car battery checked before each winter."

Macs keep the gears and pulleys pretty well hidden. This is under-the-hood stuff for the technically inclined; the rest of you can skip it.

Where to Go from Here

Hey, it's a Mac. You're set. If you do have problems not covered here, lots of resources are available to help you (see Chapter 18). You can also visit my

Web site, `www.ditchmypc.com`. I'd be happy to hear from you directly at `switchtomac@ditchmypc.com`, and would love to know what you think of this book and how it could be improved, but I cannot promise individual advice.

Meanwhile, use your new Mac to build a Web site, create a business, solve the world hunger problem, write the great novel of the twenty-first century, produce your first feature film, meet some cool people, or just have fun. After all, the rest of your computing life has just begun.

Part I

Informed Switching Starts Here

The 5th Wave · By Rich Tennant

"He saw your MacBook and wants to know if he can check out the new Mac OS X features."

In this part . . .

Perhaps you are fed up with Windows and are ready to try something different, or maybe you're a happy Microsoft user who is curious to read what silly justifications someone might come up with for switching to a Mac. In this part, I suggest some reasons I find compelling and address common objections. Then, I introduce you to the Mac family and help you figure out what to buy when you're ready to take the plunge.

Chapter 1

Why Switch? Demystifying the Mac Mantra

- -

- -

Apple's Macintosh computers aren't perfect. They won't cure bad breath, save your marriage, or fix a bad hair day. Apple has had its share of product recalls. Talk to enough Mac owners, and you'll find one who thinks he got a lemon and wasn't satisfied with Apple's service. You can probably find a cheaper computer that will do what you really need. The vast majority of computer users get by using Microsoft Windows, and you can, too. So why even think about switching?

Macs offer you a far better experience; that's why. In big ways, such as security and industrial design, and in countless little details, Apple makes the extra effort to get things right — right for the user, not some corporate purchasing department. For those of us who spend a good part of our lives in front of a video display, those easier-to-use controls, well-thought-out software choices, and better hardware fit and finish all add up to create a tool that lets us do what we want and doesn't get in our way. For more casual users, Mac's simpler design means less head scratching while you figure out how you did that task the last time.

Life is too short for Windows aggravation. Computers are now integral parts of our lives: We use them for work, for play, to communicate, to find mates, to shop, to express ourselves, to educate our children, and to manage our money. They help us fix our homes, cure our diseases, and even clean out our attics. No one has time to fuss over them, fix crashes, fight viruses, clean out hard drives, figure out why the printer won't work, reload the software, or press Ctrl+Alt+Delete. We need computers to be there when we want them. And for the most part, Macs are. Macs just work.

Microsoft isn't run by a bunch of idiots. The company is run by some very smart people, and they hire top-notch engineers. Just getting a product as complex as Windows out the door takes extraordinary talent. But Windows is designed for corporations. A Microsoft engineer revealed on his blog that one of the company's corporate users had 9,000 programs for Windows. The user simply couldn't afford to update them for new releases. Microsoft Windows has to support all the old software that is out there. Apple is better able to let go of the past and is therefore more nimble in developing new ways to make your life easier.

Apple sees its mission as harnessing the rapid advances in computing hardware to create revolutionary new products that improve our lives. The Macintosh, the iPod, and the iPhone are each filled with groundbreaking innovations. They are cool to look at and to own. Why buy boring?

Be Happy You Waited

In many ways, now is an ideal time to switch to Macs. Windows users who upgrade to the new Vista operating system will have a lot of new stuff to get used to anyway. So one way or another, a switch is in your future. If your PC is more than a year or two old, you'll probably have to buy a new computer or do a major upgrade of your existing hardware to run Vista — the PC industry is counting on it. Meanwhile, Apple has just gone through a major transition in its product line that makes Macs much more attractive to Windows users. All new Macs now run on Intel microprocessors, the same ones that power most Windows machines. In fact, any Mac sold today is a full-fledged, strictly kosher PC, one that can run the Windows XP and Vista operating systems as well as any PC on the market. So if you must run some software that is available only for Windows, you can use it on a Mac too. Yeah, you'll have to buy and install Windows separately, but I walk you through that in Chapter 13.

Steve Jobs' other company

For ten years, Apple CEO Steve Jobs moonlighted in another job: running Pixar Animation. There have been many movie studios in the history of film, but few have produced eight smash hits in a row: *Toy Story 1* and *2; A Bug's Life; Monsters, Inc.; Finding Nemo; The Incredibles; Cars;* and *Ratatouille.* All were critically acclaimed box office successes that made extensive use of the very latest in computer animation technology. But the key to their popularity was subordinating the gee-whiz special effects to the telling of a compelling story. Want to know what makes Macs different? Rent one of these movies.

Take Your Best Shot

The question of which is a better personal computer, a Macintosh or a Windows PC, provokes passion matched by few other controversies. Were the world less civilized, Apple fans would long since have been burned at the stake by more numerous Windows users fed up with hearing how great Macs are. Instead, the debate rages over claims that Macs are not a suitable choice because they're too this or can't do that. The following sections outline the principal objections.

"Macs are too expensive"

If you are looking for the absolute cheapest computer you can find, you are reading the wrong book. As of this writing, you can buy a new Windows XP computer for as little as $300. But when you price higher-end configurations from name-brand manufacturers — ones that match what you get standard with a Mac — the difference in price is less and often disappears. In the United States, you can buy a complete and very usable Mac desktop setup for under $600, assuming that you already own a suitable display, keyboard, and mouse; you can buy an excellent MacBook laptop for about $1,100.

The arguments for buying a Mac are based on quality and total cost of ownership, not initial purchase price. Few people boast about how cheap their car is or how little they spent for their home entertainment center. A cheap product that causes you years of aggravation is no bargain.

"Switching is too hard"

I'm not saying that switching from Windows to a Mac is painless. If you have been using Windows for a while, you are used to its idiosyncrasies. You made a big investment in learning how to use all that Windows software, not to mention what you paid for it. You may find some aspects of the Mac hard to get used to, though I guide you through all this in Chapter 4. But on the whole, it's not that bad. Macs and Windows PCs have more in common than they have differences. All in all, I think you'll find a switch worth the effort.

"I'll be left with no software"

Many Windows advocates claim that less software is available for the Macintosh. The standard smart-aleck Mac user answer is, "Yeah, we really miss all those viruses and spyware programs." But some truth to this objection exists.

Certain highly specialized programs in many fields only run in Windows. If equivalents exist for the Mac, you might have fewer choices. On the other hand, thousands of software titles are available for the Mac, and they cover the needs of most users quite well.

Some great software is available only for the Mac. Every new Mac comes with Apple applications for e-mail, instant messaging, address book, calendar, and of course, iTunes. Apple's iLife suite, also included, has programs for photo management, making movies, burning DVDs, creating Web sits, and even composing your own music. New Macs that have a built-in display (laptops and iMac desktops) all have a built-in camera and include powerful video-conferencing software that works with industry standards.

The Mac OS X operating system is built on top of UNIX, and Apple follows the Single UNIX Specification. This means that a large amount of software developed for UNIX and Linux operating systems can run on your Mac, including many popular, free, open source packages. Much of that software does not run in Windows.

Finally, as I mention earlier in this chapter, Macs can also run Windows, so you can still run the odd program for which an equivalent isn't available on the Mac.

"Macs are dying out"

Macs *were* close to dying a decade ago. Their share of the personal computer market was less than 3 percent. However, their share has been climbing steadily, and at last report was 7.6 percent in the United States. But that isn't the whole story. Consumers buy only about 37 percent of the total PCs sold. The rest are purchased by corporations — think of all those PC-based cash registers you see in stores and restaurants. Add in all those office workers who have no say in the computer they use. Apple has very little presence in the corporate world. Most companies restrict Macs to the creative departments. So that 7.6 percent of total sales may represent up to 20 percent of the consumer market — people who buy the computer for their own use. And Apple's share is growing. More than half of all new Macs are purchased by people who were using Windows before.

"Macs are not expandable"

Since the earliest days of the IBM Personal Computer, PCs have come in big boxes that a user could open to install expansion cards or to add memory and hard drives. Steve Jobs horrified the techie end of the PC world when he built the original Macintosh as a self-contained unit that users were not supposed to open. Apple later relented and offered the Mac II, which had expansion slots — six of them — but few users filled them. So instead, Apple developed a blazingly fast expansion port, called FireWire, that lets users attach high-performance devices without opening the box. The PC world responded by developing its own fast expansion port called USB 2.0, which Apple then adopted as well. All new Macs offer both these ports, allowing a wide range of accessories to be attached just by plugging them in. Macs also offer networking and wireless capabilities. For those who think they must have expansion cards, the top-of-the-line Mac Pro comes in a big box that you can open to install the same PCI Express expansion cards that modern PCs use. But I don't think most of you will ever need to do that.

See Chapter 2 for an introduction to the Mac models currently available.

"Macs don't comply with industry standards"

Early in Apple's history, Steve Wozniak, a cofounder of Apple and its engineering genius, came up with a clever way to squeeze more bits onto a floppy disk (an early form of portable data storage for you youngsters). Unfortunately, this design made floppy disks written on early Macs unreadable on IBM PCs. That gave Apple a reputation of being an odd duck, from a standards standpoint, which it has never been able to shake completely, even though it later added PC-compatible floppy drives and is now exemplary in sticking to industry standards. Indeed, Apple was the first to popularize now-ubiquitous computer industry standards such as WiFi wireless networking and the Universal Serial Bus (USB). Other standards gobbledygook that Macs support include Gigabit Ethernet, Bluetooth, IEEE-1394 FireWire, PCI Express, ExpressCard/34 (see Chapter 3 for more details), and now the Intel microprocessor architecture. Apple's Web browser, Safari, now also available for Windows, carefully follows Internet standards — more so than Microsoft's Internet Explorer.

"I need Windows for work"

So run Windows XP or Vista on your Mac. You will have to buy a copy, which is an added expense. But both run fine on a Mac, and you can still use Mac OS X when you're not working. With third-party virtualization software, you can run both operating systems at the same time, with Windows applications appearing on the Macintosh OS X desktop alongside native Mac applications. I tell you more about how all this works in Chapter 13.

"Macs are a poor game platform"

True, more games exist for the PC, but plenty are available for Macs, many of the top titles too. And many more are coming. Electronic Arts and id Software now support Macs. Macs come with built-in networking for multiplayer games. How much of your life do you want to spend playing video games anyway? Sorry, dumb question.

Will Apple license OS X for other PCs?

A perennial question in the Apple-watching community is whether Apple will license its OS X operating system to run on other PCs. With Apple's switch to Intel processors, there is no technical reason why this could not be done. Indeed Apple has to go to some lengths to discourage clever programmers from modifying (hacking) OS X to run on personal computers sold by other manufacturers. One scenario has Apple mimicking Microsoft's strategy and selling OS X to anyone to run on any computer that meets minimal standards. A perhaps more likely scenario might be licensing OS X to one or two manufacturers who would produce computers complementary to Apple's current link, a sub-notebook, perhaps. At the moment there is every indication that Apple will keep OS X to itself and continue to play its high-end branding strategy, but Steve Jobs is known for surprises.

"Vista will kill Apple"

Microsoft spent five years and billions of dollars developing its new Vista operating system, in part to end the scourge of computer viruses and spyware that have plagued the PC world for over a decade. I hope Microsoft finally got it right. In the same period, Apple has been devoting its energy to improving its OS X operating system from the user's perspective. While Vista was gestating, Apple released a series of improved versions of OS X, code-named Jaguar, Panther, Tiger, and Leopard — someone in Apple likes big cats. Microsoft still has catching up to do, but it has indicated that Vista may be its last big operating system release. The race may be too exhausting for Microsoft. Still, Microsoft will have to find some way to keep up with Apple.

Considering All Aspects — Advantage Apple

Standard business school theory says that a company that sells the most product can't be stopped because it just gets better and better at what it does, to the point where no one can catch up. But Apple has adopted some strategies that give it some important advantages that let it win against the competition provided by Microsoft.

One neck to wring

Microsoft sells its Windows operating system to dozens of companies that make personal computers. This has some benefits in that competition among these

PC vendors keeps prices down, but it also means that Microsoft has to support a bewildering number of different hardware designs and components (displays, hard drives, communications adapters, processor chips, and so on). And this includes not just all the variations currently being sold, but products no longer on the market but still in use, including PCs made by companies no longer in business. Outside of a brief flirtation with licensing in the mid-1990s, Apple has maintained complete control over the design and manufacture of products that use its software. This *vertical integration* greatly simplifies Apple's development efforts, allowing it to bring out new versions of its operating system much more often than Microsoft has been able to.

Vertical integration also has benefits for customers in terms of reliability and service. If you have a problem with hardware or software, Apple has a strong incentive to fix it. With the computer, operating system, and much of the software supplied by a single vendor, Mac users don't have to worry about being shuttled from company to company. ("I'm sorry, but you'll have to contact Fly-by-Night Software to solve your movie-editing problem; it makes that application.") Regardless of the problem with the extensive suite of software that comes with a Mac, it's Apple's problem. There is only one neck to wring.

Apple is the industry thought leader

Anyone who follows the high-tech industry is used to reading articles about amazing new technologies that are going to revolutionize our lives, and then never hearing about them again. One of Apple's roles in the computer industry is to pick and choose among those new ideas. For the most part, technologies that Apple picks get adopted by the rest of the industry, particularly Microsoft. Apple may not have invented the graphical user interface, WiFi wireless networking, or the universal serial bus, but Apple's adoption of these technologies made them industry standards. Apple users get the good, new stuff first.

Appearances matter

Sometimes you *can* judge a book by its cover. Sometimes function follows form. Early on, Steve Jobs, Apple's CEO, recognized that aesthetics matter. The original design team that created the first Macintosh computer included a fine artist who was involved in everything from graphical interface design to the artwork on the cardboard box that the Mac came in. When Jobs returned to Apple in 1996, he restored artistic quality to prominence at Apple. From the original lollipop colored iMac to the latest iPod, Apple's products have won awards for excellence in industrial design.

Quality industrial design means more than arranging all the buttons and jacks in a pleasing way. It means questioning each feature and eliminating unnecessary doodads. The result is something that isn't just easy to look at but is easy to understand and simple to work with.

A case in point is the Apple Remote that comes with each Mac. Remotes for most consumer products rival an airplane cockpit in complexity; Apple's has just six buttons.

Looking forward, not backward

Apple's leadership in technology extends beyond picking winners. Apple is also the company that decides when to tell a technology, "You're fired." Apple was the first to introduce 3½-inch floppy disks on personal computers and the first to drop them as a standard feature. Other technologies that Apple was the first to drop include the RS-232 serial port and the dialup modem. You can still get these features as external add-ons if you really need them, but Apple realized that most of us no longer do. Letting go of old technology wards off the feature bloat that plagues the computer industry. Unneeded features increase complexity and make machines harder to use and more prone to problems.

Getting top-notch products

Apple makes money on the products it sells. Unit for unit, Apple is the most profitable company in the industry. How does the company do that with such a small share of the market? The same way that Mercedes-Benz or BMW or Armani does — by branding. Apple doesn't sell products that are interchangeable with products sold by half a dozen other companies. It sells something unique — products sufficiently superior for which customers willingly pay a bit more. The benefit to you as a Mac buyer is the simple reality that no company can keep such an enviable position in the long run without delivering top-notch goods. You do get what you pay for.

Innovating with the enemy

For most of the personal computer era, the Intel Corporation, inventor of the microprocessor and creator of the x86 series of microprocessors that power most PCs, was closely allied with Microsoft. The term *Wintel* was coined to describe a Windows-compatible PC, a contraction of Windows and Intel. Over time, however, the interests of Intel and Microsoft have diverged somewhat. Other companies, particularly AMD, have cloned the x86. Microsoft keeps its software compatible with all current x86 machines. That limits Intel's ability to innovate. Microsoft will not readily adopt new features introduced by Intel that are not supported by other microprocessor makers.

In 2005, Apple announced that it would be partnering with Intel. Now all new Macs use Intel chips. While Apple says it based its decision on the computers Intel already had on the drawing board, Intel's *microprocessor road map,* strong hints have surfaced that Apple expects to take advantage of unique innovations from Intel in the future.

iPod and iPhone

Apple's runaway success with the iPod personal music player, introduced in 2001, has given the company the kind of market dominance that Microsoft has enjoyed in the PC market.

Apple's iPhone has been hailed as a revolution in personal communications. It combines a four-band phone that uses the worldwide GSM standard, allowing its use anywhere, with iPod music and video technology and direct Internet access via WiFi or cellular phone links. Apple includes its OS X operating system in the iPhone, with a well-integrated and easy-to-use interface, all in a spectacularly elegant package.

Apple gives away a version of its iTunes music software that runs in Windows. Apple is betting that iPod and iPhone customers who use Windows will be impressed by iTunes's ease of use and will give the Macintosh a closer look when they are ready to upgrade their computers.

Switching Sides

The Mac-versus-PC debate ranks as one of the great emotional divides in the modern world. Just because these feelings are whipped up by marketing departments doesn't mean that they lack emotional impact. Your computer choice forms part of your personal identity. Mac users have a reputation for a certain smugness. (You just got a virus? You mean like a cold?) Much of that is defensive, of course. It's no fun being a minority in a PC-dominated world. (You bought a what? Are they still making those?) Few other choices we make in life can be as self-defining — perhaps religion, political party, and sports-team allegiance. People who move from New York City to Boston invariably suffer mental scars inflicted by changing baseball allegiance from the New York Yankees to the Boston Red Sox. Some never recover and have to live the rest of their lives in sheltered halfway houses, eking out a living writing books for novices about technology.

An optional brief history of Apple

You don't need to read this sidebar to make your decisions, but no book on switching to Macs would be complete without a little history of how the Macintosh got where it is today. Writing about computers allows one to tell stories no fiction publisher would print. None of the science fiction magazines that warped our formative minds dared to predict the level of computing power beneath our fingertips or in our shirt pockets. But no high-tech story is as compelling as the legend of Steve and Bill, two kids from the West Coast of the United States who revolutionized the world.

Apple Computer was founded on April Fools' Day, 1976, by three young men: Steve Jobs, Steve Wozniak, and Ronald Wayne. Their original mission: Sell low-cost circuit boards on which hobbyists would build their own computers, based on the newly invented microprocessor. That mission quickly changed when Jobs found that a local electronics shop wanted more fully assembled systems and gave him an order for several dozen of them. The price of Apple's first product, the Apple I, was $666.66. That sum would buy you a vastly more capable Mac mini today. Adjusted for inflation, it would come out to about $1,900 in 2007 dollars, enough for a MacBook Pro or high-end iMac.

The Apple I used a 6502 microprocessor, considered easier to program than the early groundbreaking devices from Intel, and featured a BASIC interpreter. BASIC is a particularly simple computer language invented by a Dartmouth professor, John Kemeny, to help teach programming. A young programmer named Bill Gates dropped out of Harvard — horrifying his parents — to start a business selling software to the fledgling microcomputer industry. He chose the imaginative name *Microsoft* for his venture. A BASIC interpreter

for microcomputers was Microsoft's first product, and Apple was among its earliest customers. The choice of corporate names was prophetic: a utilitarian contraction versus a friendly fruit icon.

The Apple II quickly supplanted the primitive Apple I and propelled Apple Computer to early leadership in personal computing. Dan Bricklin wrote VisiCalc, the world's first spreadsheet program, for the Apple II. If you crunch numbers for a living, imagine what the world was like when a spreadsheet was just a wide piece of ruled paper on which calculations were recorded one at a time by hand, and you can appreciate the impact of VisiCalc.

Microsoft got its big break when International Business Machines decided to try its hand at making a personal computer and chose Gates' company to supply the all-important operating system. While IBM is a well-respected name in computing today, back in the 1970s, it pretty much owned commercial computing. Almost every major corporation in the world used IBM computers. Young computer professionals were told by older hands that no one was ever fired for buying IBM. While some Apple IIs had made their way into the corporate world because of VisiCalc, they were soon replaced by beige boxes sporting IBM logos, a Microsoft operating system called DOS, and an even better spreadsheet program — Lotus 1-2-3.

The Apple II was a hard act for Apple to follow. Apple made two disastrous attempts, the Apple III (a souped-up Apple II) and the Lisa. The Lisa was a machine ahead of its time, pioneering the use of a mouse to move a pointer on the screen and letting users initiate actions by manipulating icons representing programs, data files, hard drives, and so on. But this *graphical user interface* could not overcome a $10,000 starting price, and few Lisas were sold.

Jobs, fed up with the increasingly corporatized development environment at Apple, led a renegade team to develop a more affordable computer, based on much of the same technology as Lisa. The new Macintosh was announced during the 1984 Super Bowl with what is perhaps the best television commercial ever made. You can see it at www.uriahcarpenter.info/1984.html.

Besides its mouse and graphical user interface, the Macintosh was packaged as a single unit with a built-in, high-resolution — for its time — black-on-white screen that crisply displayed what would eventually print on paper. IBM PCs offered green letters on a black background in just one font. The higher-quality Mac display enabled a "what you see is what you get" document-creation process and started the desktop publishing revolution. The Mac also introduced 3½-inch floppy disks, and its Motorola 68000 microprocessor could address more memory than the Intel 8086 in the IBM PC, allowing the use of more sophisticated programs.

Microsoft hedged its bets by developing software applications for the new Mac, including a word processing program called Word and a spreadsheet called Multiplan. Jobs and Gates personally negotiated a contract that let Microsoft sell a simplified version of a graphical interface called Microsoft Windows 1.0. When Microsoft later released a full-blown graphical user interface in Windows 3.0, Apple sued, but the courts ruled it was covered by that one-page contract. Word became the flagship word processor for Windows, and Excel drove out 1-2-3.

Jobs left Apple in 1985 after some disagreements with the board of directors and started a

new computer company, NeXT. NeXT built a graphical interface on top of an operating system called UNIX that was originally developed by the American Telephone & Telegraph Company (ATT). UNIX was popular with computer researchers because of its flexible design and because a version with source code was available.

Apple continued to introduce more powerful versions of the Macintosh, adding hard drives, laser printers, and high-resolution color displays. Its share of the personal computer market continued to decline relative to IBM PCs and their clones. In 1994, Apple switched from the Motorola 68000 series microprocessor to the PowerPC chip, jointly developed by Motorola, IBM, and Apple. The PowerPC was designed to allow programs to run faster than those for the Intel chips, but the theoretical advantage never materialized as Intel chip engineers used innovative techniques to keep up.

In 1997, Apple acquired NeXT and Steve Jobs rejoined the company, soon taking the helm. A year later, he reinvigorated Apple's sales with the iMac, an all-in-one computer that echoed the original Macintosh. A flat-panel version appeared in 2002. Apple soon replaced its OS 9 operating system, whose lineage goes back to the first Macintosh, with a new system, OS X, based on the NeXT operating system. The iPod was launched in 2001.

In 2005, Jobs ended the personal computer microprocessor wars when he announced that Apple would switch to Intel microprocessors, a transition completed in 2006. In 2007, Jobs introduced the Apple TV (TV), extending the Apple brand to the living room, and the spiffy iPhone, hoping to set a new standard in mobile communication.

This kind of psychological trauma doesn't have to happen to you just because you switch computer platforms. Think of it this way. The PC really won the great war. Apple was forced to abandon the Motorola processor family and convert to Intel. Macs are now just PCs in a more stylish package with some better software. You're not abandoning your mother's cooking, just sampling a different cuisine.

No matter what I say, you probably won't completely escape the emotional side of switching to a Mac. When you feel the shame of betrayal and the pangs of guilt coming on, repeat this mantra: *"It's just a computer. It's just a computer. It's just a computer. . . ."*

Chapter 2

Meet the Mac Family

. . . .

. . . .

Switching to a Macintosh means getting a computer manufactured by Apple Inc. No one else currently makes Macs. If you found shopping for Windows PCs a bit bewildering, you are in for a pleasant surprise. Apple has only a few models in each category, and each model generally has a name. Apple gave up using four-digit model numbers to name their products years ago. If you love having many vendors to choose from and lots of catalogs to look through, with the prospect that *something* is always on sale, the Apple experience might take adjusting to. In this chapter, I touch on the various Mac models and related products currently available. In Chapter 3, I point out your options, including memory size and disk capacity, and help you figure out which model is best for you, overall.

From time to time, Apple upgrades its products, drops old models, and introduces new ones. Check www.apple.com for the latest specifications.

Checking Out the Common Features

Apple typically offers three or so versions of each model: a lowest-price basic version, an intermediate version, and a loaded version. Certain features are common to all current Mac models, including the following:

✔ **Processors:** All models use fast Intel microprocessors with two or more processor cores, similar to those that are used in most PCs. They all support 64-bit operation, allowing, at least in theory, main memory greater than 4GB, though not all models let you install such large memory. Unlike with Microsoft's Vista, you don't need a special 64-bit version of the operating system to take advantage of this capability. Mac OS X is 64-bit ready and also supports older, more common, 32-bit applications.

Apple typically offers a couple of faster processor options for each Mac model. I don't list the processor speeds for the various models because they keep changing — for the better. Intel publishes a "roadmap" of its planned processor improvements at www.intel.com/products/roadmap.

As with PCs, Macs come with two types of memory. Random Access Memory (RAM) stores programs and data while the computer is actively processing them. All Macs come with at least 1GB (one gigabyte) of RAM. Having more RAM lets you do more things at once and is especially important if you work with very large files such as video files. The hard drive is for long-term data storage. A bigger hard drive means more space for music, photos, and video files.

✔ **Software:** All Macs come with OS X software, and all Macs except the Apple Xserve servers include the integrated iLife suite of digital lifestyle applications. I introduce you to OS X in Chapter 5. The iLife suite is the subject of Chapter 11, and I describe other software goodies that you can get for Macs in Chapter 12.

✔ **No dialup modems or floppy drives:** Apple dropped the practice of including a built-in dialup modem when it switched to Intel microprocessors. Instead it sells the Apple Modem, a small external modem, as an accessory. Macs have not had internal floppy drives for several product generations. External USB floppy drives are available from third parties.

✔ **Wireless networking support:** All new Macs have provisions for wireless networking using the WiFi and Bluetooth standards, and most models have it built in. Apple was the first computer company to embrace WiFi, using Apple's own brand name, AirPort.

This wireless support is especially handy in Mac laptops because WiFi hotspots are now in lots of places — coffee shops and public libraries, train stations, airline terminals, hotels, shopping centers, and even doctors' waiting rooms. With an Apple laptop under your arm, you're never out of touch.

The Bluetooth networking is a short-range wireless personal networking scheme that connects to nearby electronic devices. Bluetooth connects your Mac to wireless keyboards and mice. If your cell phone has Bluetooth, you can synchronize your OS X address book with your cell phone and can even use your cell phone to connect to the Internet if your phone and cellular carrier support such use.

✔ **Wired networking support:** All have Gigabit Ethernet jacks for wired networking and connecting to high-speed cable and DSL modems. See Chapter 9 for more on networking the Macintosh way.

✔ **Multimedia:** Most Macs come with an Apple Remote that lets you control them via Apple's Front Page software for comfy media viewing.

Apple is also tying its wagon to the high-definition (HD) video revolution that's underway. Its displays are normally set up with a 16:10 aspect ratio, suitable for HD video.

In other areas, you'll find some slight differences among the models, but not many. The basic versions of the mini and MacBook have optical disc drives that can read and play CDs and DVDs, but can't burn a DVD. Apple calls this a "combo drive." The other versions, including all the "Pro" models, can burn DVDs too, incorporating what Apple calls a SuperDrive. Apple is expected to introduce Blu-ray disc players in the near future, so this pattern is likely to repeat for them.

Other discriminators between models are screen sizes for laptops and iMacs, memory, and hard drive space. The more expensive models also have faster processors, though the difference is generally not dramatic — maybe 20 percent or so.

In the sections that follow, you take a closer look at how the various Mac models are suited for different tasks and uses.

Connecting on the Go with Your Apple Laptop

Laptops are the most popular Mac models. Compact and elegantly designed, they're seen more and more at meetings where clunky Windows laptops used to predominate.

One thing that sets Apple laptops apart is their built-in iSight video camera. It's located on the lid, above the display, along with an omnidirectional microphone. Coupled with easy, high-speed Internet connectivity, and OS X's iChat communication software, these cameras let you videoconference from just about anywhere. You can turn off the camera for ordinary audio phone calls if you prefer. No one needs to know what you look like first thing in the morning.

Speaking of the lid, it's kept closed by a magnet — you find no mechanical catch to break. And that's not the only magnetic feature of Mac laptops. The power cord is magnetically attached, too. Apple calls it MagSafe because it's designed not to pull your laptop off the table if you trip over the cord. MagSafe is a fine example of Apple's attention to detail.

Apple divides its laptops into two product lines, the MacBook and the MacBook Pro.

Traveling light with MacBook

MacBook is Apple's less expensive laptop line. It is built into a sturdy plastic case, snow white for the two lower-cost models and black for the most expensive. It's thin and lightweight. Goes anywhere, does anything.

If you really can't make up your mind about what Mac to get, get a MacBook.

The MacBook uses Intel's integrated GMA X3100 Graphics Media Accelerator that's good for most uses, including video and photo editing, but it's not ideal for 3-D gaming. Figure 2-1 shows a white MacBook. MacBooks are a bit more than an inch thick (2.75 cm) and weigh 5.2 pounds (2.36 kg).

Details, details

Each MacBook includes the following:

✔ Glossy widescreen display with 1280 x 800 screen resolution, measuring 13.3 inches (338 mm) diagonally. The display is set up for a 16:10 aspect ratio and is suitable for high-definition (HD) video.

✔ Intel Core 2 Duo processor with 1GB of RAM. Two SO-DIMM slots support up to 2GB of RAM. More RAM helps you work with bigger files and do more things at once. I discuss how much RAM you need in Chapter 3.

✔ Intel GMA X3100 graphics processor. I explain what you get with the low-, middle-, and high-end graphics processors in the section "Getting the Right Graphics Processor," later in this chapter.

✔ Mini-DVI video out. You can see full native resolution on the built-in display and up to 1920 x 1200 pixels on an external display, with the second display either extending your desktop or duplicating what's on the built-in screen, for use with a projection screen, for example.

Figure 2-1:
The MacBook in white, showing video-conferencing with three other people.

Photo courtesy of Apple, Inc.

✔ Full-size keyboard, including 12 function keys, 4 arrow keys, and an over-laid numeric keypad.

✔ Scrolling trackpad for cursor control. Apple's trackpad is precise and supports two-finger scrolling, tapping, double-tapping, and dragging.

✔ AirPort Extreme built-in WiFi wireless, supporting 802.11a, b, g, and draft-n.

✔ A dual-layer-burning SuperDrive on the higher two models and a combo drive on the lowest. Both are slot loading, so you have no slide-out tray to break.

✔ Standard models offer up to 120GB of hard drive space, but you can order your MacBook with up to 200GB of storage. *Hard drive space* is the memory you need to store your pictures, music files, and more. I discuss how much to get in Chapter 3.

✔ Bluetooth 2.0 + Enhanced Data Rate (EDR).

✔ FrontRow infrared remote control.

✔ Stereo speakers.

✔ Lithium-polymer battery that provides up to six hours of battery life.

✔ Power supply that runs on 100–240 volts AC, 50 to 60 hertz, up to 60 watts. Meets U.S. EPA Energy Star requirements. Uses MagSafe connector.

Ports

All the MacBook cable connections line up along the left side. See Figure 2-2. These include the following:

✔ MagSafe power connector.

✔ Gigabit Ethernet.

✔ Mini-DVI external video.

✔ FireWire 400 port, which enables you to transfer pictures and video quickly, if your camera supports FireWire. You can also use it with higher-performance FireWire external hard drives.

✔ Two USB 2.0 ports, which you can use to plug in any number of devices, including a mouse, external drives, flash memory cards, a printer, and more.

✔ Combined optical digital audio input/audio line in — 3.5-mm minijack.

✔ Combined optical digital audio output/headphone out — 3.5-mm minijack.

✔ Kensington cable lock slot for physical security.

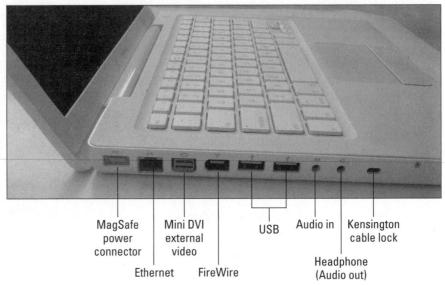

Figure 2-2:
Connections
to the
MacBook.

MagSafe
power
connector

Mini DVI
external
video

USB

Audio in

Kensington
cable lock

Ethernet

FireWire

Headphone
(Audio out)

MacBook Pro

The MacBook Pro is the more expensive laptop line, with a number of features that set it apart from the MacBook. These include the following:

- ✔ A choice of display screen sizes, 15 or 17 inches.

- ✔ An aluminum case. Aluminum is stronger per pound (or kilogram) than the plastic used in the MacBook case.

- ✔ Faster processors with more memory.

- ✔ More powerful graphics chip with full 3-D support.

- ✔ Faster FireWire 800 port along with a FireWire 400 port.

- ✔ Two USB 2.0 ports on the 15-inch model, three on the 17-inch model.

- ✔ ExpressCard/34 slot.

- ✔ Backlit keyboard for easy use at night.

- ✔ Heftier, 85-watt AC power module. It can also power a MacBook, but the power module that comes with the MacBook isn't powerful enough to supply the MacBook Pro.

Figure 2-3 shows a 17-inch MacBook Pro running Apple's FinalCut Pro video editing software.

Figure 2-3:
The 17-inch
MacBook
Pro.

Photo courtesy of Apple, Inc.

Details, details, details

Each MacBook Pro includes the following:

✔ Glossy widescreen display with 1440 x 900 screen resolution, measuring 15.4 inches (381 mm) diagonally, or 1680 x 1050, measuring 17 inches (432 mm) diagonally. The 17-inch model can be ordered with a higher resolution of 1920 x 1200. The 15-inch model weighs 5.4 pounds (2.45 kg), and the 17-inch model weighs 6.8 pounds (3.08 kg). Both are 1 inch thick (2.59 cm).

✔ Intel Core 2 Duo processor. Two SO-DIMM slots support up to 4GB of RAM.

✔ NVIDIA GeForce 8600M GT graphics processor. The more expensive model adds additional graphics memory; see the section "Getting the Right Graphics Processor," later in this chapter, for details.

✔ 120GB hard drive on the 15-inch model; 160GB hard drive on the 17-inch. You can order your MacBook Pro with up to 200GB of storage.

✔ Dual-link DVI video out, which you can use to connect your Mac to your HDTV.

✔ Full-size backlit keyboard, including 12 function keys, 4 arrow keys (inverted *T* arrangement), and an overlaid numeric keypad.

✔ Scrolling trackpad for cursor control. Apple's trackpad is precise and supports two-finger scrolling, tapping, double-tapping, and dragging.

✔ AirPort Extreme built-in WiFi wireless, supporting 802.11a, b, g, and Draft-N.

✔ A dual-layer-burning slot-loading SuperDrive.

✔ Bluetooth 2.0 + Enhanced Data Rate (EDR).

✔ FrontRow infrared remote control.

✔ Stereo speakers.

✔ Lithium-polymer battery that provides up to six hours of battery life.

✔ Power supply runs on 100–240 volts AC, 50 to 60 hertz, up to 60 watts. Meets U.S. EPA Energy Star requirements. Uses MagSafe connector.

Ports

The MacBook Pro cable connections include the following:

✔ MagSafe power connector

✔ Gigabit Ethernet

✔ Mini-DVI external video

✔ FireWire 800 port

✔ FireWire 400 port

✔ Two USB 2.0 ports (three on the 17" model)

✔ ExpressCard/34 slot

✔ Combined optical digital audio input/audio line in — 3.5-mm minijack

✔ Combined optical digital audio output/headphone out — 3.5-mm minijack

✔ Kensington cable lock slot for physical security

Starting Small — the Mac mini

The mini is Apple's least expensive Macintosh model. As its name implies, it's quite small, about the size of an external CD or DVD drive. It is aimed, in part, at PC users who are considering switching to Mac, as it does not come with a keyboard, mouse, or video display. It can work with most video monitors. You can also use your USB keyboard and mouse if you like, or you can order new ones from Apple.

The mini's small size — 6.5 inches square by 2 inches high — and unobtrusive package fit in almost anywhere and make it ideal for living room home entertainment centers. Apple has adopted its quiet styling for other products, including the Airport Extreme base station and the Apple TV. In Figure 2-4, you can see the mini as well as the FrontRow IR remote control (on the left).

Figure 2-4:
The Mac mini and FrontRow remote control. The mini weighs less than three pounds.

The mini is not designed for user servicing — you need a putty knife to open its case — but many people have developed interesting modifications that customize it for fun or specialized uses. See *Mac mini Hacks & Mods For Dummies,* by John Rizzo, with contributions from yours truly (published by Wiley). Some interesting ideas described there include the following:

- Upgrading the hard drive, optical drive, and RAM
- Building a home theater around a mini
- Automating your home with the mini
- Using the mini in the kitchen
- Installing a mini in your car (maybe even a Mini)
- Modding the mini's case
- *Overclocking* a mini (that is, running it faster than Apple recommends)

The mini has an Intel Core Duo 2 processor with up to 2GB of memory and an Intel GMA 950 graphics processor. The low-price version has a 80GB hard drive and a slot-loading combo drive — it reads CDs and DVDs and writes CDs, but can't write DVDs. The high-price version has a SuperDrive that can burn DVDs. You can special-order one with a 160GB hard drive. Both models include AirPort WiFi networking, Bluetooth, and FrontRow IR remote control.

The mini's power button and all cable connections are on the back. These include the following:

- Power connector for cable from separate power adapter
- Gigabit Ethernet
- FireWire 400 port
- DVI external video
- Four USB 2.0 ports

✔ Combined optical digital audio input/audio line in — 3.5-mm minijack

✔ Combined optical digital audio output/headphone out — 3.5-mm minijack

✔ Kensington cable lock slot for physical security

Getting It All in One Box: The iMac

Apple's iMac continues a tradition that goes back to the first, revolutionary Macintosh — packaging the computer and display as a single unit. Having it all in one box means a single power cord, fewer connecting cables, nothing to tuck under the desk, and less clutter all around. And who couldn't do with less clutter in their lives?

The current iMacs take this idea one step further. All you have on your desk is what looks like an ordinary flat-panel display. Well, not quite ordinary: With an aluminum case and sculpted stand, it's well turned out. But that's all there is. The computer is tucked inside the display. All the connections are in the back. Figure 2-5 shows the two iMac model sizes: 20 inches and 24 inches.

Figure 2-5:
The iMac
family.

Photo courtesy of Apple, Inc.

Although the computer is out of sight, it has plenty of mind. The iMac can keep up with most desktop machines out there.

Like Apple's laptops, the iMacs sport a built-in iSight camera for videoconferencing and chat. Both have Intel Core 2 Duo microprocessors, AirPort WiFi, Gigabit Ethernet, built-in microphone, audio in and out, and FrontRow IR remote control. Both come with a keyboard and Apple's Mighty Mouse, which are wired, but you can order wireless models.

Both have three USB 2.0 ports and two FireWire ports, one 400-MHz, and one 800-MHz port. All the ports are neatly lined up along the bottom-left of the

iMac as you face the rear. No groping under the desk to get at cable connections. The wired Apple keyboard has two more USB 2.0 ports.

Note that the lower-cost model is good enough for most ordinary uses. The
next model up offers a faster CPU, larger hard drive, and a faster graphics
processor for not that much more money. See the section "Getting the Right
Graphics Processor," later in this chapter, for the advantages of more powerful graphics. The spectacular larger screen on the 24-inch model lets you
have more open windows on-screen when you're doing complex tasks like
editing a video or researching a paper. I love mine.

Maxing Out with a Mac

If you have a big budget and need lots of computing power, Apple has the
answers. In the following sections, you find out about the stand-alone Mac
Pro and the rack-mounted Xserve.

Mac Pro

As its name suggests, the Mac Pro is Apple's most capable Macintosh, with
dual Intel Xenon quad-core processors and room inside for 3 terabytes (3TB)
of hard drive and 16GB of RAM in eight DIMM slots that incorporate error-
correcting codes (ECC) for greater reliability.

While most Macs are designed with the expectation that their cases will
never be opened, the Mac Pro is a major exception. It's built into a full
tower–sized case that opens easily to gain access to most Mac Pro components. Figure 2-6 shows the Mac Pro all buttoned up, while Figure 2-7 shows
the cabinet splayed open to reveal its insides.

And, also unlike other Macs, you have room for expansion. The units contain
four hard drive bays, and you can install dual SuperDrive optical drives. And
you have your choice of these three graphics cards:

- NVIDIA GeForce 7300 GT with 256MB of GDDR2 SDRAM, one single-link
  DVI port, and one dual-link DVI port

- ATI Radeon X1900 XT with 512MB of GDDR3 SDRAM and two dual-link
  DVI ports

- NVIDIA Quadro FX 4500 with 512MB of GDDR3 SDRAM, two dual-link DVI
  ports, and one stereo 3D port

Figure 2-6:
The Mac
Pro.

Three additional full-length PCI Express (PCIe) slots are available for plug-in cards, which allow expansion of your Mac's capabilities. These are the same type of expansion cards used in newer PCs. They are not, however, compatible with the older PCI, PCI-X, or ISA cards. The PCIe slots can hold high-speed communications cards, such as fiber channel, or up to three more graphics cards. Three hundred watts of power are available just to power these cards. The whole Mac Pro can draw 12 amps at 120 volts — half that at 240. If your office is a bit chilly, convince your boss that you need one of these puppies, fully loaded, and it will keep you toasty warm.

The Mac Pro has two connector panels, a main one in back and a smaller one in front. The rear panel includes the following:

- ✔ FireWire 400 port
- ✔ FireWire 800 port
- ✔ Three USB 2.0 ports
- ✔ Two independent Gigabit Ethernet ports
- ✔ Optical digital audio input and output Toslink ports
- ✔ Analog stereo line-level input and output minijacks

Photo courtesy of Apple, Inc.

Figure 2-7:
The
Mac Pro
opened up.

The front panel conveniently supplies the following:

- ✔ A second FireWire 400 port
- ✔ A second FireWire 800 port
- ✔ Two more USB 2.0 ports
- ✔ Stereo headphone minijack

Perhaps surprisingly, WiFi and Bluetooth are options on the Mac Pro.

Now serving OS X — the Xserve

People who buy servers — the computers that provide the information we consume for the Internet — consider different factors than consumers in making their purchasing decisions. Issues such as reliability, packaging density, hot-swappable components, and remote management become paramount. Server owners want their machines to be up all the time. When something like a hard drive or power supply fails, they want to replace it without shutting the machine down. The server is often located in expensive server-farm real estate, and the space it takes up becomes an issue.

Apple's server offering is called Xserve, and you'll find that it offers appealing answers to each of these criteria, especially that of space. Apple's Xserve is a 1U device, which means that it's quite thin and maximizes the number of Xserves that can fit in a single rack. That makes server farmers happy — more cows in the barn. Figure 2-8 shows three Xserves and an Apple RAID storage unit in a minimalist rack.

Figure 2-8:
Three
Xserves and
a RAID.

Photo courtesy of Apple, Inc.

Back in the nineteenth century, as the railroad and telephone industries got going, folks realized that a lot of electrical equipment had to be installed in their offices. Mounting equipment in vertical "relay racks" with side bars spaced 19 inches apart became a standard that is still used today. Even the location of the screw holes is standardized, and the devices that fit in these racks have heights measured in "units" or Us. The shortest height unit that can still span a pair of standard mounting holes is designated 1U.

Each Xserve features the following:

- ✔ Dual Intel Xenon CPUs.
- ✔ Up to 32GB of ECC RAM, banked in four channels for high memory throughput.

✔ ATI Radeon X1300 PCI Express graphics processor card with mini-DVI output.

✔ Two available PCI Express slots, one of which can also take an older PCI-X card instead.

✔ Hot-pluggable SATA and SAS mass storage.

✔ Combo optical drive, SuperDrive optional.

✔ One FireWire 400 port on the front panel.

✔ Two FireWire 800, two USB 2.0, and two Gigabit Ethernet ports in back.

✔ Also lurking in back is an old-fashioned DB-9 serial port. Most commercial server-hosting facilities use DB-9 serial ports for console monitoring from a remote station using KVM technology. They are also needed for some uninterruptible power supplies.

✔ Optional second power supply for redundancy.

✔ Integrated processor for lights-out management and supporting software.

✔ A license for Mac OS X Server software, with no limit on the number of clients.

✔ Optional 24/7 AppleCare service.

Xserve RAID

Xserve RAID is a storage solution companion to Xserve, though it can be used with PCs and UNIX servers. You might be interested in RAID if you store large amounts of data, say for video editing, and want higher disk performance or greater reliability. Xserve RAID stores up to 10.5TB of data in 14 hot-swappable Apple Drive Modules and connects to servers via two high-speed 2GB Fibre Channels. To keep the cost per gigabyte down, Apple uses Ultra ATA drives, each with its own channel, instead of the more expensive SCSI drive used in competing systems.

Xserve RAID supports RAID levels 0, 1, 3, 5, 0+1, 10, 30, and 50. These are different ways to combine multiple drives to increase reliability, data speed, or both. Dual hot-swappable power supplies are available. The unit is 3U high.

South Park uses Xserve RAID, so if you don't buy one, Kenny will die in the next episode.

Xsan

Xsan is Apple's Storage Area Network (SAN) software. A storage area network aggregates all the disk drives in the local-area network into a single entity, allowing all servers to access that data at the same time. It can support up to 2 petabytes of data. That's 2,000,000 gigabytes.

Getting the Right Graphics Processor

In modern personal computers, a graphics processor takes over from the central processing unit much of the work of generating visual displays. Some are designed to perform the intricate mathematical calculations needed to render three-dimensional objects realistically at speeds fast enough to keep up with real-time game play. Apple supports a variety of models in its Macintosh line:

- **The low end:** Apple's low-end models, the iBook and Mac mini, use a GMA graphics processor from Intel that is integrated with its support chip set for the Core Duo processor line. These graphics processors are fast but are not designed for 3-D game play. To a large extent, Apple's dual CPU design, even in low-end models, makes up for this because the second CPU can perform the 3-D calculations fairly rapidly. If you're mostly doing light 2-D graphics, this type of processor should meet your needs.

- **The middle portion:** Mid-range machines and the Xserve come with graphics cards from ATI including the ATI Radeon X1300, the ATI Radeon HD 2400 XT, and the ATI Radeon HD 2600 PRO. You'll appreciate the better quality of these processors if you are a casual player of 3-D video games or visit 3-D virtual reality worlds such as Second Life, but they might not be enough for the really serious game play or professional video work.

- **The high end:** If you're serious about your graphics processor, the Mac Pro blasts graphics out with top-end PCI Express graphics cards. You get your choice of the following:

    - An NVIDIA GeForce 7300 GT with 256MB of GDDR2 SDRAM, one single-link DVI port, and one dual-link DVI port

    - An ATI Radeon X1900 XT with 512MB of GDDR3 SDRAM and two dual-link DVI ports

    - An NVIDIA Quadro FX 4500 with 512MB of GDDR3 SDRAM, two dual-link DVI ports, and one stereo 3D port

    NVIDIA and ATI, now owned by AMD, vigorously compete for king of the graphics hill. Each has loyal fans. You likely have used one or both of these companies' products in your PC experience, and you may have your own opinions. The highest-performance cards have two dual-link DVI ports allowing them to drive two HD displays simultaneously at full resolution. Virtual reality becomes more real than life.

Adding On and Filling In

Apple is judicious in the choice of peripherals and other accessories it provides. For example, although it was among the first to sell laser printers, it no longer brands its own printers, but supports most models made by others. Apple does offer displays and other hardware, software, and support packages, which may come with your Mac or which you can purchase as an add-on. The following sections explain the more popular options to help you decide what you might want — or want to ignore.

Apple displays

Apple sells several attractively styled flat-panel displays:

- ✔ 30-inch Apple Cinema HD Display, 2560 x 1600 resolution
- ✔ 23-inch Apple Cinema HD Display, 1920 x 1200 resolution
- ✔ 20-inch Apple Cinema Display, wide-aspect 1680 x 1050 resolution

The displays are packaged in anodized aluminum with a narrow bezel, so you can put two displays right next to each other. All models have a FireWire 400 hub and a USB 2.0 hub, each with two ports. The video signal connects via a DVI cable, so these displays work with properly equipped PCs as well.

An optional VESA mounting kit is available from the Apple Store that meets the Video Electronics Standards Association (VESA) Flat Display Mounting Interface (FDMI) standard, allowing you to attach your Apple display to a third-party mounting device.

AirPort Extreme WiFi base station

Apple's AirPort Extreme is technically a WiFi wireless access point, or base station, which connects computers and other devices in your home or office without running wires. As usually installed, you run an Ethernet cable from the back of the AirPort Extreme, shown in Figure 2-9, to your high-speed Internet modem — cable, DSL, or satellite. If you are in a school or office with a direct Internet connection, plug your Ethernet cable into it.

Figure 2-9:
AirPort
Extreme
from the
back.

Photo courtesy of Apple, Inc.

AirPort Extreme supports all current WiFi standards, including 802.11a, b, g, and Draft-N. This means that it should work with just about any WiFi-equipped computer and other WiFi devices, such as the iPhone and Apple TV. It supports all the WiFi security standards — WEP, WPA, WPA2, 802.11X, Radius, and so on — and includes a firewall. You can set permissible times for access for each authorized computer, which is great for limiting kid access.

AirPort Extreme does more than just supply high-speed Internet to any WiFi device within range, which by the way is about 150 feet (50 meters), though your footage may vary. In the rear, as shown in Figure 2-9, it has three local Ethernet ports so that you can hook up computers that require a wired connection. It also has a USB 2.0 port that lets you attach a printer that can be shared by your network. Or, you can attach a USB hard drive that is then shared over the network. What's that? You want both a printer and a hard drive? Don't be so greedy. Okay, Okay. But you need to get a USB 2.0 hub. They're inexpensive, and you can then have multiple printers and multiple hard drives. Go wild.

The AirPort Extreme is styled like the Mac mini and the Apple TV. It fits in the same footprint as the mini, 6.5 inches (165 mm) square, and weighs 1.7 pounds (0.753 kg). It comes with an AC power adapter, but runs off of 12 VDC, so you can put one in your car to run a WiFi network at your next geek picnic.

AirPort Express, a WiFi relay

The AirPort Express is smaller and simpler than the Airport Extreme. Kind of like the Latte Grande at Starbucks — it's the small model. While it can function as a WiFi base station to share an Internet connection, it's intended more as a relay and interface to your stereo so that you can pipe music from iTunes to your home entertainment system. It supports the 802.11b and g signaling speeds.

AirPort Express has just four connections:

✔ An AC wall plug — just stick it in any outlet

✔ An Ethernet port

✔ A USB port

✔ A combined optical digital audio output/headphone out — 3.5-mm minijack

The USB port supports a shared printer. The audio port can connect to your stereo. You just need a 3.5-mm stereo phone plug–to–RCA phone plug adapter cable. You can get one from the Apple Store or your local Radio Shack. If you have more than one sound system, you can install multiple AirPort Express units.

The AirPort Express looks like the Apple laptop power supply (see Figure 2-10). It even has the same "duck's head" snap-off power connector. You can take the AirPort Express in your suitcase and use it to create a WiFi network in your hotel if the hotel only has wired Internet.

Figure 2-10:
The AirPort Express plugged in.

Photo courtesy of Apple, Inc.

iPod

If you have not heard of Apple's iPod portable music player yet, please return this book for a full refund. They're everywhere and are revolutionizing the music business. The iPod currently comes in three models, shown in Figure 2-11:

- ✔ The diminutive video iPod, with a tiny built-in hard drive (in either 30GB or 80GB capacity) and a 320 x 240 color screen. It plays music, movies, TV shows, your photographs, and audio books, and it can serve as a portable hard drive for computer data.

- ✔ The even smaller iPod nano, with 2GB, 4GB, or 8GB of solid-state memory.

- ✔ The tiny iPod shuffle, with 1GB of flash memory. It's so small that it is almost dwarfed by its built-in clothing clip.

I talk more about the iPod and its mother ship, the iTunes Store, in Chapter 11.

Photo courtesy of Apple, Inc.

Figure 2-11:
The iPod
family.

iPhone

Apple's acclaimed iPhone is four devices in one:

- ✔ It's a four-band GSM cell phone. GSM is the cell-phone standard used in most countries of the world.

- ✔ It's a 2-megapixel still camera.

- ✔ It's a 4GB or 8GB video iPod with an even bigger screen, 320 x 480, that fills almost the entire front of the unit.

- ✔ It's a new type of device, a portable Internet communicator, that talks WiFi, Bluetooth, and EDGE (Enhanced Data Rates for GSM Evolution).

While most mobile phones, even "smart" phones, use a minimalist operating system that limits the types of applications they can support, the iPhone uses the OS X operating system. It runs a version of the Safari browser that can access and display the real World Wide Web, not just made-for-mobile mini-pages. Figure 2-12 shows the front of the iPhone.

The front of the iPhone is a multitouch pad like the ones on Apple laptops, allowing novel interactions such as adjusting the size of a photo by pulling or pinching it with a pair of fingers.

Photo courtesy of Apple, Inc.

Figure 2-12:
The iPhone.

Apple TV

Apple TV is a box that bridges your Macintosh and the Internet with your big-screen home entertainment center. It has a 40GB hard drive inside to automatically store movies and TV shows that you've downloaded to your iTunes library. You can also display your photos at high definition in your living room. Apple TV connects your home computer network (Mac or PC) to your living room electronics suite in several ways:

- ✔ High-Definition Multimedia Interface (HDMI) for high-definition video and audio
- ✔ Component video for older TVs
- ✔ Optical audio for the latest sound systems
- ✔ Analog RCA stereo audio for just about any home audio system ever made

✔ 10/100 BASE-T Ethernet if you prefer a wired connection to your computer

✔ USB 2.0

✔ AirPort/WiFi 802.11n for fast access to your wireless network

✔ Infrared receiver for use with the Apple Remote — one comes with the Apple TV

The Apple TV is styled like the Mac mini, as you can see in Figure 2-13, but is a bit larger: 7.7 inches (197 mm) square. It weighs 2.4 pounds, a bit more than a kilogram. Its power cord connects directly to a wall outlet or a power strip, with no space-hogging power adapter. We don't need *their kind* in our living rooms.

Support

Apple doesn't just sell hardware. It supports that hardware (and software) as well. Most Apple products come with 90-day free telephone support and a one-year warranty on the hardware, subject to the usual fine print that says it's limited and doesn't cover products hurled into active volcanoes or used to stop stampeding elephants, and other forms of abuse. In my experience, Apple gives customers the benefit of the doubt.

Figure 2-13: Apple TV hooked up to a high-definition television.

Photo courtesy of Apple, Inc.

The following sections introduce you to the three big support programs Apple offers as add-ons.

AppleCare

AppleCare extends the phone service and warranty that come with your Mac, usually to three years, but always check the terms before you buy.

Service policies are a form of insurance. If they are priced properly, you pay a bit more for the policy than your losses are likely to be on average. But "on average" is the kicker. If something goes wrong with your computer after the warranty expires, repairs can be very expensive — often a good fraction of the cost of a new machine. Portables, like laptops and iPods, take a lot of abuse. For a new Mac user, I think the free phone support and the peace of mind justify the added cost.

OS X upgrades

OS X is included with new Macs. The version you get has a number, such as 10.5.2. Here's what that number means:

- ✔ The 10 refers to OS X, X being the Roman numeral ten.
- ✔ The .5 is a major release; 10.5 is also known by its Apple not-so-secret code name Leopard.
- ✔ The .2 is a minor upgrade, known as a point release, that typically includes bug fixes, minor enhancements, and support for new hardware.

Apple traditionally provides point releases and other minor changes, such as security patches, for free via its Software Update service. You get notified about the availability of such changes once a week unless you change the settings.

Expect major releases every 18 months to two years. Apple charges for these; in the past, they've cost about $129. You've also been able to buy a family pack with five licenses for about $200. When an upgrade comes out, it's usually a good idea to wait a bit to see whether there are negative reviews or whether the upgrade breaks programs you use. But Apple's upgrades have been relatively painless, and the added features are usually worth the expense. So expect to buy an upgrade at least once in the life of your Mac.

.Mac

Apple's .Mac, pronounced *dot-mac,* is an online service that's integrated with Mac OS X. It is not an Internet service provider, but it does offer e-mail, chat, groups, Web page hosting, a photo and video gallery and 10GB of storage space. It currently costs $100 per year, and a family pack is available. Keep in mind, though, that you can often find a lower price for .Mac by shopping around, such as at Amazon.com.

The Internet-based storage service is called iDisk, and it shows up on your computer's desktop along with your local disk storage. You can use it to back up files or to share files with others, who can log on to a guest area.

The .Mac service enhances several applications in the Apple iLife suite, which is the subject of Chapter 11. It can also be used to synchronize two or more computers' address books and appointment lists. And photocasting lets you send pictures to other Macs — perfect for grandparents. See Chapter 14.

Application software offerings

While Macs come with an impressive array of easy-to-use applications that are ready to go, Apple sells a number of additional software tools. These break down into three groups, roughly by price and power.

Small, extra-cost upgrades

Apple has a few of these, including QuickTime Pro and JamPacks, that add additional music and tools to GarageBand.

Advanced applications

These typically sell in the $80 to $300 price range and are suitable for quality, commercial work. They include the following:

- ✔ **iWork:** Apple's office suite that includes the Pages word processor and page-layout program, Numbers spreadsheet, and Keynote, Apple's answer to Microsoft's PowerPoint presentation software.

- ✔ **FileMaker:** A database application that is also available in a fully compatible version for Windows.

- ✔ **Final Cut Express HD:** A big step up from iMovie, the video-editing component of iLife, Final Cut captures, edits, and outputs HDV (high-definition video).

- ✔ **Logic Express:** A powerful music-creation package.

- ✔ **Aperture:** Apple's top-of-the-line solution for professional photographers.

Pro applications

These applications are world-class solutions that hold their own against any solution on the market and are generally less expensive than their top competitors:

✔ **Final Cut Studio:** Everything you need to edit and post-produce a full-length feature motion picture or a TV series. Movies edited in Studio have won an Emmy and received one Oscar nomination so far. The package includes the following:

- Final Cut Pro: With native HDV and real-time editing
- Color: Adjust the tone and color values of your film
- Compressor: Convert between formats
- DVD Studio Pro: Make professional DVD masters

✔ **Logic Pro:** Powerful music composition tool I don't begin to understand.

✔ **Shake:** Advanced digital compositing.

Server software solutions

Mac makes a mean server version of OS X, and the full version is licensed without the per-seat head tax that brand-M imposes. Server products include the following:

✔ Mac OS X Server

✔ Xsan Storage Area Network (SAN) for Mac OS X

✔ Apple Remote Desktop

✔ WebObjects for Java server applications

✔ FileMaker Server, which doesn't require OS X Server

Chapter 3

Deciding What to Buy

*B*uying a computer can be a bewildering experience. Stores are stuffed with oodles of models in different shapes and sizes, and they are offered in a wide range of prices. Many of the options you are asked to select involve stuff that only a geek could love, like how many bytes of RAM to get (what if I don't like lamb?) or what the hard drive capacity is (what if I prefer a soft drive?).

Computer store sales staff can be helpful, but all too often they give questionable advice. Many are not that knowledgeable about the latest features and software. Sometimes they receive financial incentives to sell those models in stock that aren't moving.

Buying a Macintosh simplifies things quite a bit. Apple only has half a dozen or so models and relatively few options for each. It doesn't sell cheap "lowball" models that require expensive upgrades to do anything useful. Apple's lowest-price models can more than meet the needs of most users.

Still, you need to make choices, and you're generally best off making your decision — or at least narrowing it to a couple of possibilities — before you go off to the store or log on to Apple.com. In this chapter, you find tips that can help you decide what type of Mac suits your needs. (If you skipped the preceding chapters, be sure to check out the detailed introduction to the different models in Chapter 2.) Switching to a Mac may also impact how you connect your computer accessories and access features that you need, because your new Mac is likely an upgrade to better technology, and some ports and options on new Macs are different from those on older Windows computers. In this chapter you find the most important things you need to know, and I provide a final section that helps you decide where to buy.

Selecting a Conversion Strategy

Time to take a deep breath. Before I get into which model and what options to get, I want you to think about what you're trying to accomplish, and consider the best way to get exactly what you want (I'm just talking about computers here — don't get excited). There is more than one way to peel an Apple.

To begin with, answer the following questions honestly (the mind-reading chip in the spine of this book is automatically disabled when you are on this page, so no one will know your answers):

 ✔ **How often do you use your computer?** Less than once a week, several times a week, every day, hours each day?

 ✔ **What do you use your computer for?** Crunching numbers in a spreadsheet, writing *For Dummies* books, surfing the Internet, communicating with friends, looking for soul mates, downloading music, playing games?

 ✔ **What new things would you like to use it for?** Organizing photos, developing a Web site, podcasting, editing movies?

 ✔ **Where do you use your computer?** In a den or office, anywhere in the house you feel like, at work, at work and at home, on the road?

 ✔ **What's your budget?** Under $1,000, $1,000 to $2,000, or whatever it takes?

Depending on your answers, you have several different switching approaches to consider. I try to group them sensibly and give the categories cute, easy-to-remember names.

Taking it slow

No need to rush things. The Mac mini is perfect if you're the cautious type who wants to convert gradually and not spend a lot of money. Start out with worry-free Internet surfing and switch over additional applications as you get more comfortable with OS X. Of course you can use the spiffy iLife applications that come with the Mac mini as soon as you set it up. Taking it slowly can be the lowest-cost conversion strategy. It assumes that you already have a fairly up-to-date PC set up with a good-quality CRT or flat-panel display. All you really need to buy is a Mac mini. The tiny mini does not take up much room — it's not much bigger than an external CD burner. Just find a spare outlet for it on your power strip.

If you don't have a compatible USB keyboard and mouse, you can add those to your shopping list — literally. Many supermarkets now carry these accessories. For extra convenience, purchase something called a USB KVM switch.

These switches allow you to share a keyboard, mouse, and display between two computers (more expensive KVM models can support more than two computers). With a KVM setup, you can be working on the PC and, by pressing a special key combination on your keyboard, quickly switch to the Mac, check a Web site, and return to the PC with another key press. Be sure to buy a USB KVM switch, not the more common PS/2 type. (This assumes that your PC is new enough to have a USB port. If not, you need a separate keyboard and mouse for your Mac.) I tell you more about what to get later in this chapter, and I describe how to hook up a KVM switch in the next chapter.

If you already have a WiFi wireless network with your PC, you can easily incorporate the mini into the network. If not, you may need an Ethernet router and cable — inexpensive items. See Chapter 9 for details.

Macs tend to keep their resale value longer than PCs, so you are not taking much of a financial risk with this approach. If you aren't happy with the Mac mini, you probably won't have any trouble unloading it on eBay or CraigsList.org.

Living on the go

If you travel a lot or simply like to work or be online in different parts of your house, a MacBook or MacBook Pro laptop may be just right for you. If you need to bring your computer to work and also have it at home, you probably already have a laptop, but maybe you'd like something more up to date.

The Mac laptops are complete, powerful computer systems. They are elegant looking and priced competitively with all but the cheapest PC laptops. You can buy one and still keep your PC setup intact. They can network with your PC, just like the mini, and you can even hook one up to a KVM switch when you have it at home, so you can use your keyboard, mouse, and display with the Mac laptop.

Giving your PC the heave-ho

Maybe you are the type who just dives into the pool without dipping your toe in first. You may as well plan on just replacing your PC with a new Mac. I tell you how to transfer all your files in Chapter 6. A desktop iMac can fit on your desk where the PC display now sits. If you have a good-quality video display and enough room, you can keep your display on your desk and plug it into the iMac for two-screen computing. All you have to do is tell the iMac where the other display sits relative to the iMac so that OS X knows how to match them up to allow you to drag windows from one screen to the other, across the adjacent screen edges.

If your only computer is a laptop, switching to a MacBook or MacBook Pro is pretty simple. If the PC laptop has WiFi networking, the two laptops should talk to each other without much ado. (See Chapter 9.) Otherwise, a simple Ethernet cable should do the trick. If the laptop is so old that it has no network port, you have to get a bit more creative, and I cover those details in Chapter 6.

Spending lots of dough

If you have the money, I recommend a Mac Pro with Apple's large Cinema Display — or, even better, two Cinema Displays. (Al Gore has three.) It'll knock your socks off. And while you're at it, get a MacBook Pro laptop to take with you on trips and some iMacs that other family members can use. (You weren't going to stick your kids or spouse with that old PC, were you?)

Gaming glow

Does playing computer games, particularly those with detailed three-dimensional visuals, dominate your computer usage? Your life? If so, you should avoid the lower end of the Mac line, the mini, the MacBook, and the low-end iMac. All three use a built-in Intel Graphics Media Adapter, adequate for most purposes but wimpy on the 3-D front, whereas the other iMacs, the MacBook Pro, and of course, the Mac Pro blast out 3-D imagery with more powerful third-party graphics engines from ATI and NVIDIA.

Why not Linux?

You have another way to escape the clutches of Microsoft that is cheaper than getting a new Mac. You have no doubt heard of Linux, an operating system developed by volunteer computer programmers. Linux is closely related to the UNIX operating system that underlies Mac OS X, but differences exist. Linux was once a toy for übergeeks, but it has come a long way, and some people now use it as their only personal computer operating system. You can probably use it with your existing PC hardware. But Linux still lacks the polish and ease of use of a Mac or even a Windows PC. If you are technically inclined and want to find out how operating systems work, by all means give Linux a try. But most readers of this book are better off with a commercially supported operating system. The good news is that much of the software that runs on Linux also runs on Macs. See Chapter 16.

Finding bargains

Bargain hunting is harder in the Mac world than it is in the PC world. Generally, price reductions happen most often when inventory of a product is too high or when a new product is about to be introduced. Because so many PC manufacturers exist, these supply problems happen often for PCs. Apple, however, has better control of its distribution chain and tries very hard to keep Macintosh clearance sales from happening. They still do appear, but nowhere near as often as with PCs, and even when they do, the price cuts are rarely as dramatic. If you're ready to buy a Mac, it's not worth waiting months for one of these sales. Peripheral devices such as printers, scanners, and hard drives are another matter. These are often discounted. Apple also sometimes offers refurbished Macs at its online store. These typically come with Apple's standard warranty. You can search the Apple store with the keyword refurbished to find what's on sale.

I also don't recommend buying a used Mac in most cases. There is something about unpacking a brand-new machine and setting it up that builds confidence. You know the stuff was recently tested at the factory and should work. You have Apple tech support and, possibly, the people at the retail store to call on if you have trouble. In the worst case, you can take the Mac back and get a refund. Switching from one computer system to another is a complex enough task without having to worry about possible hardware problems.

And you are not likely to get much of a bargain — Macs tend to command higher prices on the used market than PCs of comparable vintage. Also, Macs sold before 2006 use a different microprocessor, the PowerPC, or, if it's really old, a Motorola 68k series. The multicore Intel chips in current Macs are so much faster that the lowest-end new Macs can keep up with most higher-end pre-2006 PowerPC models. The 68k models are for antique computer collectors only — a fun hobby, but not what this book is about. So unless you have a friend who is giving you a spectacular deal on an Intel Mac or a fairly recent PowerPC G4 or G5 series machine *and* is willing to help you get set up, you are better off buying a new Mac.

Relaxing as a couch potat-oh

Computers are invading our living rooms. The home entertainment center is going online. Channel surfing is merging with Internet surfing. If nothing on the tube is worth watching, try YouTube. All Macs have video outputs designed to display stunning images on large-format high-definition TVs and displays. The simple-to-use Apple remote coupled with a Mac mini can let you effortlessly switch among broadcast content, Internet feed, your home movies and slideshows, and other video. Alternatively, you can buy the new $300 Apple TV (TV), which connects with Macs and Windows PCs around your house via wireless (or wired) Ethernet and lets you play downloaded digital content — movies, TV shows, music videos, songs — as well as your home videos and photos, right on your large-screen HDTV or projection system. And it's controlled by the same tiny Apple remote.

Following the KISS principle

KISS stands for keep it simple, stupid. Whichever way you go, I recommend that you start with your Mac configured pretty much the way it is when it comes out of the box. You can customize lots of settings, and you can download software add-ons. But the less of this you do, the less likely you are to get into trouble and the easier it is to obtain support. I mention a few customizations I think are worthwhile later in this book.

Parental control

I'm not a big fan of computers for small children. They will be spending too much of their lives in front of video screens as it is. But if you are getting a computer for your kid or kids, make sure that you understand how to set limits. OS X has some great features to help you enforce them. Be sure to take a careful look at Chapter 14 before buying anything.

Figuring Out What's on Your Windows Computer

Before deciding what to buy, it is worth figuring out what is on your existing computer. You'll want your new Mac to have at least the capabilities of your present computer, plus lots of room to grow. You may know some of this information and much of it may be on the sales receipt or the original box your computer came in. Of course, if you have added options and peripherals, that info may be out of date.

If you're having trouble with your PC, skip this section for now and see the section on recovering files from a damaged PC in Chapter 6.

The easiest way to get the information on your current configuration is to ask Windows to give it to you. Follow these steps:

1. **Choose Start⇨My Computer.**

   The My Computer window should appear. You should see a section labeled Hard Disk Drives. If more than one drive is shown, start with the drive labeled C:.

2. **Select your C drive and then choose File⇨Properties. (Or, you can right-click the drive and select Properties.)**

   Figure 3-1 shows the Drive C: Properties window, which tells you how much disk space is used and how much is available.

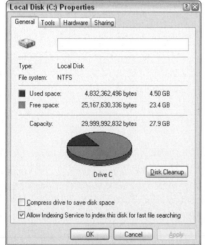

Figure 3-1:
Windows
XP Drive C:
Properties
pane.

3. **Make a note of the drive's total capacity and how much of that is used space.**

   The numbers to the right, which are shown in GB (gigabytes), are all you need. You can organize your notes in the following form:

Drive letter	<u>C:</u>_____	_____	_____
Total capacity	_____	_____	_____
Used space	_____	_____	_____

4. **When you are done, click the Cancel button to close the drive's Properties window.**

5. **Repeat this procedure for any other hard drives shown in the My Computer window.**

6. **At the bottom of the My Computer window, you should see the Control Panel icon. Click it.**

   Alternatively, you can select the Control Panel directly from the Start menu. When the Control Panel window appears, double-click the System icon.

7. **In the System pane that appears (see Figure 3-2), make a note of the following:**

   - Operating system (for example, Microsoft Windows XP)

   - Edition (for example, Home)

   - Last installed service pack (for example, SP2)

   - Manufacturer and model number

   - Speed (for example, 1.8 GHz)

   - Amount of main memory (for example, 224MB RAM)

Figure 3-2:
Windows
XP System
pane.

Navigating from PC to Mac Ports

When you're deciding what Mac model to buy (and what you can afford), you need to figure out which of the devices that you already own will work with your selected model. Unfortunately, few things about computers are as confusing and annoying as the bowl of spaghetti wiring underneath the desk. That's why here, you find a quick guide to what goes where in the Mac world. Much of it is the same as on a modern PC, but some old favorites are no longer with us. In many cases, you can get adapters to make the necessary connections; in other cases, well . . . it's time to move on.

Finding your way in the back of a Mac

When you're trying to figure out where to plug things in, the good news is that Apple keeps things simple by limiting the number of ports it uses, and has a good track record of picking the most useful ones. In the sections that follow, I summarize the ports available in new Macs currently on the market. Except as noted, the ports in this section are common to all current Macs. They are also common on late-model PCs.

If a plug won't go into a jack with a firm but modest push, don't try to force it in. Triple-check to make sure that the shapes and icons match up exactly, and then look for dirt or other obstacles in both ends.

Universal Serial Bus (USB)

Intel invented USB technology to let a wide variety of low- and medium-speed devices connect to a computer using only one type of port. Apple was the first to popularize it for use with keyboards and mice. USB is called a *bus* because more than one device can share the same port. *Serial* means all the data marches down a single pair of wires. The current version, USB 2.0, can support high-speed devices like disk drives, as well. All new Macs have two or more USB 2.0 ports. Older USB 1.0 and 1.1 devices should plug in and work fine in a USB 2.0 port.

FireWire

Apple created a different serial bus, called FireWire, to support connecting high-speed devices; it is also known as IEEE-1394. It comes in two speeds: 400 megabits per second (Mbps) and 800 Mbps. A number of camcorder manufacturers adopted FireWire 400 (Sony calls it i.Link), but USB 2.0 is almost as fast and many low-end video recorders now use USB 2.0. All Macs have FireWire 400 ports. High-end Macs also sport a FireWire 800 port, which uses a different connector, although 800 to 400 adapters are available and inexpensive.

Ethernet

Ethernet is the most poplar technology for getting computers to talk to each other over a wire. Ethernet came out of the same Xerox lab that developed the graphical interface that the Mac first popularized. Ethernet is available in 10-, 100-, and 1,000-Mbps versions. Macs support all three.

Ethernet connectors look like fatter versions of the connectors used on most telephones in North America. Just like the telephone connectors, you find a little, easy-to-break plastic tab you have to squeeze to get the connector out. Be gentle.

Don't plug your telephone line into this port. Current Macs don't have built-in telephone modems. Apple sells an external modem that plugs into a USB 400 port.

Digital Visual Interface (DVI)

Older (analog) methods of sending signals to displays limit the quality of pictures that can be shown. DVI sends images to the display in digital form, preserving their full fidelity for viewing on flat-panel computer displays and high-definition televisions (HDTVs). The iMac and MacBook use a variant called the mini-DVI connector. Apple sells inexpensive converter cables that let you hook up DVI and mini-DVI ports to most digital and analog video displays, including most large-screen television sets.

Audio input and output

All Macs come with two little round jacks that look like the earphone jacks on a portable radio or an iPod. One of them is just that and is marked with a tiny pair of earphones. The other is a *line-in* jack that accepts audio from other devices. Both accept ⅛-inch (3.5-mm) stereo plugs, and you can buy a wide variety of cables, adapters, and other accessories that work with these at your local Radio Shack. But these diminutive jacks are much cleverer than that. They also can work with newer optical digital audio devices that use a standard called *TOSLINK,* which is becoming more popular in the world of consumer electronics. If you shine a light down the little hole, you can see the tiny optical port in the center shining back at you.

Infrared

Infrared (IR) is a form of invisible light that is used in most remote controls that come with televisions, stereos, and other devices. When you press a button on the remote, it projects a beam of invisible light out the front that is coded with a signal that tells the TV or other device what button you pushed. A magic spot on your TV or device receives these IR signals, and if you point the remote in its general direction, the device should do what you wanted. Macs come with their own Apple Remote, so they have a magic spot too.

WiFi and Bluetooth

Strictly speaking, WiFi and Bluetooth aren't ports in that there is no place to connect a wire. That's because they support *wireless* communications. WiFi is mostly used for networking computers within a home or office, and is essentially Ethernet without wires. Bluetooth has a shorter range and is mainly for connecting small devices. It is used for wireless keyboards and mice and for wireless headsets that can be used with cell phones. Macs generally support both, though they are optional on the Mac Pro.

ExpressCard/34 (MacBook Pro only)

ExpressCard/34 is a new standard for expansion modules, which are basically cards that you can slide into personal computers, though they're mostly used with laptops.

Only the MacBook Pro series has an ExpressCard/34 slot. Figure 3-3 shows a MacBook Pro with an ExpressCard/34 card installed to access Verizon wireless Internet service. Accessing wide-area networks is probably the most common use for the ExpressCard/34 slot.

Figure 3-3: Express Card/34 for wide-area networking installed in a MacBook Pro.

As the name implies, the cards are 34 mm wide, about two-thirds the size of a credit card. They replace an older standard known as CardBus PC card, or PCMCIA card. You can also find bigger ExpressCard/54 cards (54 mm wide), but no current Apple models support them. See www.expresscard.org for more info on what devices are available in this format. But before buying one, make sure the manufacturer offers Mac drivers.

PCI Express (Mac Pro and Xserve only)

Peripheral Component Interconnect Express (PCI Express or PCIe) is the newest, blazingly fast incarnation of the classic open-the-cover-and-plug-a-card-in-the-motherboard expansion model. Only the Mac Pro and the Xserve currently have these slots. The Pro has four of them, one of which is typically occupied by the graphics card. You can use them to add more graphics cards or for ultra-high-speed communications cards, and they're handy for other specialized applications. These capabilities excite video producers and serious gamers, but if you don't know why you need expansion cards, you probably don't.

PCI Express is not compatible with the older PCI or PCI-X cards. Xserve has one slot that can accept a PCI-X card.

Ports that require an adapter for Macs

If you have a device with a connection type that a Mac does not support directly, you might still be able to connect your device using an adapter. This section covers the types of connections that Macs no longer support, but that you can still use with an adapter. By adding the adapters you need to your list of items to buy, you'll be able to get your new Mac setup running quickly, with less hassle.

Before you buy any adapter, make sure that the manufacturer supports the latest version of Mac OS X. Many don't support Mac at all, and some only support Mac OS 9 or old versions of OS X. Also realize that when an adapter maker says that it supports OS X, it doesn't guarantee that your printer, scanner, or digital bread maker will work perfectly. If you are buying new stuff, avoid peripherals that require an adapter if at all possible.

Apple Desktop Bus (ADB): The way older Mac keyboards and mice connected back in the twentieth century.

Camera memory cards: Some PCs come with slots where you can plug in the memory cards used in digital cameras and some camcorders. Many different types are available, and Apple apparently chose not to clutter its spiffy boxes with half a dozen camera card slots. USB adapters that accept most card types are inexpensive and readily available. Anyway, it's usually easier to hook up your camera via a USB cable.

Fiber Distributed Data Interface (FDDI): A high-performance data network that sends information over optical fibers instead of wires. You'll need a Mac Pro or Xserve and a PCI Express FDDI card, which Apple sells and supports.

High-Definition Multimedia Interface (HDMI): HDMI input is standard on most flat-panel and high-definition televisions. While many also allow analog input, HDMI is the input to use if you want the video quality you are paying those big bucks for. Apple sells adapters that let you connect a Mac to that HDMI port. You'll be amazed when your Mac's display fills your living room wall.

Musical Instrument Digital Interface (MIDI): This music-industry standard was introduced in 1983 for connecting musical keyboards (the ones with black and white ivories, not the kind you write e-mail on). Apple's Core Audio offers strong MIDI support in software. Many new MIDI devices use USB or FireWire interfaces and work directly with Macs. Older instruments may have a 5-pin DIN connector and, yup, you'll need an adapter.

Modem: Macs no longer come with a dialup modem port (the type that you can plug a phone line into). Apple sells a modem built into a short cable that plugs into a USB port for about $50. Other USB modems are on the market, some cheaper, but make sure that they support Mac OS X.

Parallel printer (IEEE-1284): This printer interface is also known as a Centronics port, named after a long-defunct company that made printers for minicomputers back when Richard Nixon was president. If you have a printer you love that only talks parallel port, Keyspan.com makes a USB–to–parallel port adapter that supports OS X.

PS/2: The second-generation IBM PC introduced these ports for connecting keyboards and mice. Lots of PCs still come with PS/2 keyboards and mice. See the next section in this chapter for details on what works and what doesn't.

RCA audio: This simple connector (which dates back to the early 1940s) is common on home audio systems. Radio Shack sells a cheap cable that plugs into your Mac's 3.5-mm stereo audio output and has a pair of RCA plugs at the other end that can go into your stereo. For RCA video, see S-Video, later in this section.

Small computer system interface (SCSI): Apple popularized this interface for hard drives with the Mac Plus, and SCSI (pronounced *scuzzy*) is still used in high-end applications. However, Apple has long since adopted the Serial ATA standard used by most PC manufacturers. USB-SCSI adapters are available, but they generally do not work with OS X. Ratoc Systems, Inc. (`www.ratoc systems.com`) sells a FireWire-to-SCSI adapter that it claims does work with OS X. It's a tad pricey, and it uses the latest UltraSCSI connector, so you may need special cable for first-generation SCSI devices. That old SCSI scanner better be worth it.

Serial port (RS-232, RS-422): Apple largely dropped serial ports in favor of USB ports when it introduced the first iMac. (A serial port is provided on the Xserve's back panel because the server world expects one.) Several companies sell USB–to–serial port adapters. Try Keyspan.com and Serialio.com. You can also buy Bluetooth-to-serial adapters that let you control serial devices without running wires.

S-Video: Apple sells an inexpensive adapter that converts your Mac's video output to S-Video and composite video (an RCA jack), the two most common analog television standards. With one of these adapters, you can show your photo collection on any TV with a video input jack.

Video Graphics Array (VGA) and Super VGA: VGA and SVGA are by far the most popular ports for connecting older analog computer monitors. Apple offers adapters that connect VGA/SVGA displays and other devices to the Mac's video output port. This adapter is free with some Mac models and an extra-cost (about $20) option with others.

Stuff that won't work

You may have some plug-in cards that do specialized things in your PC. Sorry, but the following ones won't work on a current Mac. (A few are usable with some older Mac models, but that's beyond what I can cover here.) Much of the functionality these cards were used for, such as Ethernet networking, is built into Macs, and USB and FireWire devices replace other uses.

- ✔ Industry Standard Architecture (ISA)
- ✔ Extended Industry Standard Architecture (EISA)
- ✔ Micro Channel architecture (MCA) and NuBus
- ✔ PC card, also known as a PCMCIA card (but see the section "ExpressCard/34," earlier in this chapter)
- ✔ Peripheral Component Interconnect (PCI)
- ✔ Accelerated Graphics Port (AGP)

Using Your Old Equipment with a Mac

If you've been a PC user for a while, you probably have purchased a number of accessories. Some of them may be usable with your new Mac, saving you the expense of buying new stuff. Whether a particular device is Mac compatible depends on its port interface — the type of cable you use to hook it up to the computer — and whether Mac software is available that works with the device.

You might also consider the device's age and whether your new Mac will offer a different and improved way of accomplishing what your old, familiar accessories do. Older devices may not have that much life left in them, and worse, they may simply be obsolete. Maybe you have a SCSI Zip drive. The storage capacity of a Zip drive was very impressive in its day, but it is dwarfed by the capacity of a cheap CD-RW disc that is usable in any Mac, so it may not be worth finding an adapter that lets you hook it up to your new Mac unless you have a large collection of Zip disks — and even then, you're probably better off copying them to your PC and then transferring them to the Mac. Or, you could look for a Zip drive with a USB connection. It should work on a Mac with no fuss.

I can't possibly discuss every combination of Mac model, non-Apple device, and software version, so check with the device manufacturer where possible.

Displays and projectors

If you are buying a mini or Mac Pro, using the display you have can save you money. High-end displays often cost more than a computer. Even if you're buying a Mac with a built-in display, an extra display is handy. Macs can use them as an extension to the desktop area, letting you drag an icon or window from one screen to the other. Or, you can set up the second display to mirror what you are seeing on your main display — handy for letting others see what you are doing. (Select System Preferences from the Apple menu and click the Displays icon to set all this up.)

The following sections help you assess what you need in order to connect your Mac to commonly used displays.

Flat-screen displays and HDTVs

Flat screens work fine with Macs, including those with a built-in display. The same goes for flat-panel or high-definition television sets. The only question is whether to connect your Mac to your flat-screen display or HDTV using a digital or analog interface (that is, the port available where you connect the cable from your Mac to your display). In either case, make sure that you have the right adapter cables. Digital and analog interfaces are described as follows:

- **Digital interface:** Digital connections generally produce better results. For a digital interface, you'll need to check what video output connector your Mac has (see Chapter 2) and what connector or cable your display has. You may need more than one cable. For example, if you choose a MacBook or iMac, which comes with a mini-DVI port, and your HDTV has an HDMI connector on the back, you'd need to get a mini-DVI to DVI cable and a DVI to HDMI cable. Check the booklet that came with your display and the booklet that came with your Mac for details about your specific equipment. Also, see the list of connector types in the section "Navigating from PC to Mac Ports," earlier in this chapter.

- **Analog interface:** You'll need a VGA adapter that you plug into the DVI port on your Mac. Some Macs come with these adapters; otherwise, order one from Apple.

CRT displays

CRT (cathode ray tube) displays are rapidly going the way of the dinosaur, perhaps for the same reason: They are too big and consume too much energy. Still, if you have a good-quality display and a tight budget or if you need the richer color fidelity that CRTs offer for high-end graphics work, using that old CRT might make sense. The good news is that almost all computer-grade CRTs produced since the 1990s use a VGA cable that should work fine with Apple's VGA adapter.

Otherwise, you should replace that CRT with an iMac, saving you acres of space on and under your desk — and you'll have no display cables to worry about.

Projectors

Big-screen projectors and PowerPoint presentations dominate business communication these days and are rapidly taking over our schools. We hate to contribute to this cultural disaster, but the truth is that most projectors work with a Mac. Most take VGA, so you'll need that VGA adapter.

Keyboard and mouse

When deciding whether you can use a keyboard or mouse you already have, here's the short version of the story:

- ✔ **If you have a two-button scroll-wheel mouse with a wire coming out of it that has a USB connector** — a flat rectangular metal plug about the size of a fingernail — at the other end, that is something worth keeping.

- ✔ **If you have a Windows keyboard with a USB connector,** it will work fine, but a couple of keys are labeled differently from Mac keyboards, and that may make it more trouble than it's worth.

- ✔ **If you have a cool keyboard, mouse, or other pointing device that you really like** — wireless maybe — read on for the longer story.

- ✔ **If you have some old piece of junk,** skip this section and buy something new.

Connections, connections

The first thing to consider is how your keyboard and mouse connect to your PC. The three most common methods are a USB cable, a PS/2 cable, and wireless:

- ✔ **USB** cables should work just fine with your Mac.

- ✔ **PS/2** connectors are round and have a pastel-colored shell. PS/2 won't work with your Mac directly, but adapters are available. Be sure that you get the kind of adapter that converts PS/2 devices to USB and not the other way around, which is much more common. Also make sure that the manufacturer supports Macs.

  These days, many manufacturers only make USB keyboards and mice and include an adapter that converts it to PS/2. So you should take a closer look at what you think is a PS/2 plug to see whether it is just one of these adapters, in which case you're in luck — just pull the USB plug out of the adapter and plug it into your Mac.

- ✔ **Wireless** devices have a built-in radio transmitter instead of a wire. The receiver is often in a finger-sized pod that plugs into the computer, or it can be built in. Some devices transmit using technology that's proprietary to the maker; others use Bluetooth. Most Macs come with Bluetooth inside (it's not included in the lowest-cost iMac, and it's an option on the Mac Pro), and Bluetooth devices generally work with Bluetooth-equipped Macs, at least at some basic level. But you may need special software to take full advantage of this feature on a Mac. A wireless device that uses a USB receiver module and a proprietary transmission scheme may need special software as well. Check with the manufacturer in either case.

Relics of days gone by

The mice and keyboards that came with computers in the 1980s used an RS-232 serial port connection. These are useless. Old Apple USB keyboards work fine on current Macs. If you have an older Apple keyboard or mouse with a round plug (Apple Desktop Bus), you can get an ADB-to-USB converter, but it is probably not worth the bother.

Keyboard layout

Mac keyboards have two special keys in the lowest row, to the left of the spacebar. One is labeled *option,* and to its right is a key with an Apple logo (🍎) and a fan symbol (⌘), known as the *Command key* in Apple-ese. On PC keyboards, these two keys are the Windows key and the Alt key, respectively. If you just plug a PC keyboard into a Mac, the Windows key works as the Command key, and the Alt key works as the Option key. Unfortunately, their positions are reversed from where they are on Mac keyboards. Because you are new to the Mac way of doing things, you don't need this tactile confusion. You can buy a piece of software called DoubleCommand (`doublecommand.sourceforge.net`) that lets you reverse these keys.

If all this seems more trouble than it's worth (I think so), get a Mac keyboard. Figure 3-4 shows the keyboard on a MacBook laptop, with its special keys.

Figure 3-4:
MacBook
keyboard.

KVM switch

A KVM switch lets you share your keyboard, video display, and mouse between two computers — more than two with fancier KVM models. Some KVMs also let you share a set of audio speakers or headphones. Two types of KVM switches are available, based on the type of connection they use for the keyboard and mouse: USB and PS/2. *Only buy a USB KVM switch.* Most recent PCs accept a USB input for the mouse and keyboard.

Many USB keyboards and mice come with a USB-to-PS/2 adapter. These aren't general-purpose converters, however. The USB keyboards and mice are smart enough to also talk PS/2, and the adapters just take the wires from the USB connector and jigger them into a PS/2 plug. Don't expect one of these adapters to convert the USB output of your KVM switch to PS/2.

Printers, scanners, and fax machines

If you'd like to use your current printer, scanner, or fax machine with your new Mac, you may not have to buy anything extra or you may need an adapter. The following tips can help you figure out what you need to do:

- ✔ If your PC printer is of reasonably recent vintage and connects with USB, Ethernet, or WiFi, it will probably work with your Mac with very little fuss. Macs come with oodles of drivers for current devices installed, though it never hurts to check for updated drivers at the printer manufacturer's Web site.

- ✔ Older printers with a parallel port require a USB–to–parallel port adapter, and chances of them working are a bit more iffy.

- ✔ All-in-one units generally work, but some features, like receiving faxes to your hard drive, may not work with the Mac. (Get an Apple USB modem if your all-in-one's fax feature won't play Mac.)

The mantra again is to check with the manufacturer. Apple has a handy page with links to major printer manufacturers' support pages: www.apple.com/macosx/upgrade/printers.html.

The scanner story is pretty much the same. Recent USB and FireWire scanners should be fine. Older SCSI devices need a pricey SCSI-to-FireWire adapter and still may not work. Check with the manufacturer. Your mileage may vary.

I talk about how to set up printers in OS X in Chapter 5.

External hard drives and flash drives

External hard drives and flash drives are those storage devices you can plug into your computer with a USB or FireWire connection. If you have one, you know how handy it is for storing backups or transferring files. USB and FireWire external hard drives should work fine, even if they've been formatted for your PC. Just plug them into the appropriate Mac port and a drive icon will appear on the desktop, which you can then click to access your files. The same goes for USB flash drives.

All Macs come with at least a CD burner. Apple markets DVD burning as the *SuperDrive* option. If you have a USB 2.0 or FireWire DVD burner, it will probably work with your new Mac. But if you plan on burning many DVDs, it's probably worth the extra expense to get the SuperDrive option.

An external DVD reader or burner can come in handy if you want to watch DVDs from countries outside your zone. (The movie industry has obnoxiously chopped the world up into six zones, and Macs can only play DVDs from one zone.)

Internal drives

Because new drives have so much more capacity than those from even a couple of years ago, reusing internal hard drives may not be worth the bother. If you do have an internal drive you'd like to use in your new Mac, you can also buy hard drive enclosures that let you install your PC's internal hard drive and then plug it into your Mac via USB 2.0 or FireWire.

Networking devices

Most of the hardware you use to create a home network (technically called a *local area network* or *LAN*) for sharing broadband Internet access should work with a Mac. This includes the following:

✔ **Ethernet switches and routers and Ethernet cabling:** This is the equipment you use to create a network with wires.

If you do decide to buy a new Ethernet router or hub, be sure to get a model that supports at least 100Base-T speeds (1000Base-T is blazingly fast but expensive and probably more than you need). If you own older 10Base-T equipment, you can use it if you like.

✔ **Cable modems and DSL modems:** These are the modems that come with high-speed Internet connections from your cable or digital subscriber line (DSL) provider, respectively. In all likelihood, you won't need any different hardware to use your existing Internet connection with your Mac.

✔ **Wireless routers and access points:** This is the hardware you use to set up the popular WiFi wireless networking. The 802.11b, g, and n standards also work with a Mac. The *n* version is the fastest, and *b* is the slowest.

WiFi networks work at the speed of the slowest device on the network, so an older laptop that only supports 802.11b is best left off when not needed.

Another, less common WiFi standard, called 802.11a, operates in a different frequency band from the *b* and *g* modes. The radios in WiFi-equipped Macs can operate on the 802.11a band as well, but Apple does not officially support this option.

Digital cameras and camcorders

Macs and OS X provide extensive support for digital photography. Macs work with most digital cameras and support the *RAW mode* that high-end cameras output when you want the best-quality images from them. The most common way to connect a camera to your Mac is via a USB cable. If you want to read your camera's memory card directly, get an inexpensive USB memory card reader. Macally.com sells an ExpressCard Media Reader that works with a MacBook Pro. (For details about ExpressCard technology, see the section "ExpressCard/34," earlier in this chapter.)

Digital video recorders are also well supported. Some use USB 2.0 and others use FireWire, though manufacturers may call it IEEE-1394 or i.Link (Sony's brand name). Both work fine on a Mac. The movie-editing software that comes with new Macs also supports the new High Definition (HD) camcorders, so you're ready for the latest in videography.

Cell phones and PDAs

The main reason anyone connects his or her cell phone or PDA (personal digital assistant) to a computer — either with a cable or wirelessly with Bluetooth — is to synchronize the address book and calendar. This feature can be a lifesaver if you lose your phone or switch services and get a new phone.

If you're looking to sync your phone with your Mac, a Bluetooth radio is built into most Macs (it's an option on the Mac Pro). If your phone or PDA supports

Bluetooth, too (most new models do), you can connect wirelessly to Macs. Other devices can connect via a USB cable.

Also, every Mac comes with Apple's iSync software, which lets you match (synchronize) your Mac's address book and calendar with those on your cell phone or PDA. The iSync software supports over 100 models of cell phones and PDAs. You can find a list of supported models at `www.apple.com/macosx/features/isync/devices.html`.

Of course, if you decide to upgrade your phone as well as switch to a Mac, Apple's iPhone works great with Macs.

PC cards

PC cards, also known as PCMCIA cards, are about the size of credit cards, though a bit thicker, and are designed to plug into special slots on PCs, primarily laptops. The good news is that many of the capabilities that PC cards were typically used for, such as adding Ethernet, are built into Macs or can be added in other ways, such as with the Apple USB modem.

If you need to add functionality to your Mac via a card, you have a couple of options:

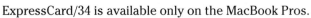

 ✔ **Get a MacBook pro with ExpressCard/34:** ExpressCard/34 slots are basically the latest version of the PC card technology. With the introduction of the Intel-based laptops, Apple switched to this newer standard. ExpressCards, which are a little smaller than PCMCIA cards but have much faster connections to computer's innards, are becoming available for many other uses, because newer PC laptops come with ExpressCard slots, too.

ExpressCard/34 is available only on the MacBook Pros.

 ✔ **Get a USB PC card reader that works with your card:** If you depend on a PC card for what you do, this may be your only choice. You insert your PC card into the reader and then plug the reader into your Mac via the USB port.

Portable music players

Needless to say, iPods work hand in glove with Macs — after all, Apple makes both.

Most other music players can operate as USB so that you can at least transfer music files in a open format (like MP3) to the player. Non-Apple players don't play songs purchased from the iTunes Store directly under OS X; however, you can burn a playlist to CD and then read it back in and transfer the files to your player.

Microsoft's Zune music player does not even have this USB option. Some third party may create a way to transfer files between Macs and Zunes, and of course, you can run Windows on the Mac and transfer files that way. But if you're seriously considering purchasing a Mac and a Zune, you may be reading the wrong self-help book.

Miscellany

You probably have accumulated a pile of computer-related stuff. Some of it is still useful, and other bits can be given away or tossed out.

Power strips and surge protectors: You always need more of these.

USB and FireWire hubs: These let you connect more than one device to a single port. Don't forget to save the matching power supply, if you have one.

Uninterruptible power supply (UPS): Some of these connect to your computer to tell it to shut down when the power goes out. Check with the UPS manufacturer to see whether it has Mac software to support this feature. If not, you can still use it to supply backup power.

Computer furniture: A desk is a desk, and switching to a Mac can free some space on one, but if yours doesn't have a good ergonomic design (see www. apple.com/about/ergonomics) or just looks terrible, it may be time for an upgrade.

Cables: Ethernet, USB, and FireWire cables are worth hanging onto. Serial, SCSI, and proprietary cables can go. The ubiquitous 3-pin power cords used with most desktop PCs (IEC-C13) don't fit Macs except the Pro. One or two are always handy to keep around, however.

Blank discs: Keep full-size blank CD-Rs and DVD-Rs. The mini and credit-card size ones don't work in the Mac's slot-loading drive (don't even try it), though they may work in an external optical drive. Blank floppy and Zip disks can go unless you work with folks who still use them and can get hold of an external drive that supports them. (Save one floppy to show your grandchildren.)

Floppy disk holders: Holders for the ancient 5¼-inch floppy disks are great for CDs and DVDs. Holders for 3½-inch disks are good for organizing little tchotchkes like flash drives, the Apple remote, camera memory cards, small cable adapters, and so on.

Printing supplies: You can use your printer paper, address labels, and ink or toner cartridges for your printer, if you're keeping it.

Getting Ready to Buy

I think you're ready to decide what to buy. You've reviewed the different approaches to switching and considered what items you could use from your PC. I told you about the different Apple models in Chapter 2. It's time to take out a sheet of paper and work up a couple of configurations that meet your needs, compare them to your budget, and pick one. The rest of your computing life begins today.

Choosing options for your new Mac

All the Macs that Apple sells are complete, usable systems, but some options and accessories are worth considering. Apple typically stocks three or four configurations for each model, and you can custom-order additional options. The following sections walk you through the key decisions you'll need to make when you order.

Processor speed

Apple charges a little extra for the fastest versions of the Intel processors it uses. Computer reviews tend to dote on 10 percent differences in speed. Most users will hardly notice the difference. All Macs have more than one central processing unit (CPU) — the part of the chip that carries out program instructions. Most have two, but the highest-performance models have four or more. If you don't know why you would need that much processing power, you probably don't.

Random access memory

Random access memory (RAM) is where your computer temporarily stores information so that the CPU can quickly (in billionths of a second) access the data while it is working on that data. Other terms used include DRAM and SDRAM. When your computer runs out of RAM, it writes data it hasn't used in a while to the much slower hard drive.

Adding memory reduces the need for these memory swaps and can typically improve performance more than getting a faster chip. The 1GB of RAM (one billion or so characters of information) that new Macs come with is adequate. Getting 2GB is better.

Hard drive size

Hard drives are where your computer retains information that you wish to keep. If you plan to manage your photos, movies, and music on your Mac, or if you plan on running Windows, you'll want lots of hard drive space. You can buy an external drive — and you'll want one for Apple's Time Machine backup feature — but it's handy to have your main files in one place. On some models — the Xserve, the Mac Pro, and surprisingly, the low-end MacBook — adding a bigger drive is easy, but most models require a technician to install one. Bottom line: It's worth spending a little more for a bigger hard drive, but save some money in your budget for an external unit, too.

SuperDrive, yes or no?

The lowest-priced Macs in the mini and MacBook series come with *combo drives.* These drives can read CDs and DVDs, including playing movies, and can burn (write) recordable CDs, but they cannot burn DVDs. The next step up in price includes what Apple calls a *SuperDrive,* which does all the above *and* burns DVDs. If you plan to make movies on your Mac, you'll want the SuperDrive. They are also great for backups, because DVDs store much more data than CDs do.

DVD technology was developed in the mid-1990s, and the electronics industry is ready to replace it. Unfortunately, the industry has not agreed on a single format to replace it. Two main contenders have emerged: Sony/Panasonic's Blu-ray Disc (BD) and Toshiba's HD DVD. Apple has announced it supports Blu-ray, and Microsoft is pushing HD DVD. The twentieth century was marked by three great conflicts: democracy versus fascism, capitalism versus Communism, and VHS versus Betamax. We'll see how this conflict plays out.

Selecting other accessories

It's best to get your computer configured the way you want it when you buy it. You can buy other accessories with your purchase or later, when you need them.

Modem

Current Mac models do not include a modem. If you need dialup Internet access at home or on the road, or if you need to send fax documents from your computer, you'll want to get Apple's tiny USB modem, which sells for about $50.

AppleCare

Macs typically come with a one-year warranty and 90-day free phone support. You can extend the warranty and phone support by signing up for AppleCare. Although you can do this anytime before the warranty expires, extending the warranty when you buy is best; otherwise you may forget. Alternatively, mark your iCal calendar about a month before the warranty expires (see Chapter 11).

Apple could change its terms, so verify the warranty info in this section before you buy — don't take my word for it.

ProCare

For about $100 per year, Apple sells a premium service plan called ProCare that offers a number of improvements over the standard warranty. You can buy it only at an Apple retail store (not online). It entitles you to personal training, priority repairs, advance registration at the in-store Genius Bar, and a yearly preventive maintenance tune-up. (You find out more about the Genius Bar in the section "Visiting the Apple store," later in this chapter.)

If you also purchase your Mac at an Apple retail store and get ProCare as part of the package, the folks at the Apple store can set up your Mac for you, including transferring files from your PC to the Mac. The PC has to be working and must have an Ethernet port and at least Windows 98 — and of course, you have to schlep it in. Be sure to request complete setup service when you purchase your Mac; Apple only gives you a ten-day period in which to ask for it.

.Mac

.Mac is Apple's data storage and sharing service, offered on an annual subscription basis at $99 per year. You get an e-mail address ending in .mac and 10GB of online storage that shows up as another hard drive on your desktop and that you can use to store your Web site, photo and video gallery, calendar, and backup files, all subject to a terms-of-service agreement (no naughty stuff). Many iLife programs have features that take advantage of .Mac if you have it. Apple typically offers new Mac customers a 30-day free trial, so you can check it out before buying.

Printer deals

When you buy a new Mac, you are typically offered a reduced price or rebate on a new inkjet printer. Sometimes the rebate covers the purchase price of the printer, so even if you already own a printer, it may be worth getting a new one as a spare or to give to someone else.

There is no such thing as a free lunch, however. Printer manufacturers sell their printers cheap and force you to buy ink or toner from them at prices that work out to a few cents per page for a text document to a half-dollar or more for a color photograph — in effect, a tax on every page. New printers often come with "starter" cartridges that print fewer pages than a purchased cartridge, so you might as well buy a cartridge with that new printer and save yourself a trip to the store.

Most inkjet printers use ink that runs when wet, but some are more smearproof than others. Ask to have a sample page printed and apply a drop of water or saliva to the printing. If you need a relatively waterproof print, it's best to go with a laser printer.

If you have a printer you like and it is supported by OS X, it might be best to forego the printer deal and shop for a new one when you need it.

Microsoft Office

Microsoft Office is still the most widely accepted tool for creating text documents and spreadsheets. You can safely send documents back and forth between the Macintosh version of Office and the Windows version. If you feel you need Microsoft Office, say for work or school, check on whether special deals are available with the purchase of a new Mac. Unfortunately, you cannot transfer your Windows license to OS X.

External hard drive

If you don't already own one, get a high-capacity external hard drive — at least 120GB worth. They're pretty much a "must-have" if you want to get decent use out of Apple's Time Machine backup software. They're also handy for transferring large files. External hard drives offer capacities in the quarter-terabyte (250GB) range for under $150. You can buy a terabyte (1,000GB) for under $400. You should get one with both FireWire and USB 2.0 interfaces, giving you maximum flexibility, because you can use USB 2.0 with your PC and the faster FireWire with your Mac.

Flash drive

If you don't already have one of these tiny, inexpensive USB mass storage units, it's time you got one. They are also known as thumb drives. A typical unit is shown in Figure 3-5, with a peanut for comparison. There is nothing like knowing you have the files you need in your pocket. Get at least a 1GB unit.

Figure 3-5:
A flash drive and a peanut. The USB plug is at the top.

How big is a gigabyte?

The international metric-system prefix *giga* means 1,000,000,000 — a billion in North American English — so a gigabyte is a billion bytes, right? Well, in the computer world, it's not so simple. A gigabyte (or GB) sometimes means that, and sometimes it means 1,073,741,824 bytes. (You can make any geek's day by asking him why.) The latter version is always used for RAM. Hard drive manufacturers tend to mean 1,000,000,000 bytes. It's kind of the opposite of a baker's dozen — they put one less donut in the bag. Pretty much every manufacturer does this the same way, so you aren't being cheated. And you should buy at least twice as much hard drive space than you think you'll need, so none of this really matters.

External floppy drive

If you have a collection of 3½-inch floppies, your best bet is to read them all onto your PC's hard drive and then back them up, either directly or to your Mac when you transfer the rest of your files (see Chapter 6). But if you've accumulated too many of them, don't want to spend the time, or still use them to exchange data, get an external USB floppy drive.

Networking equipment

If you already have high-speed Internet access and maybe even a home network, your Mac will plug right in. If not, see Chapter 9, where I tell you about the various options:

- **Wireless:** If you are buying a laptop or just don't want wires strung all over your den, consider getting a WiFi router. Apple's offering is called the AirPort Extreme Base Station (AirPort Extreme is Apple's name for the 802.11g WiFi standard). However, just about any 802.11g router will do.

- **Ethernet (wired):** If you plan to use wired networking, check to see whether you have an extra Ethernet port available on your router or cable modem. If not, you might need an Ethernet router. Getting one that also includes WiFi doesn't cost much more, however.

Another handy accessory is a USB hub, a small box that multiplies the number of USB devices you can plug in at the same time. You may already have one, but make sure that it supports the faster USB 2.0 standard. If not get a new one.

Travel accessories

If you are getting a Mac laptop and plan to travel with it, here are some other accessories worth considering:

✔ **Airplane power adapter:** If you take long plane trips, you might want to get Apple's airplane power adapter. Many airlines provide laptop power outlets, though less often in economy seating. You can find out what seats on your flight have power adapters at www.seatguru.com. Note that the Apple adapter powers your laptop but does not charge its batteries.

If you are traveling to other countries, the good news is that the power adapter that comes with Mac laptops runs on any AC power source in the world — 100–240 volts, 50 or 60 hertz. However, you may need to buy a travel adapter to plug it in. You can get these at Radio Shack and many travel stores. You don't need the transformer type.

✔ **Three-way extension cord:** Those of us who travel spend untold hours in airports, and most of them only have a few power outlets, usually located for the benefit of the cleaning crew. When you do find a pair of outlets, another road warrior has probably already claimed them for his laptop and cell phone. But most people are willing to share the outlet if you ask nicely and produce your three-way cord.

✔ **Security cable:** If you plan to use your Mac laptop at work or school, consider buying a security cable that lets you lock it up when you have to leave it unattended. You can find a variety of such locks at Kensington.com.

Shopping for Your New Mac

You're probably fed up with choices by now, but you have one more decision to make: where to buy your Mac. Here's the gist of it: You can buy online or in a traditional "brick and mortar" store, and you can do either directly from Apple or from an independent retailer. There are pros and cons for each, and the sections that follow can help you decide.

Wherever you go to buy your Mac and accessories, make sure that you take a list of all the specs and accessories you know you'll need, based on the information you gathered earlier in this chapter. Your list should include not only what Mac model you want, but also how much RAM you need, what size hard drive you want, and what options you'll choose (such as whether you want a SuperDrive or a higher-end graphics card). By having all these notes at the ready, you're much more likely to stay within your budget (if you have one) and get no more or no less than what you need.

Shopping at your local computer store

The nice thing about going to a computer store is that you can see the various models before you make your final decision. You can also ask the friendly salesperson questions and maybe even get useful answers. Assuming what you want is in stock, you get to take your new toy home with you. And if you have a problem, most stores have a place where you can talk to someone face to face (ask your salesperson to show you the service department before you buy).

Not all computer stores carry Macs. Apple is pretty choosy about which establishments it does business with. It doesn't want Macs stacked along the wall with all the Windows models in a department staffed with salespersons pushing the PC that happens to be on sale that week. You can find a list of authorized Apple resellers near you at `www.apple.com/buy`. And call ahead to see whether what you want is in stock.

Visiting the Apple store

Frustrated with the way its computers were being sold, in 2001, Apple defied conventional business wisdom and started building its own chain of computer stores. Designed with Apple's usual panache, and propelled by the success of the iPod, this venture has made its customers and stockholders very happy. If you choose to buy your Mac at an Apple store, you'll find that the stores are well stocked with most Apple models, attractively displayed — although you probably won't see an Xserve, and the inexpensive minis are usually tucked away in a corner. The stores carry lots of accessories, both from Apple and third parties — printers, external hard drives, carrying cases, software, games, and of course, iPods, iPhones, Apple TVs, and the growing list of Apple consumer electronics.

The coolest thing about the Apple store is the Genius Bar, a section staffed with people who know their Macs and can answer your questions. After you buy your Mac, if necessary, the Genius Bar can take your hardware for repair. If the store is busy, and it usually is, you'll have to sign in and wait a bit. Most stores give you a pager so that you can shop elsewhere or visit the food court if the Apple store is in a mall, as many are. You can visit the Genius Bar and bring in your Mac to the Apple store for service regardless of where you purchased it originally. You'll have to pay for service, of course, if your Mac is no longer under warranty or is not covered by AppleCare.

Look for the Mac logo

Macs work with most USB, FireWire, and networking devices — printers, scanners, wireless base stations, and so on — so don't be afraid to try what you already own. But if you are buying new equipment, make sure that the package says it is designed for Mac and OS X. If you do, you are more likely to get a product that works with little or no fuss. And if you run into problems and don't find the solution in this book, you are more likely to get useful help from that vendor's customer service if the box says that it supports Macs.

Apple claims that a large chunk of the population of North America is within a 45-minute drive of an Apple store. And you find Apple stores in many other parts of the world as well. You can find the ones near you at www.apple. com/buy.

Buying your Mac online

Assuming that you already have an Internet connection, buying online can be very convenient. Pick out the model you want, enter your shipping address and credit card number, and in a day or so, depending on how cheap you were about shipping, your computer arrives. If you don't have an Internet connection or your PC is so riddled with viruses that you don't trust it with your credit card, most online stores also have toll-free phone numbers and even printed catalogs that you can request.

Surfing to Apple's online store

You can buy all the products Apple makes from its electronic Apple store at www.apple.com (or by calling 1-800-MY-APPLE). You can even watch the latest Apple TV ads.

The online Apple store is your best bet if you want to buy a build-to-order configuration. Select the Buy Now option on the model you want, and you are presented with all the possible options for that model. Of course, you are not committed to buy anything until you enter your credit card information and confirm your order.

Other online retailers

A number of other online stores sell Macs, including Amazon.com, Macconnection.com, and Maczone.com. Again, you can find a full list at www. apple.com/buy. These stores sometimes offer discounts or deals on extra memory. They may only stock the more popular configurations, however.

If you live in the United States, you may be able to avoid paying sales tax by purchasing from one of the independent online stores. The independent store has to collect sales tax only if it has a business presence in the state where you live.

Part II
Making the Switch

The 5th Wave   By Rich Tennant

"It's been two days, Larry. It's time to
stop enjoying the new computer smell
and take the iMac out of the box."

In this part . . .

You did it. You got a Mac. Now what? This section guides you through setting up your new Mac and introduces you to Apple's OS X operating system. I suggest ways to move over your files and help you deal with the most important applications you need to get started.

Chapter 4

The Big Day: Setting Up Your Mac

• •

• •

Congratulations! You've done it. You bought a Mac. A new world is about to unfold. Apple does an excellent job of making the task of setting up a new Mac simple and painless, and it usually is. But computers are by far the most complex consumer product ever sold, and things can go wrong. Also, some simple preparations can make the setup process smoother and much less stressful. So resist the temptation to rip open the package, and read on.

Unpacking and Setting Up

You are now ready to unpack your new Mac. (I know some of you did this as soon as you got it home, but please gather all the pieces in one place and pretend you didn't.) I hope you notice the attractive presentation. Apple has elevated packaging to an art form, with everything snugly in its place. I also hope you notice the tiny manuals that come with the Mac. They explain the basics but leave plenty of demand for aftermarket books such as this one. Thanks, Apple.

Getting organized

First thing to do is to make room for the new machine and clear away the clutter on your desk or work table so that you can keep track of everything. Next, find a shoebox or plastic storage container so that you'll have a place to store the discs, manuals, and other bits of stuff that come with the Mac. A friend of mine services computers in his apartment complex and is forever telling people to put the discs and papers in a safe place when he sets up a new computer. When he has to go back sometime later, his clients can never find the stuff. So think of a place you'll remember and write it down here, in the margin of this book.

Hooking up your computer

It's time to put your computer together. Looking through the manual that comes with your Mac for the latest info is always a good idea, but the following sections provide a quick guide on what to do, depending on your computer model.

iMac

The iMac is an easy setup. Apple once ran an ad showing a 7-year-old putting an earlier model together. If anything, the task has become easier. I don't recommend letting a 7-year-old lift an iMac out of its box, however, particularly if you bought one of the bigger screens. The largest weighs almost 25 pounds (11 kg), and you really don't want anyone to drop it. Don't be ashamed to ask for help.

Your iMac comes with a keyboard and mouse. Plug them into the USB ports located on the back, and plug the power cord into the power socket on the back of the iMac. Plug its other end into an AC wall outlet or power strip. If your power strip has a switch, make sure that it's set to On. You're done.

MacBook and MacBook Pro

Apple's laptops require very little setup. Plug the power adapter into an AC outlet or power strip. At the other end of the power adapter, you'll find the MagSafe power connector. Remove its little plastic protective cover and then just hold it horizontally and bring it near the power receptacle, located on the left side of your laptop, near the display hinge. When it's close, it snaps together as though it were magnetic — because it is. It doesn't matter which side of the MagSafe connector is up; it works properly either way. The MagSafe connector has a tiny light, and when you first apply power to your new laptop, the light should show green and then promptly switch to orange, indicating that it's charging the batteries. When the battery is fully charged, the light turns green again.

A good friend of mine trashed a nice Apple PowerBook, the predecessor of the MacBook Pro, by tripping over the power cord, sending her laptop crashing to the floor. It never booted up again. The MagSafe connector is designed to prevent such tragedies by popping out if tugged, without imparting a big enough jerk to pull the laptop off a work surface. Still, pulling on the cord is not the best way to unplug the MagSafe connector from your machine. Apple recommends that you grasp the connector itself and pull, but that sucker sticks on tight. The easy way to get it off is to gently lift it from the bottom — it tilts up pretty easily — and then pull it out.

While you are waiting for me to tell you to press the On button, take a moment to examine the power adapter. After you take off all the clear plastic wrapping, you should see two little tabs on either side of the power cord that swing out to form a cradle on which you can wind up the power cord. Also, at least in North America, there are two power blades that swing out and plug directly into a power outlet. They are mounted in a small module that Apple calls a *duck's head,* which you can pull free and replace with the longer power cord that comes with the Mac (see Figure 4-1). The U.S. power cord has a grounding plug, so if you are working in a place with older wiring, the duck's head may be more convenient, because it fits into just about any outlet.

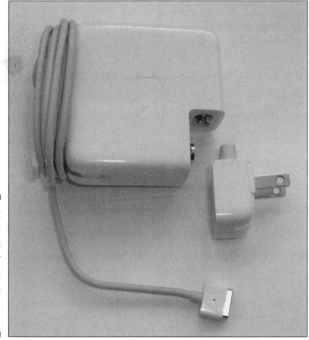

Figure 4-1:
The MacBook power supply with "duck's head" detached.

Mac mini, Mac Pro, and Xserve

The top and bottom of the Mac line are both a little more complicated to set up because neither has a built-in display; you have to supply your own and hook it up to the computer. That brings up the ugly question of adapters.

Both the Mac mini and the Mac Pro have DVI video output connectors and come with a DVI-to-VGA adapter. The Xserve comes with a mini-DVI–to–VGA adapter. If you are hooking up to a high-definition TV (HDTV), you probably need a DVI-to-HDMI cable. Apple sells one, but you might use Google to search for a less pricey model. DVI and HDMI cover most of the displays on the market, but you may have something different; check your display's service manual.

The Mac Pro is heavy — 42 pounds (19 kg) — but it has conveniently placed carrying handles on the top that make it easier to lug about. The Xserve is designed to fit into a standard 19-inch electronics rack. It weighs up to 38 pounds (17 kg), depending on options, and comes with the necessary mounting hardware, but consider getting a technician to help you install it.

Network

If your PC is connected to the Internet using a WiFi wireless network, you're all set. If you have a wired Ethernet network at home, plug your Mac into it. You likely have such a network but don't know it. If you have high-speed Internet (via cable TV, DSL, or satellite) and your PC is connected by a wire with a plug that looks like a telephone plug but is fatter, that's what you have. You need an Ethernet router or switch to share this connection. If you forgot to buy one, don't worry. You can unplug the connection from your PC and plug it into your Mac for now and pick up a router the next time you're near a computer store, or you can order one online.

KVM

A KVM box lets you share a keyboard, video monitor, mouse, and speakers between your Mac and your PC, as shown in Figure 4-2. Hooking up the box involves a lot of wires, but the idea is simple enough. With luck, you got a USB KVM. It should say so on the package. If it doesn't, or if it says PS/2, return it and get a USB unit.

You plug your monitor, keyboard, mouse, and speakers into the KVM box; normally, the monitor and speakers each have only one possible connection. You should find two USB jacks, one for the keyboard and one for the mouse, but it shouldn't matter which goes where. You also have two sets of cables — more if you bought a multiport KVM. One end of each cable goes to the KVM box; the other end of each cable has a set of plugs. The plugs on one cable go to your PC; the other cable's plugs connect to your Mac. Plug the speaker cables into the speaker outputs of each computer, and plug the USB plug — you should see only one per cable — into an available USB socket. Finally, you have a VGA video plug to contend with. The one on the PC cable should find a matching jack on the PC. For the Mac cable, you need a DVI-to-VGA adapter or a mini-DVI–to–VGA adapter (see Chapter 3).

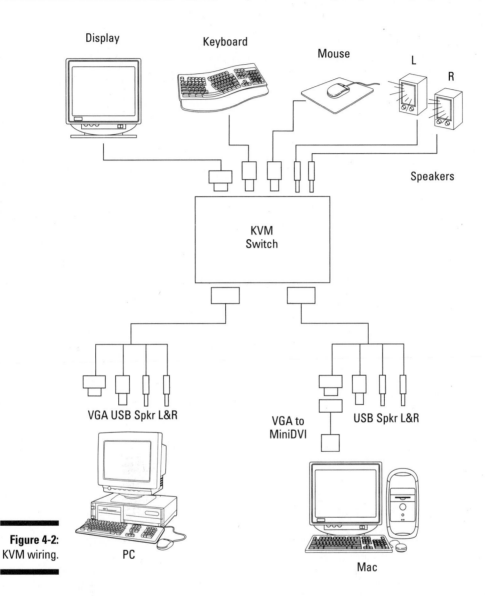

Figure 4-2:
KVM wiring.

After you have everything set up, switching between the Mac and PC should be easy. Check the manual that came with your KVM box for the details on which method it uses to control the switching.

Finding the On switch and turning it off

The power switch on most Macs is a round, white, or silver button marked with the *discus interruptus,* a circle broken at the top with a short, vertical line. This is actually the international symbol for a *soft power switch,* one that tells the equipment to go on or off but doesn't actually control the power directly.

As with a Windows computer, you should always tell your Mac to turn itself off when possible, lest you lose data or damage the operating system. The Shut Down command is located on the Apple menu (the one headed by the Apple logo). After you choose Shut Down, you're asked whether you really want to shut down your computer. If you choose Restart, you get a similar message.

OS X is a very stable operating system, but if it doesn't seem to be doing anything after you tell it to shut down, you can try a couple of things. First, be patient; some programs, particularly Apple's Safari Web browser, can take a while to quit. Also, look at your screen to see whether any application is asking whether you want to save a file, for example.

If all else fails, you have two last-resort options: You can hold down the power button for about six seconds, and if that doesn't work after a couple of tries, remove the power cord or, on a laptop, remove the battery. Restore power and press the power button, and you should be back in business.

Configuring Your New Mac

You're almost ready to turn on your Mac. But before you do, I recommend that you gather some information so you have it ready during the initial setup.

Collecting information you need

After you get your Mac plugged in and turned on, your Mac starts asking you a bunch of questions. Things go more smoothly if you have collected the answers ahead of time, so the following sections discuss the information you need. With a few exceptions, you can change the information later, but you might as well get it right the first time, if you can. Make notes of your choices in the margin of this book (assuming you're not still browsing in the bookstore).

Name

This sounds straightforward enough. But give some thought as to how you want your name presented: Mary Smith, Mary Ann Smith, M. Smith, M. A. Smith. If you are setting up the computer for a youngster, you might not want to include his or her last name, but don't use a too-cute nickname the child will outgrow in a couple of years. If the family is sharing the computer, remember that you can easily set up individual accounts for each member. The first account should be the person who is going to be in charge (the *administrator*) of the computer, though this can be changed later and you can have more than one administrator.

Short name

This entry is the name of your *home directory,* and it can't be easily changed. Your Mac proposes the full name you gave, all in lowercase letters and with no spaces. I suggest you pick something shorter, such as `msmith` or `mas`.

Password

This is the password you use to log on to your Mac. You are asked for it at other times, too, such as when you install new software or change security settings. You could use the password you've used for everything else in your life, but I suggest you pick something stronger. The security of your computer begins with a well-chosen password. When you get to the screen that asks for the password, look for a little key icon next to the password entry box. Click it, and OS X suggests a password. Pick one of its suggestions, write the password down, and keep it in a safe place. I explain why and give some tips on other easy ways to make up a password and not forget it in Chapter 10.

WiFi network name and password

If you already have a WiFi network, your Mac will probably pick up yours, along with a couple of others if you live in a built-up area. It helps to know your network's name. If you have WEP or WPA security enabled, you need your WiFi password, passphrase, or key. If you have long forgotten those, see Chapter 9 for information on how to reset your access point and set up new security.

If you are setting up a new WiFi network, look over Chapter 9 to decide whether you need to enable security. If so, see Chapter 10 for how to generate a strong passphrase to protect your network. Might as well have that ready before you begin.

Apple ID

If you already have an iTunes account, you have an Apple ID and password that lets you sign in to the iTunes Store to buy music and play music you've purchased. Take a moment to look them up and make a note of them.

Internet account information

You'll want to have the following information handy:

- ✔ Your Internet service provider
- ✔ Service type: Cable, DSL, Satellite, Dialup, Other

- ✔ Account name
- ✔ Password
- ✔ The ISP's customer service number
- ✔ If dialup, the number your computer dials

E-mail service information

If you check your mail online using your browser — say, if you have an account with Yahoo! or Gmail — you needn't do anything. Otherwise, check the Web site of your e-mail service to see whether it has any special instructions for Mac users. Keep handy the following info for every e-mail service you plan to use:

- ✔ Provider name
- ✔ Customer service number
- ✔ E-mail address
- ✔ E-mail password
- ✔ Type of account: POP (the most common), IMAP, or .Mac
- ✔ Mail server address
- ✔ SMTP server address

Getting through the Startup Wizard

Finally, it's time to press that power button. As your Mac powers on, you'll hear a soft *boing* that's long been part of the new Mac experience. Next, follow these steps:

1. **When the Select Main Language screen appears, choose the language you prefer.**

   You see the message Starting Mac OS and then a "Welcome" video. You are then asked to select the country or region you are in. If you chose English as your main language, the Mac presents English-speaking countries. (If you are somewhere else, select the Show All check box to view the compete list, including Heard & McDonald Island and the Holy See.)

   Either way, make your choice and click the Continue button.

2. **Answer the wizard's question, "Do You Already Own a Mac?"**

   You are asked this question because you can transfer your info from another Mac by using a FireWire port. If you're upgrading from another Mac, see Chapter 16. Otherwise, click the Do Not Transfer My Information button and then click the Continue button.

3. **Select your keyboard layout.**

   Select U.S. or Canada (you can add other keyboard versions later), and then click the Continue button.

4. **Select a wireless service.**

   Things start to get exciting now. If you have WiFi at your location and you aren't using exotic security tricks to make your network invisible, your WiFi base station should show up on the screen, along with any others your Mac has found.

   If you have security enabled, you need to know the WEP or WPA password or key to connect. If all goes well, at this point you are now online. If you're not, don't worry; just move on for now. I go over networking your Mac in more detail in Chapter 9.

5. **Enter your Apple ID and its password if you have an iTunes (or a .Mac) account. Click the Continue button.**

   You can skip this step and enter this info later using iTunes or the .Mac pane in system preferences.

6. **Supply the requested registration information, and then click the Continue button.**

7. **Continue with some optional questions from the wizard. (You can decide whether Apple is being too nosy.)**

   The questions include where you will use the computer and what "best describes what you do."

   Deselect the Stay in Touch check box if you don't want e-mail announcements. Then, click the Continue button.

8. **In the Set Up This Account screen of the wizard, verify the account name and enter your password.**

   Make sure that the account name is the one you want. This is one thing you can't easily change later; you have to rebuild the whole computer. Enter the password you prepared (twice). If you didn't have a password ready, click the key icon next to the password entry field, and Password Assistant suggests some passwords. Pick one and write it down on a slip of paper that you will keep in a safe place. (See Chapter 10 for more on how Password Assistant works.) Finally, click the Continue button.

9. **Select a picture, if you want, for this account.**

   If you have a Mac with a built-in camera — iMacs, MacBooks, and MacBook Pros have one — the Startup Wizard now offers to take your picture to use as an icon for this account. You can retake the photo if you don't like the results, and you can change it later by choosing System Preferences⇨Accounts. Alternatively, you can choose from a picture library.

Maintaining parental control

I'm not a big fan of computers for small children. The kids will be spending too much of their lives in front of video screens as it is. But if you are getting a computer for your kids, make sure that you understand how to set limits. OS X has some great features to help you enforce them. Be sure to take a careful look at Chapter 14 before setting up your computer. That chapter has suggestions about keeping your kids safe in cyberspace.

10. **Select a time zone, click the Continue button, and then set your date and time, if necessary.**

    Macs come set to Pacific Standard Time (PST) and Cupertino-USA, Apple's hometown. Click the map or select the closest city from the list shown. After your time zone is set, the date and time displayed are likely to be close to correct. If you are connected to the Internet, your Mac will set itself using a time server traceable to the U.S. Government's atomic clock.

Are we there yet?

If all went according to plan, you should see an OS X desktop waiting for you to work or play with. And if you have a modern Internet hookup, you should be online as well. I give you an introduction to OS X in the next chapter. Later chapters tell you more about getting online, setting up e-mail, moving your files over, increasing your security level, and solving any problems you may encounter. You also find out more about the various neat things you can do with your Mac. Chapter 20 suggests some creative (and some mundane) things you can do with your old PC.

Dive on in!

Chapter 5

Mac OS X for Windows Users

. . . .

. . . .

As a PC user, you are already familiar with an operating system called Windows. It is a complex piece of software developed by Microsoft, and some version of it comes with most personal computers that are sold today, with one big exception. Apple doesn't sell its Macs with Windows software. Instead, Apple equips its Macintosh computers with Apple's own operating system, called Mac OS X. Apple pronounces it *Oh Ess Ten,* as in the Roman numeral ten. (Apple's previous operating system was OS 9.) Apple's computers are stylish and well made, but OS X is the main reason to get a Mac. (You can have Windows on your Mac in addition to OS X, but you have to buy it and install it yourself or find a vendor who will install it for you.)

Apple and Microsoft are locked in a battle over which company can produce an operating system that offers a better experience for the user. Both companies are forced to keep improving their offerings. Most Mac users believe that Apple keeps coming out ahead.

PC and Mac: We Have a Lot in Common

Microsoft adopted many of the features of Mac OS when it created Windows, so you will find much that is familiar when you try OS X. The fundamental idea is pretty much the same. The operating system stores data as files that have names; organizes files in a hierarchy of folders; runs applications; talks to external devices such as printers, scanners, music players, and cameras; and connects to other computers via local-area networks and the Internet.

You interact with the computer using a graphical user interface (GUI) that presents a simulated desktop on the screen, with icons you can move around and click. Information appears in rectangular windows, and you can select from pull-down menus. You use a pointing device, such as a mouse or track-pad, to move a cursor around the screen. The cursor is normally an arrow, but it sometimes changes its shape to reflect what is going on.

Over the years, the computer industry has adopted numerous standards to ensure that different products can work well together. Nowadays, Apple is at the forefront of this process, adopting most standards and frequently contributing some new ones that other companies adopt. Here is a quick rundown of the alphabet soup of standards that Mac OS X shares with Windows and other operating systems:

- **Input/output:** USB, FireWire/IEEE-1394, Bluetooth, TOSlink audio, and PCIe (Pro and Xserve)

- **Networking:** Ethernet, TCP/IP, WiFi, HTTP, S/MIME, POP mail, LDAP, RSS, and Bonjour

- **File systems:** Apple's HFS+, Microsoft FAT, Microsoft NTFS (read-only), NFS, ISO 9660 CDs, UDF 1.5 DVDs, and 3.5-inch HD floppy (with external drive)

- **Data formats:** ASCII, Unicode, UTF-8, MP3, PDF, JPEG, MPEG, TIFF, and H.294

- **Software standards:** UNIX 03, LP64 64-bit, OpenGL graphics, BSD, POSIX, X11, CarDAV calendaring, SOAP, DHCP, BootP, PPPoE, EFI, x86, Java, and Ruby on Rails

- **Security:** AES, HTTPS, RADIUS, SSL/TLS, SSH, WEP, WPA, and WPA2

This isn't a complete list, and I don't expect you to know what all these geeky acronyms mean. I explain the more important ones in Chapter 3 and other ones as I go, and you can check the glossary for the rest. But I'm about to dive into all the differences, and I want to emphasize how much overlap exists between the two operating systems. After you get used to a few new concepts and some different terminology, you'll feel right at home using OS X.

Adjusting to the Differences

You do, of course, encounter differences between Windows and Mac OS X. Some are merely a matter of terminology. Others just take getting used to, and a few you might find annoying. For most of those annoying issues, I point out ways to accomplish what you want to do in a reasonably familiar way.

Comparing Windows-speak with Mac-speak

Computers seem to run on jargon. Many of the buzzwords used on Macs are exactly the same as those used in Windows: files, users, log on, log out, open, close, shut down, help, and most networking and Internet terms. Terms used to describe the graphical interface are mostly the same, too: menu, check box, dialog box, radio button, dragging, clicking, and double-clicking. Table 5-1 provides the equivalent terms or types of programs for each platform.

Table 5-1	Windows Terms versus Mac Terms
Windows	*Mac OS X*
Control Panel	System Preferences
Ctrl+Alt+Delete	Option+⌘+Esc
Exit (Alt+FX)	Quit (⌘+Q)
Internet Explorer	Safari
My Computer	Finder
My Documents	Documents folder
My Music	Music folder
My Pictures	Pictures folder
Notepad	TextEdit
Outlook Express	Mail
Recycle Bin	Trash Can
Settings	Preferences
Shortcut icon	Alias
Taskbar	Dock
Hourglass cursor (busy signal)	Spinning beach ball (busy signal)
Windows Explorer	Finder window
Windows Update	Software Update

Some things, thankfully, have no equivalent in the Mac world. No activation is required to use OS X; you can skip registration if you like. You find no Windows Genuine Advantage checking up on you, and no animated paper clip offering inane help (unless you are using Microsoft Office). And you won't run into DLL files or any equivalent of the Windows Registry, both notorious sources of problems.

Seeing the big picture: The desktop and menus

After you've answered all the startup wizard's questions, you see the Mac desktop, as shown in Figure 5-1.

The basic idea is the same as the Windows desktop. Most of the screen is filled with a pattern or image that's like a tablecloth on which you see various icons that represent files, storage media, and applications. You also find an arrow cursor that you can move around using the mouse or trackpad. You can move icons around by placing the arrow cursor over them, clicking the mouse or trackpad button, and holding down the button as you move the cursor.

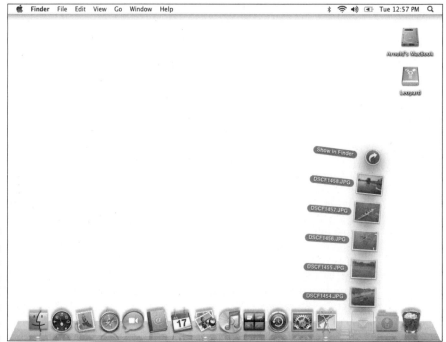

Figure 5-1:
The
Macintosh
OS X
desktop
screen.

The big differences between the Mac and PC desktops are at the top and bottom. All OS X menus appear at the top of the screen, and each application has a different menu. The menu shown is for the application whose window is in front — that application is said to *have focus* or to be the *current application*. The first menu on the left is headed by an Apple logo (🍎) and is called the Apple menu, naturally. It has system-related stuff. The next menu over is headed by the name of the current application (Finder, in Figure 5-1). That menu is where you find entries for changing preferences and quitting the application. Continuing from the left, you typically see File and Edit menus that work much like the corresponding Windows menus. The Help menu is always on the right.

At the bottom of the screen, you see a bunch of largish icons (you can make them smaller, as explained later in this chapter). This area is called the *Dock* and roughly corresponds to the Windows taskbar. Each icon on the Dock represents an application or folder; you click an icon once to start or open it. If you don't know what an icon represents, move your cursor over it and a label appears. Open applications have a little black triangle underneath their corresponding icon on the Dock. You add applications and folders to the Dock by dragging them there. Click on a folder or *stack* on the Dock and its contents spring out in a graceful arc as shown in Figure 5-1, or as a grid, if there are too many items. I say more about menus and the Dock in the following sections.

Pointing the way — the mouse and trackpad

One of the great divides between Apple and Microsoft was over whether computer mice should have one or two buttons. You may think it bizarre that adults would fret about such a thing, but the debate invoked great passions. Apple touted the simplicity of having a single button, avoiding the need to explain what each button does. Microsoft eventually found a good use for the second button — the one on the right. It displays menus of possible actions appropriate to the window in which the right-click occurred. Later, scroll wheels appeared, allowing users to move up and down in a window using intuitive finger action. Apple added similar functions to its operating system and eventually introduced its own multibutton mouse, which it named Mighty Mouse.

Mighty Mouse comes with the iMac and Mac Pro. You can order a wireless Bluetooth version as an option. At first glance, this mouse looks like a single-button mouse with a tiny ball toward the front. The ball acts like a scroll wheel, but it can command horizontal as well as vertical scrolling. The top of the Mighty Mouse is a single shell. To perform a right-click, you press only on the right half of the shell. Regular (left-) clicks, the most common action, can be on the left or both sides simultaneously. The scroll ball can also be pressed down to signal a third type of click, and each side of the Mighty Mouse has a button that you squeeze to represent a fourth click. So Apple has gone from one button to four, but in a way that still looks like one.

If your Mac came with a Mighty Mouse, by all means give it a try — I think it's pretty slick. But if yours didn't or if you find the Mighty Mouse too confusing, I suggest that you stick with a standard, two-button, USB, scroll-wheel mouse. If you already have one you like, great. If not, go buy one. Wired (as opposed to wireless) optical mice are inexpensive, and almost any will do fine. Just plug it in to a free USB port or your USB hub. You don't even have to turn off the computer. Apple keyboards have extra built-in USB ports (one on the left and one on the right) for the mouse. No setup is necessary. Apple software uses the left button for primary clicks, the scroll wheel to scroll up and down, and the right button to bring up context-sensitive menus, just as Windows does. If you're a left-handed user, you probably will want to switch the buttons by using the Keyboard & Mouse pane in System Preferences.

Apple's laptops, the MacBook and MacBook Pro, also feature a single button located below the trackpad. PC laptops generally have two buttons. You can signal a right-click on a Mac laptop by holding down the Control key and clicking the one trackpad button. Another way is available, however. Apple's trackpad is clever enough to notice when you have two fingers resting on it instead of just one. Moving two fingers up and down on the trackpad makes it work like a scroll wheel. You can also tell your laptop to interpret a click as a right-click when you have two fingers resting on the trackpad. To do so, choose System Preferences from the Apple menu (in the upper-left of your screen) and then choose Keyboard & Mouse. Select the Place Two Fingers on Trackpad and Click Button for Secondary Click check box and then close the window. Note that Apple can't even say the words *right-click,* but that's what I call it whenever I want you to make it happen. Of course, you can use your two-button USB mouse with your laptop, too. Just plug it in.

The key to keyboards

Apple's keyboard layouts look very much like standard Windows keyboards. The biggest difference is in the two keys on either side of the spacebar. On a PC, the keys closest to the spacebar are labeled Alt; the next ones over sport a Windows logo. On a Mac, the keys closest to the spacebar have an icon (⌘) that looks like a four-bladed propeller or electric fan. The Mac world calls them the Command keys; they both have the same function. (You can also see an Apple logo, , on the Command keys for reasons that go back to the Apple II days.) The next one over is the Option key (⌥).

The Command key (⌘) is used in almost all keyboard shortcuts. It's one of the most important things to know about the Mac.

Another key that may not be familiar to PC users is at the upper-right on Apple keyboards. It's the eject button (⏏) for the optical drive (that reads and writes CDs and DVDs). You see the same symbol on the eject button on home audio devices. Continuing to the left on stand-alone keyboards, you find a key with a speaker symbol; this key turns the system sound on and off. It's a mute button, in effect. It is followed by two keys that raise and lower the volume.

The keyboards built into Apple laptops and Apple's wireless keyboard have fewer keys than Apple's wired stand-alone keyboards. No separate numeric keypad is available. You can use a group of keys on the right side as a keypad by activating the *Num Lock* function (press Control+F6). On many Mac keyboards, the sound-control keys, screen-brightness, and other controls are on the function keys.

Backspace versus Del versus Delete

Fasten your seat belts for this one. The large key at the right end of the numeral row on PC keyboards is labeled Backspace. Of course, it doesn't really back space; the left-arrow key does that. Instead, the Backspace key deletes the character to the left of the insertion point, which is the blinking vertical line that tells you where in a block of text you are editing. Long ago, Apple decided to label this key Delete, because that is what it really does. The problem is that PC keyboards have another, regular-sized Delete key in the group above, or sometimes next to, the arrow keys. This Delete key deletes the character to the *right* of the insertion point. Back when Apple was less concerned about playing nice with PCs, it omitted this key. Later, when Apple switched to connecting by USB for its stand-alone keyboards, the second delete key came back, labeled del or delete. It also has a standard delete symbol on it which looks like a boxy arrow pointing right with an x in it. The big Delete key doesn't have a symbol on it, though one exists, and it has the same boxy arrow pointing *left*. The Apple laptops don't have a second delete key, but you get the right delete function by holding down the function key (fn) when you press the Delete button.

Keyboard shortcuts using the Command key versus the Ctrl key

Keyboard shortcuts are little incantations combining a couple of key presses that let you carry out a task without having to plow through the menus. PCs have two kinds of keyboard shortcuts. For some, you hold down the Ctrl key and a letter key; for others, you press the Alt key and type one letter from each menu item name — often, but not always, the first letter. Mac keyboard shortcuts are like the first type, but you use the Command key (⌘) instead of the Ctrl key. Following are examples of Mac keyboard shortcuts:

Keyboard Shortcut	Action
⌘+C	Copy
⌘+X	Cut
⌘+V	Paste
⌘+A	Select All
⌘+F	Find
⌘+G	Find Again
⌘+S	Save
⌘+Z	Undo

Replacing the Ctrl key press with the Command key (⌘) also applies to most Ctrl key shortcuts in programs such as Microsoft Office.

The letters in keyboard shortcut combinations are always shown capitalized in this book and on-screen, but the Mac recognizes the lowercase versions as well. Thus you can type either ⌘+Q or ⌘+q to quit (exit) the program.

Although the Mac OS X menu layout appears to be intuitive and easy to follow, it's fair to say that Apple gets a little carried away with shortcuts. There are dozens of them. Don't try to remember them all. The most important shortcuts are the ones already mentioned, many of which you probably already know from Windows. Pick up others as you need them, and take advantage of the Cheat Sheet in the front of this book.

OS X displays the available shortcut for each menu item right in the drop-down menu itself. Some combinations use different and even multiple control keys. Apple uses other symbols in addition to the ⌘ symbol and symbol to indicate these keys. Here is a quick guide (also see the Cheat Sheet):

- ✔ **Option:** This key (⌥) often modifies a shortcut or menu item by telling it to do more. So, for example, ⌘+W closes the front window. ⌥+⌘+W closes *all* windows for the front application. Shortcuts can be complex. The shortcut in TextEdit for Edit⇨Paste and Match Style is ⌥+Shift+⌘+V.

- ✔ **Control:** This key's symbol (∧) looks like a hat. The key is pressed in combination with a mouse click to mean right-click.

- ✔ **Shift:** Either the right or left Shift key (⇧) may be used, but caps lock has no effect on shortcuts that include a Shift key.

- ✔ **Escape:** This key's symbol (⎋) looks a lot like the power button icon, but it's different. The line is at an angle and has a little arrow pointing out. Escape is a shortcut for Cancel in dialog boxes.

Keep it simple

You have oodles of ways to customize Mac OS X using system and application preferences, and you can download software that gives you even more possibilities. I recommend restraint. Don't customize OS X more than necessary, particularly when you are first getting used to working with it. The closer your Mac software is to its out-of-the-box configuration, the easier it is to get help when you have a problem, whether it's from this book, from Web sites, or from Apple customer service.

Many other Mac keyboard shortcuts exist. Open the Apple menu and choose System Preferences⇨Keyboard & Mouse and then choose Keyboard Shortcuts to see a list. The Keyboard & Mouse pane has many other options for customizing your input experience. Explore, but don't get carried away.

If you have difficulty holding down combinations of keys, you can activate the sticky keys feature in the System Preferences⇨Universal Access pane. See Chapter 14 for other accessibility tips for people who have difficulty using computers.

Keying in special characters and other languages

Macs let you input text in a wide variety of languages. On the menu bar at the top right, you should see a little national flag, corresponding to the language of the keyboard you selected during the startup process — for example, stars and stripes appear for the U.S. keyboard. If you click this flag, a menu of options appears. Select Show Character Palette. You can browse through all the characters available on OS X — there are thousands of them. Click the small triangles next to Character Info and Font Variation to discover the name of each character and which fonts contain it.

You can add keyboard layouts for other languages from the Apple menu by choosing System Preferences⇨International and then choosing Input Menu. Each language you check shows up as a menu option under the flag icon on the menu bar.

Select Show Keyboard Viewer from the flag menu, and a small keyboard corresponding to the language you chose appears. You can enter characters with it by clicking its buttons.

Mac windows versus Windows windows

This section refers to windows spelled with a lowercase *w* — those rectangular boxes on your computer's screen where all the action happens. Again, the basic idea in OS X is similar to what you are used to in Microsoft's operating system. You see a title bar at the top of each window, with colored buttons that you can click. From left to right, *red* closes the window, *orange* minimizes it — the window slurps down to the Dock — and *green* resizes it to make better use of the screen. You move a window by clicking the title bar and dragging with the mouse. A scroll bar and slider appear on the right side. You can also adjust the window size by dragging a corner — only the lower-right corner on a Mac, but any corner in Windows.

May I See the Menu, Please?

As already mentioned, the menu bar in OS X is at the top of the screen, not in each window. The menu you see changes depending on which application's window is at the front. You change which application window is in front either by clicking a window that is behind the one in front or by clicking the application's icon on the Dock.

You can see a summary of all the applications that are open by holding down the Command key (⌘) and pressing the Tab key. As shown in Figure 5-2, you see a translucent bar with icons for each running application. Release the Command key, and the selected application comes to the front. Keep holding the Command key down and press the Tab key repeatedly to cycle through all the applications. This feature is similar to that performed by pressing Alt+Tab in Windows. If you hold down the Command key and press the accent-tilde key (`~) — it's just above the Tab key — OS X cycles through the open windows of the front application.

Figure 5-2:
The ⌘+Tab
display.

Getting to know the Apple menu

The leftmost menu is always the Apple menu, and it always offers the same set of choices, regardless of which applications are in use. Those choices are as follows:

> ✔ **About This Mac:** Provides a quick summary of your computer's configuration, including memory, processor, and operating system release. Choose More Info for an excruciatingly complete rundown of everything in, on, or attached to your computer, including its serial number.

✔ **Software Update:** Gets you the latest versions of the software that came with your Mac. Your Mac will check for updates every week automatically unless you change the setting, labeled, unsurprisingly, Software Update, in the System Preferences pane.

✔ **Mac OS X Software:** Takes you to Apple's Web site, where you can download neat stuff — some free, some not.

✔ **System Preferences:** The equivalent of Control Panel in Windows. It's where you can see and change the numerous settings associated with OS X system software. Figure 5-3 shows the main window that you see when you choose Systems Preferences, with all the icons that you click to complete specific settings chores.

Figure 5-3:
The main System Preferences window.

✔ **Dock:** Lets you control the size, location, and behavior of the Dock. Depending on your choices, the Dock can be your best friend or be truly annoying. The option I like best is Turn Hiding On, which moves the Dock off the screen until you steer you cursor all the way to the bottom edge, at which time the Dock pops up, ready to do your bidding. Move your cursor away from the bottom of the screen, and the Dock hides itself again.

✔ **Recent Items:** Offers a quick way to get back to the application, document, or server that you were just using. You can tell OS X how far back the Recent Items lists should go in the Appearance pane under System Preferences. The default is ten items.

✔ **Force Quit:** Lets you kill any application that is not responding to commands (see Figure 5-4). Yes, Mac applications freeze just as Windows applications do. Commit to memory the Force Quit keyboard shortcut: Option+⌘+Esc. You may need it if you can't get to the menu for some reason. It's the Mac equivalent of the Windows "three-finger salute": Ctrl+Alt+Delete.

Figure 5-4:
The Force
Quit
window.

> ✔ **Sleep, Restart, Shut Down, and Log Out:** These commands perform the same tasks as they do in Windows. Apple provides only one sleep option; there's no separate hibernate nonsense. You control the sleep settings in the Energy Saver pane of System Preferences.

Application menu

The menu to the right of the Apple menu has the same name as whichever application is in front, and looking at the menu is the easiest way to find out just which application is active, if more than one is open. As with the Apple menu, this menu's contents are essentially the same from application to application. The top item brings up the About screen for the application, which gives the application's version number, copyright notice, and anything else the application's developers want to tell you.

Other menu choices to expect are as follows:

> ✔ **Preferences:** Choose this menu item to change the application's settings. It's one of the most important menu items to know about for PC-to-Mac switchers.
>
> ✔ **Hide and Hide Others:** These items (and their keyboard shortcuts) are handy to keep in mind when your screen gets cluttered. Keep pressing ⌘+H until the application you want is in front; press Option+⌘+H to hide the rest.
>
> ✔ **Show All:** Brings all windows for this application ahead of any other applications' windows that you may have open.
>
> ✔ **Quit (and its shortcut, ⌘+Q):** Tells the program to terminate; it's equivalent to Exit in Windows.

The Finder's application menu is where you empty the Trash.

File and Edit menus

For most applications, the next two menus from the left are the File and Edit menus. These closely resemble their Windows counterparts. One big difference is that the Quit command is not on the File menu; instead, it's on the application menu, to the left. This is one of the more annoying differences between Windows and OS X. Just remember the ⌘+Q shortcut and avoid the aggravation. Also, Preferences, the OS X equivalent of Windows' Settings, isn't on the Edit menu. It's on the application menu.

When you save a new document for the first time or choose Open or Save As from the File menu, you see a dialog box much as you would see in Windows XP when doing the same things. Figure 5-5 shows many of the navigation features of this window, including the sidebar with your favorite destinations and the option to select between list and column view.

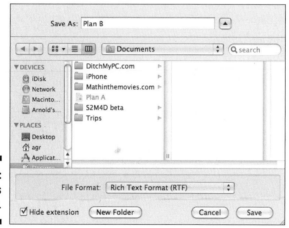

Figure 5-5:
The Save As
dialog box.

If you see the shortened version of the Save As dialog box (shown in Figure 5-6) rather than the full version (shown in Figure 5-5), click the little triangle button to the right of the filename text field toward the top of the dialog box to bring back the full dialog box.

Figure 5-6:
The stunted
Save As
dialog box.
Note the
down
triangle.

Help and Window menus

The Help menu is located to the right of the menus associated with the application, just as in Windows. To the Help menu's left, you usually find a Window menu, similar to that found in many Microsoft Windows applications. The Window menu lists which windows the application has open and lets you bring the one you want to the front.

Applications typically have several other menus between the Edit and Window menus; these are usually organized in ways that should be familiar to Windows users.

Filing Away in OS X

Files in OS X are similar to files in Windows or any other operating system, with one exception that you probably don't need to know about. So skip the next paragraph unless you're curious.

In most operating systems, a file is just a bucket of bits — 1s and 0s that programs can interpret as a text document, photograph, music, or whatever. The operating system is responsible for storing the file accurately and copying or deleting it if asked to, but that's it. Macs may add something called the *resource fork* to this notion of what a file is supposed to be. (*Fork* here is used in the sense of *fork in the road,* not *fork in the steak.*) The resource fork contains additional information about what is in the file that the application can use. The good news is that you probably don't have to worry about this. They're less common in newer apps, and OS X handles resource forks automatically. The files you bring over from Windows don't have resource forks, anyway.

File types

Many of the file types you are used to on the PC are supported directly by OS X: documents in Microsoft Word format, photographs in JPEG format, and music MP3s, for example. Others require additional software. Still others, particularly music files purchased under one of Microsoft's proprietary formats, such as for the Zune music player, may not be usable, except, of course, when you're running Windows on your Mac. I give you the gory details about moving files from your PC to your Mac in Chapter 6.

Filenames

Filenames in Mac OS X can be up to 255 characters long, and you can use any characters you like except the colon (:). Windows doesn't allow any of the following special characters in filenames:

> : \ / | * ? " < >

If you are planning to move files back and forth between your PC and Mac, it's a good idea to follow the more restrictive Windows naming rules so that filenames don't get mangled.

Extensions

In the Windows world, filenames have extensions — a period (.) and a few cryptic letters that are added to the end of a filename, for example, `Chapter5.doc`. The file extension tells the operating system what type of file it is so that the OS knows which program should open it. OS X uses file extensions in the same way, but it also has a separate way to know the file type and creator, using special four-letter codes for each that are stored with the file's directory entry.

Pathnames

A file is stored in a folder, which may be in another folder, which may be in another folder, and so on. Operating systems keep track of all that hierarchy using a pathname. The *pathname* lists all the folders you have to visit in turn to find your file. The names are separated by a special character. In Windows, this character is the backslash (\). For Macs — and in UNIX, in Linux, and on the Internet — the forward slash (/), sometimes called the front slash, is used. You can make nice patterns stringing them together, like so: \/\/\/\/\/\/\/\/\/\/ — but this has nothing to do with what I'm talking about.

Disks and volumes

Disk drives appear on the desktop just as files do, but with distinctive icons (see Figure 5-7). The main hard drive icon looks like the real hard drive in your computer. Unfortunately, most people have never taken a computer apart and don't have a clue what a hard drive looks like. External hard drive icons resemble an external drive, with either a FireWire or USB logo on it, indicating the manner of connection. Optical disc icons look like, well, optical discs. Flash drives look like an old external floppy drive, as do virtual volumes that appear when you open a disk image file (which has a .dmg extension).

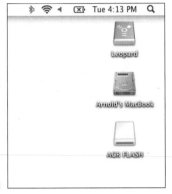

Figure 5-7:
An OS X
desktop
displaying
several disk
volumes.

The Mac way to eject or dismount one of these disk volumes is to drag the volume to the Trash. This peculiar idiom goes back to the earliest Macs. You are not deleting any information when you do this, and the Trash Can changes to an Eject icon when you are dragging a disk or volume, to emphasize that nothing is being trashed. If dragging disks to the Trash seems too weird — you've become a true Mac person when it makes sense — right-click the disk or volume icon and select Eject from the menu that appears. All ejectable volumes also appear in Finder window sidebars and have eject symbols next to them that you can click.

Aliases

Maybe you've used *shortcuts* in Windows XP. They are icons that point to some other file, program, or disk drive. Macs have a similar feature called an *alias,* which is very handy. You can create an alias by clicking the name or icon of the file, program, or disk volume you want to alias and then choosing Make Alias from the Finder's File menu. It's worth remembering the keyboard incantation for making aliases: ⌘+L. Just as in Windows, the alias icon appears with a little arrow at its lower left, and you can move the alias anywhere you want. You can even move it to the Trash if you no longer need it; the original file won't go away. Mac OS X has one big improvement over this Windows feature, however. In Windows, if you move the original file to another folder or change its name, Windows gets unhappy and doesn't know where to find the file anymore. OS X keeps track of where the file went and just does the right thing. Of course, if you delete the original file, there's not much OS X can do.

Watch out for aliases when you want to copy files to another medium, such as an external hard drive, CD-R, or flash drive. If you drag an alias, only the alias gets copied, not the file. To copy the file or folder the alias points to, click the alias and choose File⇨Show Original, or just type ⌘+R.

The Finder Is Your Friend

When you first start your computer, you find yourself in a special program
that Apple calls the Finder. The Finder is somewhat like Windows Explorer,
but it is an even more basic tool on the Mac than in Windows Explorer. You
use it all the time.

You can get to the Finder by clicking anywhere on the desktop or selecting
its icon from the Dock. Pressing F11 makes all other windows go away, and
you see only the desktop and the Finder. Press F11 again to bring everything
back.

Finder windows

You use Finder windows to move around among folders. You see a window
when you double-click a folder or choose File⇨New Finder Window from the
Finder.

As shown in Figure 5-8, the name of the folder is at the top of the Finder
window. The icon to its left is live; you can click it and drag it to wherever
you wish, just as you would the folder's icon in its parent folder.

Figure 5-8:
A Finder
window in
cover-flow
view.

Finder windows have a sidebar on the left with a list of available storage volumes at the top and selected folders at the bottom. You can customize these
by dragging folders into or out of the list area. Each Finder window has a toolbar at the top. You can select from four different ways to view files: by icon,
list, column, or cover-flow. The list view includes details such as when the file
was last modified, its size, and its kind (Word document, picture, and so on).

Folders have small triangles next to them. If you click one, the folder expands. You can expand and manipulate more than one folder this way. The Column view shows you the contents of the current folder and the folder that contains it, along with, optionally, a preview of any file you select. Widen columns by dragging the II icon below the scroll bars. You can customize the contents of the file view by choosing Finder⇨View⇨Customize View Options.

The cool new cover-flow view is based on the way iTunes and iPods display album covers to help you find the music you want, but in the Finder, cover-flow shows a preview of file contents. Click the Quick Look "eye" icon at the top of the window (or press the spacebar), and you see a readable, scrollable preview of the center file. Click the double-arrow icon at the bottom of that view and you see a full screen version. Quick Look supports text files, PDFs, movies, Keynote presentations, and Microsoft Word and Excel files. No need to open files in an application just to see what's inside.

The Finder window toolbar also has back and forward arrow buttons that are initially grayed out. As you open and close folders, these buttons let you return to a previous view, in much the same way as you would with buttons in an Internet Web browser. The Finder window toolbar also has an action menu with a gear icon that lets you choose options that are also available on the Finder menu. You can even customize the toolbar from the Finder's View menu and add additional icons. I find the Path icon particularly useful because it shows all the folders that include the current one and lets you pop back to any one of them.

The text at the bottom of the Finder window tells you how much space is left on the disk drive or storage volume on which the folder is located. This is the easiest way to find out how much disk space you have available.

Get info

Click an icon on the desktop or in a Finder window and press ⌘+I. A window appears with everything you always wanted to know about that file but were afraid to ask, including what kind of file it is, how big it is, where it is located, and when it was created and last modified. You can find much more if you click the little triangles next to other items in the Get Info window, such as Name & Extension, Open With (which lets you pick the application to open this file or all files of this type), Preview, and Ownership & Permissions. This last section lets you control who can read and who can change the file or folder. See Chapter 17 for more info on permissions.

Optical drives — CDs & DVDs

All new Macs can play and read CDs and DVDs and can write *(burn)* CDs. Macs with Apple's Superdrive can burn DVDs as well.

Most Macs come with slot-loading optical drives. These work only with full-size CDs and DVDs. Full-size discs are about 4¾ inches in diameter (120 mm, to be exact). Don't even think of trying to insert a smaller disk or one of those cute credit card–sized CD thingies. If you need to read or create smaller-format discs, get a tray-loading external drive that supports them and is Mac compatible.

Accessibility

Mac OS X has a range of features designed to provide accessibility to users with disabilities. These include ways make the mouse easier to use (including making the cursor bigger), ways to operate the computer with only the keyboard, a technology called VoiceOver that lets OS X respond to spoken commands, and the ability to attach some assistive technology devices. You find the settings for most of these features by choosing System Preferences⇨ Universal Access from the Apple menu.

Installing software

When you try to install software on your Mac, OS X asks you for a password. If more than one user has an account on the computer, only those with *administrative privileges* can install software. Chapter 10 has more on setting up accounts; also, see the section "Setting up additional accounts," later in this chapter. If you give your kids an account, don't give them admin status. That way you can control what software they are loading.

After you've given a valid password, installing software on your Mac is simple. In most cases, the downloaded file or installation disc opens as a window, such as the one shown in Figure 5-9. You then just drag the icon or folder that contains the application into the Applications folder, which normally is in the sidebar of all Finder windows. Some applications come with an install script. For those, you just double-click the install icon and follow the instructions. You may be given an option to *customize* your installation. Unless you are absolutely sure that you know what you want, installing the default configuration recommended by the software's publisher is best.

Newer Intel Macs can run software written for older PowerPC Macs as long as that software is designed for OS X. Apple uses some very fancy technology that it calls Rosetta to do this, but you don't have to do anything special to take advantage of Rosetta. Mac OS X on Intel Macs is not designed to run software written for Mac OS 9 and older editions — so-called Classic Mac software. Ways exist to get around this limitation, but they aren't easy or fully functional. I describe some in Chapter 16.

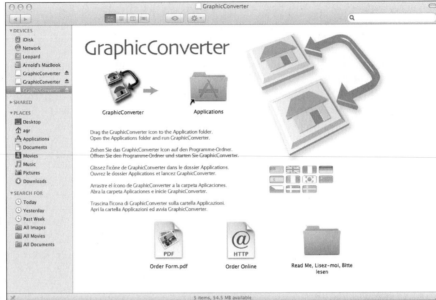

Figure 5-9:
A software
installation
screen.

Uninstalling

You uninstall software in OS X by moving the folder or icon you originally installed into the Trash. If you don't know where the program icon is, right-click any of its aliases, including the one on the Dock. Then select Show in Finder from the menu you see. If the program icon looks like a package, drag it to the Trash. If the icon is contained in a folder associated with the software, drag the folder to the Trash. In either case, don't empty the Trash until you are sure that everything else is working properly.

Printing on the Mac

Printers are the Bermuda Triangle of personal computing. Setting them up strikes fear in the hearts of most geeks. Apple has done a lot to simplify the process. It has introduced a technology called Bonjour that many printer manufacturers have adopted. Bonjour automates all the messy stuff. Also, OS X comes with drivers for dozens of printer models. So, if you have a fairly new printer, everything should go smoothly.

The first thing to do is make sure that the printer has power and is connected to your Mac. If it's a USB printer, plug it into one of your USB ports. If it's an Ethernet printer, make sure that it's connected to the same network as your Mac. If it's a WiFi printer, you don't have to do anything. Bluetooth printers may take some extra steps; check the printer's manual for instructions.

Turn the printer on. Open a short document or create one using TextEdit and try to print it. Choose Print from the File menu. Your printer's name should appear in the Print dialog box. Select it and off you go.

If your printer does not appear, choose System Preferences⇨Print & Fax and click the plus (+) icon. Wait half a minute. If your printer still does not appear in the list, click the More Printers button and select the type of printer you are using from the list at the top.

If nothing seems to work, go to the printer manufacturer's support Web site for the printer you are using and see whether you can find software for Mac OS X to download. See Chapter 18 for more printer troubleshooting tips.

Setting up additional accounts

If more than one person will be using the computer, it's a good idea to give each person his or her own account. On the Apple menu, choose System Preferences⇨Accounts. In the Accounts pane, click the plus sign (+) under the list of accounts. If the list is grayed out, click the lock icon below to unlock it. You may have to enter your password to complete this step. You'll be asked for the account holder's name, a short name that is the name of the account holder's home directory, and the password chosen for the account. The account holder can change his or her password later if desired. You can also select a picture for the account holder and specify which programs will start up automatically for that account. A parental controls section also exists. If the account is for a child, read Chapter 14 *before* setting up the account; I have lots of tips about the best way to set up an account for a child.

Backing up

The most important thing to remember about backing up is to swivel your head around and look in all directions behind you — do not rely on the rearview mirror. Wait, that's not the advice for this book. The most important thing to remember about backing up your computer is to *do it.* Regularly. Most people don't back up their data even once a month, and that isn't often enough.

National Public Radio once ran a story about a woman who worked for a company that recovers data from defunct hard drives. The company charges lots of money for this service, but it isn't successful for all customers. The woman was trained as a grief counselor, and the company hired her to break the bad new to those unfortunate customers that their precious data was gone forever.

Time Machine

Fortunately, new technology in Mac OS X 10.5, called Time Machine, makes backing up your computer easier than backing up your car. Plug an external drive into your Mac, and Time Machine asks whether you want to use it as your backup device. Agree, and Time Machine takes over, backing everything up. It works in the background so that you can carry on with whatever you are doing with your Mac.

Time Machine wakes every night at midnight and backs up everything that has changed since the last backup. You can change the time, of course, and your Mac must be on or sleeping, not shut down. Time Machine organizes the backup files by date and presents the data as a series of Finder windows stacked up behind each other, stretching into the past. You can easily cycle back to the time you want and restore the version of the file you want. If you have stuff you'd rather not back up — and I won't speculate on what those items might be — you can tell Time Machine to skip them. You can also tell Time Machine to back up to a server on your network, if you prefer. Just click the Time Machine icon in System Preferences to make all these choices. And if you're planning to back up out of your driveway, make sure that no toys, kids, or pets are behind your car before you get in.

Optical discs

Time Machine is really cool, but I still like to burn important files to CD-ROMs or DVD-ROMs every now and then and keep them in a location that's separate from where I keep the computer. I like having data on something I can touch and know won't be reused for something else.

Portable media

For short-term backup, you can't beat USB flash drives. They are tiny and inexpensive, and many can hold a couple of gigabytes of data. Having all the projects you are working on in your pocket feels good and lets you work on other computers when you need to. Another possible backup choice is an iPod, though you have to choose Enable Disk Use in iTunes and then remember to eject the iPod, as you do with any external drive, every time before unplugging it.

Backing up on the Information Superhighway

A number of services on the Internet offer large amounts of storage that you can use to back up files. Free services include Google's Gmail and AOL's Xdrive.com. Apple's $99-per-year .Mac service includes storage space. These plans offer the following advantages:

✔ They provide off-site backup — your files are safe even if your house burns down.

✔ The companies that provide these plans generally back up their servers, so you have an additional layer of protection.

If you are concerned about what's left of our privacy in the information age, you should be aware that, in the United States at least, your data enjoys far fewer legal protections when it is stored outside your premises.

Enjoying the Difference

I've concentrated on what you need to get comfortable with Mac OS X, but there is much more to know. The following sections offer a quick rundown on some of the cooler features. I cover others in later chapters.

Dashboard

Press F4 and a whole new vista of small applications appears as the screens you were viewing fade into the background. Welcome to the Dashboard. Out of the box, you only see a few programs — Apple calls them *widgets:* a calculator, analog clock, desk calendar, and weather forecast. Move the cursor over the lower-right corner of the analog clock. A little *i* appears. Click it. The clock flips over so that you can change its settings. Try the same trick on other widgets. Press F4 a second time and the Dashboard goes away, letting you resume your other work.

You can download thousands more Dashboard widgets, many for free. Just choose Mac OS X Software from the Apple menu or go to `www.apple.com/downloads/macosx`. Some of my favorites include the following:

✔ iStat Pro, a system monitor

✔ Systran language translator (as in French and German, not C++ and Python)

✔ Quotes.com stock-price service

✔ Kennedy Space Center video feed

You can even make your own widgets; see Chapter 17 for details.

Exposé

Exposé is a handy set of functions that Apple assigned to these function keys:

- ✔ **F3:** Separates all the open windows on your display so that you can pick the one you want. When you have lots of windows open, the images F3 presents can get tiny. If you hover your cursor over an image, its title is displayed legibly. Click on an image and it becomes the front window.

- ✔ **Ctrl+F3:** Does the same trick as F3 but only for the application in front.

- ✔ **⌘+F3:** Makes all the open windows scurry to the edges of the screen so that you can see the desktop. Click in the empty desktop space to see the Finder.

Pressing any of these buttons a second time restores your original view of the screen.

Spotlight

Spotlight is Apple's search tool for Mac OS X. Its icon, a blue circle with a white magnifying glass, is located on the menu bar at the upper right of your screen. Its keyboard shortcut is Ctrl+Spacebar. Mac OS X keeps an indexed database of keywords, and updates it as new files are added, so searches are fast. Spotlight starts displaying stuff as you type, so you often don't have to finish typing the word you are searching for. If you type more than one word, Spotlight searches for items that match both. If you want searches to match either item, place a vertical bar (|) between them. If you want Spotlight to exclude a word, precede it with a hyphen. So, for example, you might search for `dogs|cats -lions -pitbulls`.

You also find a Spotlight search box at the upper right of each Finder window. If you click the Save button under the search box, OS X saves the results of a search in a *smart folder,* which updates automatically as you add, change, and delete files. You can also tell Spotlight to ignore certain files using its pane in System Preferences.

Sometimes you just want to search for an old-fashioned filename. In that case, in the Finder, choose File➪Find (or press ⌘+F) and select your options.

Front Row

You've filled your Mac with music, photos, and videos. Time to kick back and let your Mac entertain you. That's where the tiny, simple Apple Remote that

Is Vista a copy of OS X?

The computer industry wouldn't be where it is today if companies didn't build upon the good ideas of others. Still, some features of Microsoft's new Vista operating system seem awfully close to a slavish copy of things in OS X. Vista has a facility that looks very much like the Dashboard, but the programs are called gadgets instead of widgets. Vista's search box is in the lower-left corner of the screen instead of the upper right, its OS X hangout. Vista color schemes seem awfully familiar to users of older versions of OS X.

The good news is that learning OS X helps prepare you for Vista. The bad news is that Microsoft's ability to innovate seems to be faltering. In the five years it took Microsoft to develop Vista, Apple released three major operating system upgrades — Jaguar, Panther, and Tiger — with a fourth, Leopard (OS X 10.5) released a couple of months after the Vista Home Edition. Some analysts are speculating that Vista may be Microsoft's last personal computer operating system, though I think that is unlikely. Microsoft will have to keep catching up with Apple.

comes with most models takes over. Click its menu button and your messy work screen dissolves into a simple screen that lets you choose which media to play, very much like the way you pick songs on the iPod. This feature, Front Row, is something you *can* take lying down.

Screen saver and desktop background

Leave it to Apple to turn the boring screen saver into a killer app. Choose System Preferences⟹Desktop & Screen Saver. The Desktop tab that appears lets you select a background pattern or photo for your screen when you are working. Make your pick and then click the Screen Saver tab. The screen saver kicks in after your computer has been idle for a few minutes (you can tell it how many minutes with the slider you see).

Apple provides several artistic displays to choose from (I like Cosmos), but the choice I like best is the Pictures folder. The screen saver randomly selects and animates pictures from your collection. You can also limit its choices to a folder or slideshow. If you enjoy taking pictures but rarely get to look at them, using this screen saver will bring tears to your eyes.

Apple has gone one step further, however. You can set things up so that you can send pictures to *someone else's* Mac over the Internet. It's a great way to let grandparents keep up with what's happening with their grandkids. See Chapter 14 for more details.

Chapter 6

Moving Files from Your PC to the Mac

In This Chapter

▶ Backing up your PC to the Mac

▶ Recovering files from a trashed PC

▶ Dealing with common file types

▶ Purging your files before disposal

*Y*ou have your Mac up and running and you've played around with OS X a bit, so you at least know how to start programs and make folders. You're ready to take the plunge and begin using your Mac for the bulk of your work. It's time to move those files off that PC and onto your Mac.

Backing Up and Movin' On

I hate to ask a deeply personal question, but when was the last time you backed up your PC? If you are like most users, it's been a while. Even if you are planning to keep using your PC, its worth moving your files to the Mac just to have another backup. The next PC virus could be your last.

I subscribe to the belt-and-suspenders approach to backing up. You should back up everything to your Mac *and* make copies of your most important files to permanent, write-once CDs or DVDs.

If you made an inventory of your PC's files, look over the inventory and add anything you may have missed. If not, now would be a good time to make an inventory. One important question your inventory should answer is how much data you need to back up. If you save mostly word processing documents and e-mail, you may well have less than the 700MB that a single CD-R optical disc can hold. If you take some digital pictures and occasionally download music, all your files may fit on a 4.7GB DVD-R. If you're an avid photographer, videographer, or music collector, you're better off using an external hard drive.

The good news is that you have many different methods by which to accomplish this moving job. I describe a bunch of ways, but you don't need to read them all. Pick one that sounds as though it might work for you and give it a try.

Ethernet or WiFi at your service

If your PC has an Ethernet port or WiFi wireless connection, you can network your PC to the Mac, set up your PC as a file server, and then copy over everything you need. This process has five steps:

1. **Connecting the Mac and PC to the same network**

2. **Enabling file sharing on the PC**

3. **Making the files and folders you want to transfer sharable**

4. **Accessing the shared folders from your Mac**

5. **Moving the files**

When it works, networking is the easiest way to transfer your files. But it's easy for some settings to get messed up along the way and hard to figure out what the obstacle is when networking becomes *not*working. You also need enough free disk space on the Mac to hold all your files. And when you're all done transferring the files, you still should make a backup copy of everything. These are the reasons I recommend using an external hard drive in most cases.

I talk more about networking in Chapter 9, but here is a quick approach to setting up your PC for file sharing. If your home network doesn't have WiFi, you need an Ethernet cable. Plug the Mac into your Ethernet router or, even better, just run an Ethernet cable between the Mac and the PC. You can borrow the one that connects your PC to your high-speed Internet modem, if you have one. Don't forget to put it back when you are done.

First, determine whether your Mac has already detected your PC on the network. In the Finder, choose Go⇨Network. Then, click the various icons in the Network browser that appears to see whether your PC's icon is among those that appear.

If you don't see your PC from the Mac, choose Start⇨Control Panel on the PC and double-click the Network Setup Wizard icon. Follow its instructions. Make a note of the name you give your computer and the workgroup name that gets assigned in the margin.

After you've set up file sharing, drag the folders on the PC that you want to access on your Mac to the Shared Folder on the PC desktop. Alternatively, you can right-click any folder you want to share and select Properties from the menu that appears. Click the Sharing tab and select the Share This Folder on the Network check box (see Figure 6-1).

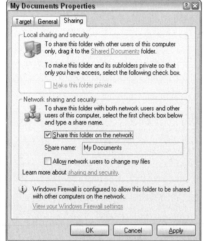

Figure 6-1: The Folder Properties Sharing tab.

On the Mac side, choose Go⇨Network and look for icons with the names you just assigned. Double-click those icons.

You should see your PC folders appear on the Mac desktop. From the Finder menu, choose New Folder. Name the folder My PC files or whatever you want. Now drag all the files you want to this folder. For extra neatness points, make separate folders for each folder you bring over from the PC, such as My Documents, My Pictures, My Movies, and so on, matching the names you used on your PC. You won't regret spending some quality time getting your files and folders organized after they are safely on the Mac. When you are done, move them all to your Mac's Documents folder.

External hard drive

High-capacity external hard drives are very affordable these days. You can buy a 1TB (1-terabyte) drive for under $400. A terabyte equals a trillion bytes, or 1,000 gigabytes, or the equivalent of 700,000 floppy disks — a stack over a mile high. You probably don't need that much, but drives a quarter of that size (250MB) sell for under $100.

Be sure to get an external drive that's labeled "for Mac and PC." These drives are usually formatted using Microsoft's FAT32 format, which both Macs and PCs handle well. If your drive is formatted in Microsoft's newer NTFS format, your Mac should be able to read it, but writing to it may be a problem. You can reformat the drive with OS X's Disk Utility after you finish transferring your data.

Plug the external drive's USB cable into your PC and copy your files to the drive. After everything is copied, shut down Windows, unplug the hard drive's data cable from the PC, and plug the cable into your Mac. The drive's letter or name should appear on your Mac's desktop. Double-click it. You can then copy everything to the Mac (make a folder for all the files first), or you can just copy the files you need and keep the rest on the external drive.

Flash memory and iPods

USB flash drives are handy for moving modest amounts of data — up to a few gigabytes. Follow the same procedure as that described previously for an external hard drive. You can also use an iPod in disk-drive mode to transfer data. The larger models hold 30 or 80 gigabytes, enough to back up many older PCs. In either case, you can again follow the same procedure as that for an external hard drive. Go to `apple.com/macosx/switch/howto/ipod.html` for tips on using an iPod to transfer files.

Burn, baby, burn — using optical media

If your PC has a CD burner or, even better, a DVD burner, you can move files by burning discs on your PC and reading them on the Mac. This approach has the added advantage that your files will be stored on a separate medium that you can put away for safekeeping. I like read-only media, such as CD-Rs and DVD-Rs, better than read-write (R/W) media because you won't be tempted to reuse it for something else. They tend to last longer, too.

Commercial solutions

Moving files is not that hard, but if you'd rather leave this task to someone else, some folks would be happy to help for a modest fee.

Apple's ProCare

Perhaps the easiest way to move your files is to sign up for Apple's $99 ProCare premium service plan when you buy your Mac at an Apple retail store. As part of the ProCare plan, the folks at the Apple store will move your files for you. You have to bring them your PC within a limited time after you buy the Mac. Ask at the store for current details.

Move2Mac

Move2Mac is a commercial file-transfer product from Detto.com that costs about $75, though it is often discounted. It comes with a special cable that you must use to transfer the files. Detto offers two types of cables. Both have a USB connector at one end that you plug into your Mac. If your PC has USB ports, you should buy the cable with a second USB connector. If the PC has a parallel printer port and is an older model, with no USB ports, or is running Windows 95 (which does not support USB), you can use the cable Detto offers with a USB connector at one end and a parallel printer port plug at the other.

You have to install Move2Mac software on both machines, so the PC must be in good enough shape to do this. Just in case it isn't, I explain other approaches later in this chapter.

Note that you cannot use a standard USB cable for installing Move2Mac software. USB is intended only to connect slave devices to an active computer, so the connector at the other end of a standard USB cable does not plug into a computer. Detto's cables have a blivit in the middle with a chip in it that lets the connection be made. The cables are only for use with Move2Mac software. You can't use the Detto cable for any other purpose, such as hooking up a printer or networking two computers.

A big advantage of using the commercial solution is that providers of these services have worked through many more moving scenarios than I have space to tell you about. Move2Mac claims to handle documents, spreadsheets, photos, music, files, folders, IE favorites, an IE home page, graphics, databases, an address book, and backgrounds.

Move2Mac does not try to convert application data files from PC format to Mac format. I discuss those issues later in this chapter. If your life is on the PC, a commercial solution may be worth the money.

Clone your PC on your Mac, virtually speaking

If you're thinking about running Windows on your Mac, consider using one of the third-party virtual hosting solutions — Parallels or VMWare — described in Chapter 13. Both allow you to copy your entire PC, operating system, applications, files, and settings to your Macintosh. Of course, you need to have enough hard drive space on your Mac to hold everything that is currently on the PC and still leave plenty of room for all the Mac stuff you want to add. And you have to determine what the licenses you have for Windows and your application packages permit. In all likelihood, you will need to remove all purchased software from the PC after you have successfully made the transition.

And make sure that you have a complete backup of everything before erasing the PC's hard drive. See Chapter 20 for suggestions on what you might do with the erased PC.

In some ways, this solution is ideal. You have your complete PC environment on the Mac — files, applications, and all your settings. On the other hand, you haven't yet transitioned to OS X; you merely have a new PC. Still, this approach allows you to take things gradually, moving one set of applications and files at a time as you are ready. Meanwhile, you can surf the Internet in safety from the OS X side of your computer.

Files on floppies, Zip disks, magnetic tape, and other media

If you have a collection of files on floppy disks, Zip disks, magnetic tape, or other obsolescent removable media, the simplest solution is to read them all onto your PC's hard drive and then move them to the Mac with your other files. If you have too many disks or tapes for this to be practical, or if you have only a few disks you really need but you're not sure which ones, a few possibilities exist. For 3½-inch floppy disks, you can purchase a USB floppy drive that can read PC floppies. You can also buy Zip drives with USB or FireWire interfaces from Iomega (`www.iomega.com`). For other media, such as 5¼-inch floppies or magnetic tapes, some companies can transfer your files for a fee, but you may be better off hanging on to your old PC until you are sure that you no longer need any of the older files.

Before sending removable media out for conversion, or working on them yourself, open the write-protect tab on the media to reduce the likelihood of accidental erasure.

Recovering Data from a Damaged PC

We all know the safe computing rules by heart. Use a good antivirus program, never open e-mail attachments you were not expecting, and back up your files regularly. Most of us aren't so careful. Or maybe your kids figured out how to get around whatever security system you set up. Anyway, your PC is barely working, if it will boot at all. What do you do?

This problem has a number of solutions; a whole industry is devoted to it, in fact. The following sections cover a couple of these solutions.

Try accessing your PC from the Mac

If your PC boots, try accessing it from your Mac using an Ethernet cable, as described previously in this chapter. Even if the PC is barely responding, the server software may still be fully functional.

If your PC is so trashed that the mouse no longer works, you may still be able to control it using Windows' accessibility tools. To do so, follow these steps:

1. **Press the Windows key on your PC's keyboard to open the Start menu.**

2. **Use the arrow keys to highlight Control Panel, and then press Enter.**

3. **Use the arrow keys to highlight Accessibility Options; then press Enter.**

4. **Press Shift+Tab and then use the right-arrow key to select the Mouse tab.**

5. **Press Alt+M to select the Use Mouse Keys check box; then press Enter.**

6. **Press Num Lock to turn on the numeric keypad.**

   You should now be able to use the numeric keypad to move the cursor around without using the mouse. The 5 key is the mouse button. Press – for right-clicking and press / to get back to left-clicking. Press Insert to hold down the mouse button for dragging and press Delete to stop dragging.

If you mess up at some point, remember that pressing Esc activates the Cancel button in dialog boxes in Windows — and in OS X.

Use the Windows System Restore program

System Restore is a Windows tool that lets you roll the operating system back to a kinder, gentler time, before all the nasties got into it. To use it, follow these steps:

1. **Save any open files.**

2. **Choose Start⇨All Programs.**

3. **Choose Accessories⇨System Tools⇨System Restore.**

4. **Select the Restore My Computer to an Earlier Time option and then click the Next button.**

5. **Select a date far enough back when you dimly remember your computer was working well; then click the Next button.**

   If this restore date works, transfer your files and perform a backup as described earlier in this chapter. If the date you chose doesn't work, you can try other dates, earlier or later.

Knoppix to the rescue

Knoppix is a complete PC operating system that fits on a single CD-R optical disc and can automatically boot up most PCs. It isn't Windows or OS X, however; Knoppix is a version of the Linux operating system. That's the bad news and the good news. It's bad news because you have enough on your hands getting used to OS X without being introduced to a third system, but it's good news because Linux won't be affected by whatever cooties your computer has. Also, you need to deal with only a few Linux commands.

You can make a Knoppix disc on your Mac that should boot in your PC, assuming that the PC hardware isn't broken and its peripheral devices are fairly standard. Knoppix can detect and use most common peripherals. However, if your PC's hard drive is encrypted, Knoppix won't be able to read it.

To make the Knoppix disc, you need a blank CD-R disc. Here's the recipe:

1. **Go to** `www.knoppix.org` **and click the English flag in the upper-left corner, assuming that** *Sie sprechen kein Deutsches.*

2. **Click the Order button and find a company in your country that sells Knoppix on a CD for a nominal fee. Or, click the Download button and select a download server located on your continent.**

   You are asked to concur with a "use at your own risk" agreement. (You expect a warranty with free software?)

   If you accept the agreement, you see a list of available downloads. You normally want the latest English version, which will have a filename that looks something like `KNOPPIX_V5.1.1CD-2007-01-04-EN.iso`. The version number is `V5.1.1`, EN means it's an English version, and `.iso` means it's a disc image. You also can download files with similar names but with the extensions `.md5` and `.sha1`. These are cryptographic signatures that enable you to verify that the files are authentic. For extra credit, download these as well. They're very short, and you might as well act as though you're interested. The `.iso` file, on the other hand, will be big — about 700MB. It just fits on a CD-R. This is not a big deal if you have a broadband connection, but plan on an overnight download if you use a dialup connection.

3. **Download the files you selected by dragging them to the desktop; do the short ones first.**

   When you have the `.iso` file on your Mac's desktop, you are ready to burn it onto the blank CD-R disc.

4. **Open the Application folder and then the Utilities folder.**

5. **Double-click the Disk Utility icon, and when the Disk Utility window opens, click the Burn button in the upper-left corner.**

6. **In the Select Image to Burn dialog box, find the** `.iso` **file, click it, and click the Burn button.**

7. **Pop in a blank CD-R and let 'er rip.**

Chill.

When the CD-R is all cooked, you see a message saying whether the burn was successful; if it wasn't, try again. When you've completed a successful burn, eject the CD by right-clicking its icon and choosing Eject from the context menu. Label the CD with a soft marking pen.

Now you can put your new Knoppix disc into the PC's CD reader and restart your PC. Knoppix takes a couple of minutes to boot, and lots of text flashes by as it does its thing, but when it's done, you should see a nice welcome screen. On the left of the screen, you see icons for all the drives that Knoppix found as it booted up. You should see an icon for your PC's hard drive if it is working. It will be labeled something like `hda1`. Double-click that icon. You should see the contents of your PC's hard drive.

If you have one, connect a portable hard drive or a flash drive to the PC. Its icon should appear on the Knoppix desktop. You can now drag files from the PC to the device you plugged in.

You can move files from Knoppix to your Mac in other ways. If you have an Internet e-mail account, such as Yahoo! or Gmail, you can log on to it using Konqueror, the Knoppix Web browser and file manager, and mail yourself files as attachments.

When you are done transferring files, right-click the removable drive's icon and select Unmount. Or, you can just shut down Knoppix by selecting Log Out from the "K" menu in the lower-left portion of the Knoppix taskbar.

If your PC hardware has a second optical drive that can burn optical discs, you can also write your files to a CD or DVD using Knoppix. Right-click in an open directory window, choose Action➪Create Data CD with K3b, and follow the instructions.

Knoppix can do a lot more, including repairing a damaged Windows file system and networking directly with your Mac, but these topics are too complex to cover here. Take a look at *Knoppix For Dummies,* by Paul G. Sery, if you'd like to do more with this powerful tool.

Should you run antivirus software before transferring your files?

PC viruses won't hurt OS X, but they could cause problems if you plan to run Windows on your Mac or exchange files with Windows users. So, updating and running your antivirus program before transferring your files is probably a wise move. However, if your PC is really on the edge, it may be best to get your important files off before running any programs. In that case, I suggest doing the file transfer twice, before and after an antivirus run. If the latter transfer goes smoothly, the first set of files can be erased.

Dealing with Common File Types

Most PC file types can be used with appropriate programs on the Mac. The following sections describe some of these file types.

Portable document format (.pdf)

The popular portable document format, originally developed by Adobe.com, is the standard display mode on OS X. The Preview program that comes with the Mac conveniently displays PDF documents. OS X can also create PDF files; it's an option you find by choosing File➪Print for most programs. You don't need to download or buy software to work with PDFs, although Adobe's Acrobat offers additional capabilities beyond what OS X provides.

JPEG photos (.jpg)

JPEG stands for Joint Photographic Experts Group, the name of the committee that pulled the format together. Macs love JPEGs. The OS X Preview displays them, and the iPhoto program stores them, organizes them, slices them, dices them, and spits out slideshows and coffee table books. Both programs come with every Mac. I discuss iPhoto more in Chapter 11, but the quick way to get your photos into iPhoto is to move the files to your Pictures folder and choose File➪Import to Library.

MPEG movies (.mpg)

The Motion Picture Experts Group came up with this family of standards for moving images. Apple's QuickTime, which comes with each Mac and is available free for Windows, is happy to screen MPEG-1 and MPEG-4 files for your viewing pleasure. Apple offers an MPEG-2 Playback Component that you can download for about $20 from `store.apple.com`. However, even with this plug-in, QuickTime won't playback audio encoded in AC3 (Dolby) format.

A free open source alternative media player, called VLC, that handles all MPEG formats is available from `www.videolan.org`.

If you are into video editing, see the discussion of iMovie in Chapter 11.

Music (.mp3, .aiff, .wma, and so on)

The iTunes program in Windows is compatible with iTunes on the Mac, so if you are using iTunes on your PC, you can transfer all the music, video, audio books, and podcasts that you have accumulated. You can also import any music or other sound files that are in MP3 format (`.mp3`). You can also import files in `.aiff` or `.wav` format. However, your Mac cannot play files in Microsoft's PlaysForSure (`.pfs`) or Zune format. These files use a digital rights management technique that is not compatible with Apple's FairPlay system.

Macs won't play Windows `.wma` files without additional software. Inexpensive solutions you can download are available from `Flip4mac.com` and `easywma.com`.

There are a number of ways to transfer your iTunes music library from a PC to a Mac. You can simply copy all the files from the Music\iTunes folder on your PC over to the Music folder on the Mac and then choose File⇨Import within iTunes. Apple recommends you use the Backup to disc feature in iTunes. You need a CD burner or, better yet, a DVD burner on your PC. See `docs.info.apple.com/article.html?artnum=302392` for details.

ASCII text (.txt) and rich text format (.rtf) files

Text files are supposed to be as simple as anything gets in computers. They are just a bunch of characters in American Standard Code for Information Interchange (ASCII) encoding. Unfortunately even these files are not so simple. The three different operating system families — Windows, UNIX, and

Mac OS — use different conventions for ending a line, or paragraph, of text. UNIX uses a line-feed (LF) character, Mac OS 9 uses a carriage return (CR), and Windows uses both (CR+LF).

The TextEdit program that comes with OS X reads text files created by Windows, UNIX, and Macs. However, by default, it saves files in rich text format (`.rtf`), which, among other things, preserves basic formatting of text. You can change the default settings to text format in the TextEdit Preferences.

Transferring your e-mail address book

If you are using an online e-mail service such as Yahoo! or Gmail, you don't need to do anything. Your address book is stored on the mail service's servers and you can access it just as well from your Mac.

Digital rights management — curse or blessing?

A popular form of entertainment on the Internet is called *trolling,* mentioning some hot-button topic in a discussion group and watching the heated controversy erupt. Few topics are more effective as troll bait than digital rights management (DRM), which is seen as either an enabling technology that allows music and movies to be enjoyed via the Internet, or as an evil, dangerous technology that allows all information to be centrally controlled by powerful interests. Both viewpoints have merit.

The rights that DRM manages are the rights that copyright law gives to content owners. When it works, DRM encrypts content and then allows decryption only on the computer or player that the copyright holder authorizes. DRM can also restrict the number and quality of copies made and the number of times content can be viewed. Providers of high-definition video using Blu-ray and HD-DVD are insisting that all computers that will show such content implement strict DRM.

Anti-DRM activists are concerned that the technology gives content creators too much power. Apple has tried to make its DRM system, FairPlay, relatively benign. You "own" content you paid for and can play it as often as you want. You can even convert purchased music into sharable MP3 files, although the process is clumsy, requiring you to first burn the tracks onto CD-Rs.

Apple's president, Steve Jobs, called for an end to DRM music in February 2007, saying, "Imagine a world where every online store sells DRM-free music encoded in open licensable formats. In such a world, any player can play music purchased from any store, and any store can sell music which is playable on all players. This is clearly the best alternative for consumers, and Apple would embrace it in a heartbeat."

If you are using Outlook Express, you can transfer the addresses using vCard records. To do this, prepare a new folder on your external hard drive or flash drive. You could call it Outlook Addresses. Start Outlook Express and choose Tools⇨Address Book. Choose Edit⇨Select All. Drag all the addresses to the folder you created. You can then import them into Apple's Mail program (see Chapter 8).

Apple offers additional suggestions on moving files at www.apple.com/lae/switch/howto.

Purging Your Files before Disposal

When you are satisfied that you have all your files safely moved to your Mac and backed up, it is time to remove data that you may not wish others to see from your PC hard drive. This may include e-mails, personal correspondence, proprietary work documents, and financial information. Sensitive information, including credit card numbers and passwords, may be stored in your computer without your knowing about it, in the form of temporary cache files and cookies. *Cookies* are blocks of information that your Internet browser often stores so that Web sites you revisit know about your past usage.

The simplest solution is to erase everything on the PC's hard drive. Doing so makes your computer much less usable if you decide to sell or donate it, however. If you still have the original discs that came with the computer, you can restore the operating system after you do the erase. You can also restore any applications you own.

Alternatively, you can just erase the data files that you are concerned about. The My Documents folder is an obvious candidate, but you must also check to see where other files may be stored. This approach is more risky, and I recommend it only if you are planning to give the computer to another family member or someone else you trust.

Removing the hard drive

A third approach, and perhaps the safest one, is to simply remove the hard drive before you dispose of your PC. This is relatively easy for a tower PC, but more tricky for a laptop. You can pay a technician at a computer store to do this for you. Of course, the computer will be much less usable without a hard drive, although it can still be used with a Knoppix CD, as previously described. If the machine is reasonably current, it may be worth it for the next owner to install a new, perhaps larger, hard drive. These drives are relatively inexpensive.

You can simply keep the old hard drive in a safe place, or you can ask the technician who removes it from your PC to install it in a USB or FireWire portable hard drive enclosure. Get one that's designed to work with Macs as well as PCs. Units that employ the Oxford chipset generally do. Putting your PC hard drive into a portable enclosure gives you yet another usable backup of your old files. It makes more sense if the hard drive is 20GB or more because it can later serve as a useful accessory to your Mac. Note that Windows NTFS-formatted disks open on OS X as read-only. Your Mac will offer to reformat the drive. Don't allow the reformat unless you're satisfied that all data is safely transferred and backed up. Then you can use OS X's Disk Utility to reformat the drive (which deletes all your files, but does not erase them fully) and use it as you wish. Disk Utility can also erase the drive after you have formatted it. Click the Erase tab and then click the Erase Free Space button.

Wiping data off your hard drive

Safely removing files from your PC is not just a simple matter of deleting them. When Microsoft Windows deletes files, it only removes information about those files from its file directory and makes the space on the hard drive available for reuse. It does not erase the data. Programs are available that can recover deleted files if they have not been erased. Even if the file has been erased only once, it is sometimes possible to recover data using highly specialized equipment.

Programs are available (see the list that follows) that can more thoroughly erase files by repeatedly rewriting them with patterns of 1s and 0s. Some do this in a way that complies with a United States Department of Defense standard that was issued some years ago. You can use the following programs:

- ✔ **SDelete:** Microsoft suggests using this free command-line program. You can see instructions and a download link at:

  ```
  www.microsoft.com/technet/sysinternals/utilities/
          SDelete.mspx
  ```

- ✔ **Eraser:** This program is also free, although a donation is suggested to help support the author. You can download it at:

  ```
  www.heidi.ie/eraser
  ```

The United States Environmental Protection Agency maintains a list of file-wiping programs, along with other computer recycling tips, at:

```
www.epa.gov/epaoswer/osw/conserve/plugin/pcthing.htm
```

Mac OS X has a built-in file-wiping utility. When you drag files to the trash, you can choose Secure Empty Trash from the Finder menu. In addition, the OS X Disk Utility can erase all your free space, so you can get rid of any files you did not securely erase.

Safely destroying your PC hard drive

Perhaps you don't want to or can't reuse your PC's hard drive but simply want to destroy it. Maybe it's so far gone that you can't access it with any program but you know it contains sensitive data that someone with the right tool and a big budget could still get at. You have a bit of a problem. It's hard to dispose of it in a truly safe and environmentally friendly way. The most widely recommended ways include melting, incineration, crushing, or shredding — yes, shredding. Some companies offer this service.

Perhaps the simplest solution is to erase it as best you can, remove it from the PC, and whack it with a sledgehammer. (Pick a safe location and wear eye protection.) Then bury the pieces in your basement.

Chapter 7

Switching Applications

· ·

· ·

*Y*our Macintosh comes complete with an impressive array of programs. But you probably have applications on your PC that you use regularly or need occasionally that do not have direct equivalents among the programs that are included with OS X. I guide you through the more common situations and point you to additional resources for others.

Processing Those Words and Numbers

Once upon a time, in the dim ages of the last century, people who wanted to produce a written document for other people to read sat down in front of a mechanical contraption called a *typewriter* that was filled with levers connected to keys arranged much the same as a computer keyboard. They even checked their spelling by looking up words in a printed book.

Today, it would be considered a form of abuse to make someone write without the aid of a good word processor. If you are working with others in an organization, you are pretty much expected to produce and be able to read documents in a format compatible with Microsoft Office, particularly Microsoft Word.

The need for Microsoft Office compatibility complicates what would otherwise be a clean, bare-knuckle-competitive relationship between Apple and Microsoft. Apple needs Office, and Microsoft makes good money selling it to Mac users. Bill Gates once half-joked that he made more money when Apple sold a Mac than when a Windows PC was sold, because Mac users were more likely to buy Office.

Many word processing solutions work with a Macintosh, ranging from the software that comes free with OS X to the full Microsoft Office for Mac suite to any number of other possibilities.

While most word processing programs can open some older formats, if you have documents that have been around a long time or were created with obsolete applications, you may not be able to read them directly from the standard Mac office suites that I describe in the following sections. MacLinkPlus, found at `www.dataviz.com`, converts numerous older types of documents to modern formats. See the DataViz Web site for a complete list.

TextEdit

The humble word processor included with OS X, TextEdit, is quite powerful, with many more features than its Windows equivalent, Notepad. You find TextEdit in the Applications folder. In particular, TextEdit can read documents produced by Microsoft Word 2003. Although TextEdit reads ASCII text files generated in Windows, UNIX, Linux, and Mac OS, unless you change its preferences, it does not save files in ASCII text format, for reasons discussed in the previous chapter. Instead, TextEdit normally saves files in rich text format, `.rtf`, a relatively simple format for styled documents introduced by Microsoft in 1987. TextEdit can also read and save documents in HyperText Markup Language (HTML), Microsoft Word (`.doc`), Microsoft Extensible Markup Language (XML), and OpenDocument formats. It can also produce PDF documents using its Print command.

TextEdit supports character formatting and the inclusion of graphics and multimedia images. Some of its more powerful features can be a little hard to find. For example, to make and edit tables, you choose Format⇨Text ⇨Table. List management features are found by choosing Format⇨Text. TextEdit allows sophisticated control of letter spacing and even speaks text aloud, but it does not support multicolumn documents. Its simple editing screen, shown in Figure 7-1, understates is capabilities.

TextEdit has full support for *Unicode,* a computer industry standard character set that includes the written characters of most of the languages used in the world today — and a few ancient ones, such as *Linear B.* (See Chapter 5 for more information on keying in special characters and other languages.) A committee is studying the addition of Egyptian hieroglyphs to Unicode. In the meantime, you can purchase the glyph processor MacScribe 2.1 at `www.macscribe.com`. The site is in French, but if you understand Egyptian hieroglyphics, you probably speak French, too.

If you want to edit HTML files in TextEdit, go to Preferences in the TextEdit menu and select the Ignore Rich Text Commands in HTML Files check box. You are also presented with this option for a particular file when you choose File⇨Open.

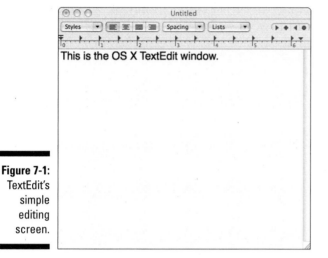

This is the OS X TextEdit window.

Figure 7-1:
TextEdit's
simple
editing
screen.

Word and Office from Microsoft

Microsoft Word and the other Microsoft Office applications — Excel for spreadsheets, PowerPoint for presentations, and Outlook for messaging — are the most widely used standards in most workplaces and schools. Microsoft sells versions of these programs for the Mac. If you frequently need to use files created by these programs, getting Word or the entire Office suite may be a wise investment. As this book went to press, Microsoft announced that Office 2008 will go on sale for OS X in early 2008. It will be file compatible with Office 2007 for Windows, just as Office 2004 for Mac was compatible with Office 2003 for Windows. If you have to use Office 2004 on your Mac, Microsoft provides a program that converts the 2003/2004 files (such as .doc for Word) to the format (.docx) that the 2007/2008 programs use. Note that Microsoft Office 2008 will not support Visual Basic for Applications. An alternative is available from www.realbasic.com.

You can buy Microsoft Word, shown in Figure 7-2, by itself, or you can buy the entire Office suite, which includes Word, Excel, PowerPoint, and Entourage, a Mac program similar to Outlook in Windows, but with somewhat different features. I discuss Entourage a bit more in Chapter 8.

Microsoft Office is pricey, especially if you are not upgrading from a previous version and don't qualify for the student version. As mentioned previously, TextEdit, which comes with OS X, can open files in Microsoft Word (.doc) format. You have other alternatives if you want full independence from the Redmond empire.

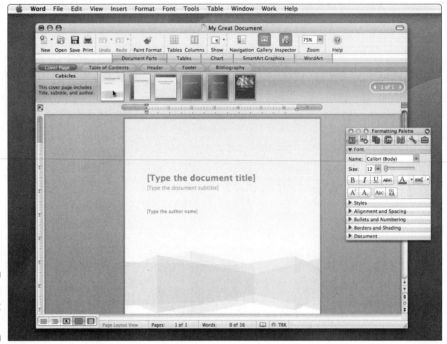

Figure 7-2:
Microsoft
Word.

If you are planning to install Microsoft Windows on your Mac and you need to work with MS Office documents only occasionally, one approach is to install the Windows version of Office in Windows and use it there. If you use the virtual technologies for installing Windows, the Office apps can be used alongside Mac apps. You can also use a program called CrossOver Mac from CodeWeavers.com (www.codeweavers.com) that runs the Windows versions of Office 97, 2000, and 2002 on your Mac without installing Windows. CodeWeaver's approach is not always perfect. See Chapter 13 for more on all these options. But if you are planning heavy use of Office, you'll be happier installing the Mac version. Get with the program, program.

OpenOffice.org

OpenOffice.org is a suite of office applications developed by the open source community that largely parallels the capabilities of Microsoft Office. It can generally read and write files in the various Microsoft formats, but is most comfortable with OpenDocument format. Oh, and it's open source and free.

OpenOffice.org says it appends the .*org* suffix to its name because someone else owns the OpenOffice trademark. The program can be used on a variety of computing platforms besides the Macintosh, including Windows, Linux, and most other forms of UNIX. OpenOffice.org consists of the following components:

> ✔ **Write:** A word processor
>
> ✔ **Calc:** A spreadsheet
>
> ✔ **Base:** A relational database management system
>
> ✔ **Impress:** A presentation program, similar to PowerPoint
>
> ✔ **Draw:** A vector graphics drawing program

NeoOffice

NeoOffice is a version of OpenOffice.org that uses Apple's Cocoa user interface, as do most other Mac programs. It's being developed by a small group of programmers, so it may not always reflect the latest version of OpenOffice.org. Download it from `www.neooffice.org`.

Installing OpenOffice.org

OpenOffice.org currently runs on the Mac using a user interface system developed years ago at MIT called X11. Apple provides X11 with OS X, but you have to install it separately. To do so, follow these steps:

1. **Insert the Install Disc 1 that came with your Mac into your Mac's CD/DVD slot.**

   Wait for the buzzing to stop. A window appears with the contents of the disc.

2. **Scroll down the window to the Install Optional Software icon and double-click it.**

3. **Follow the X11 installation instructions.**

4. **Go to** `www.apple.com/support` **to download any X11 updates and install them.**

   Congratulations! You now have X11 on your Mac, and you can take advantage of other open source programs that need X11.

5. **Go to** `www.openoffice.org` **and download the latest stable version of OpenOffice.org.**

6. **Drag the OpenOffice.org application to your Applications folder.**

Using OpenOffice.org

The X11 version of OpenOffice.org uses the same user interface on all platforms. As a result, it looks much more like a Windows program than a Mac program. The OpenOffice.org menus are in the OpenOffice.org window. You use Control-key combinations for shortcuts instead of the ⌘-key versions. A screen shot of OpenOffice.org displaying a draft of this chapter, stored as a Microsoft Word document, is shown in Figure 7-3. Note that X11 is also open as an application when you're using OpenOffice.org, and you see its menu at the top of your screen.

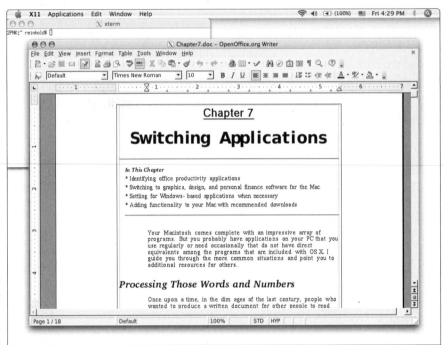

All in all, OpenOffice.org is a very powerful program, but in its X11 form, it isn't very Mac-like and takes some getting used to. It is an excellent example of both the strengths and weaknesses of open-source software.

iWork

Apple's iWork includes Pages, a word processing program; Numbers, a spreadsheet; and Keynote, a presentation program. Each is quite impressive.

Pages

Pages incorporates many of the features of a page-layout program. You don't just type and format text with pages. You create finished documents ready for printing or display on the World Wide Web or as PDF files. You can even edit images in Pages; you don't need to jump back and forth to an image editor for image adjustments. You can crop images to arbitrary shapes that you create in Pages and flow text around them. Nearly everything is editable in real time.

Pages can create tables that perform simple calculations, such as addition, multiplication, and averages. It also has three-dimensional charting capabilities, with the ability to rotate the chart image in 3-D to get exactly the effect you want. It can do mail merges, even using your address book to create personalized mailings and newsletters. And it comes with a set of templates that

Apple has designed to give your documents a professional look. To help with long documents, Pages shows detailed color thumbnails for every page in the left sidebar of your screen.

Pages can read and export Microsoft Word, HTML, RTF, and text-only files from the Mac or PC. It even supports Apple's older AppleWorks format. Pages does a good job of retaining the formatting of documents it imports.

Numbers

The world runs on spreadsheets, but they're kind of boring. Apple adds pizzazz with a flexible canvas on which you can place intelligent tables, 3-D charts and graphs, text, pictures, and whatever. Canned templates and lots of small touches make Numbers easy for non-bean counters to use. But don't worry, it can read and write Excel files.

Keynote

Keynote is Apple's attempt to one-up Microsoft's PowerPoint, which has become the primary means of business communications in the twenty-first century. There is a joke about two kidnapped businesspeople about to be executed who are offered a last request. The first asks whether he can finally give the presentation he had been working on before his capture. The second asks to be killed first so that he doesn't have to sit through one more PowerPoint presentation. Keynote is designed to make it easy to create killer presentations that don't bore the audience to death. Apple's president, Steve Jobs, claims that he is Keynote's prime customer, demanding ever-improved features for his numerous presentations. Keynote has a dizzying array of special effects, transitions, slide builds, and templates. It also calls on tools from Pages and the iLife suite (see Chapter 11) to simplify slide creation so that you can have tables that update when you change the numbers and 3-D charts that you can rotate. You can also export Keynote presentations in PowerPoint format (`.ppt`), but some of the cooler effects may not translate fully. Always be sure to preview your presentation on the machine and program you will use to give it.

Web-based office applications

In a major new trend in computing, Web sites are offering software applications, either free or for a subscription fee. All you need to use them is a computer with a reasonably modern Web browser. You don't have to download any software. You sign up for the service and access the document and the programs you need to create, and then edit them over the Internet. It works a lot like Web-based e-mail, and it's no surprise that one of the foremost vendors of this type of service is Google, but others have gotten in the act as well.

A special advantage of Web-based apps is that you can access documents stored on the Web site from any computer, anywhere you find an Internet connection. Your documents are password-protected, of course, but most sites have a way for you to share documents with colleagues and work on them collaboratively. The downside is that you cannot work when you are out of range of an Internet connection — say, when traveling with your laptop. Also, you need to have a fast Internet connection, and even then, response times can be slow.

Google Docs & Spreadsheets

Google's offerings include a word processor and a spreadsheet. Its word processor was originally called Writely and proved so popular that Google had to limit the number of people who could use it. Those restrictions have now been lifted.

If you have a Google account and password for Gmail, groups, or another Google service, you simply log on to use Docs & Spreadsheets. Otherwise, you can register for a new account with little effort. All Google requires is your e-mail address. Even your full name is optional. Docs & Spreadsheets lets you create new documents that are stored on Google's servers. You can also upload documents in Microsoft Office .doc and .xls formats, as well as .rtf, OpenDocument, and of course, plain-text formats.

You share a document with other people by entering their e-mail addresses. They receive an invitation and can see and edit your document as soon as they sign in. Multiple people can view and edit a document at the same time. The spreadsheet program even has a chat window, allowing all the editors to discuss what they're up to. You can see who made changes, when the changes were made, and what was changed. When you're done, you can leave the document on Google's server. You can also download it to your Mac in a variety of formats, including .doc, .xls, .csv, .ods, .odt, .pdf, .rtf, and .html. You can also publish your document on the Web in .html format. Figure 7-4 shows Google Docs displaying a draft of this chapter, which was uploaded to Google in Microsoft Word .doc format. Figure 7-5 shows a simple Google spreadsheet.

Other online office applications

A number of other Web sites are offering online office applications; some of these are as follows:

- ✔ **ThinkFree:** ThinkFree.com (www.thinkfree.com) offers Write, for word processing; Calc, a spreadsheet program; and Show, for presentations.

- ✔ **Zoho:** Zoho Virtual Office includes word processing, spreadsheets, and presentations. It's available free for individuals at www.zohox.com. Business users pay a small monthly fee and get a few additional features.

- ✔ **EditGrid:** This is an online spreadsheet program with strong collaboration features. It's free for personal use and requires a monthly fee for businesses. See whether you can guess its Web address.

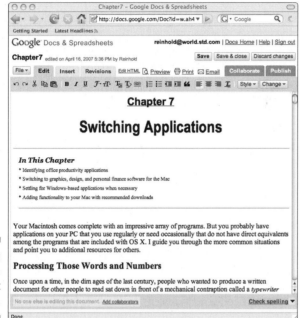

Figure 7-4:
Google
Docs at
work.

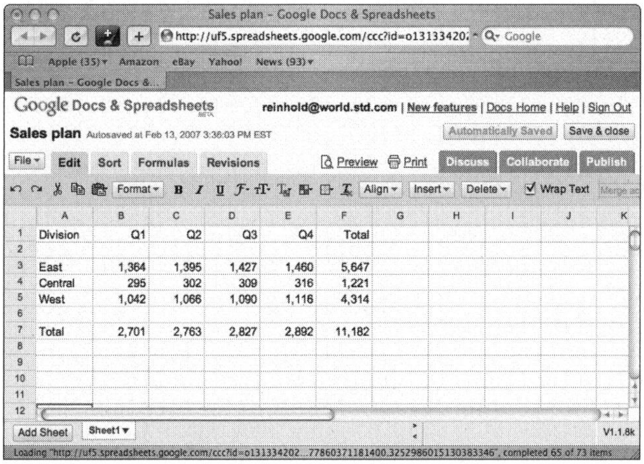

Figure 7-5:
A Google
spreadsheet.

Accessing Databases

The one major application missing from Microsoft Office for the Macintosh is Access, the Office database component. The following sections describe some alternatives to it.

FileMaker

FileMaker is a database program developed and sold by Apple. It's considered one of the better database programs out there and has a loyal following. It's easy to use (for a database) and has many powerful features. It is also available in a Windows version, and the two versions can be networked, allowing databases to be shared between users employing both platforms. The .fp7 database format is the same on both platforms, but differing fonts can sometimes cause problems. FileMaker is suitable for a range of applications from small and simple to large and complex, with Web-based access. A strong community of FileMaker developers exists. FileMaker Pro costs about $300 and numerous add-ons are available, including FileMaker Server, FileMaker Unlimited, and FileMaker Mobile. A server version is even available for Linux. FileMaker provides a white paper that compares its database to Access at the following Web site:

```
www.filemaker.com/downloads/pdf/fm_access_comparison.pdf
```

Fourth Dimension

4D (www.4d.com) offers a high-end database program that runs in OS X and Windows. It is based on a client/server model, and the program supposedly claims to support Service Oriented Architecture (SOA). It also has an active developer community that offers many plug-ins.

OpenOffice Base

The Base component of OpenOffice.org is a relational database written in the Java programming language. Its look and feel mimic Access, but it has limited ability to import and export database files, at least in the 2.0 version. It is a relatively new open source project and is still being improved. It's free with the rest of the OpenOffice.org suite. It's worth playing with or trying out on small projects. Future releases may be more suitable for mission-critical stuff.

MySQL

MySQL is the multiuser Web-oriented database that powers some of the most famous sites on the Internet, such as Craigslist.org classified ads, Flickr.com photo sharing, and the Wikipedia.org online encyclopedia. The Mac OS X server edition comes with MySQL built in. Using MySQL requires programming skills and is significantly beyond the level of Microsoft Access. For more info on the powerful tool, see *PHP & MySQL For Dummies,* 3rd Edition, by Janet Valade.

The battle of the century: OpenDocument versus Office Open XML

Ignore all those clashes of nations and -isms you see on the nightly news. The big battle of the twenty-first century may be between two proposals for what may become the primary way the history of our civilization is recorded. Computers have revolutionized the way we write. Our records are stored on hard drives and backup tapes in zillions of different formats created by software manufacturers, in part, to ensure their customers' continued loyalty. If all your documents are in a format that only your word processing vendor knows how to work well with, you are more likely to continue buying upgrades from that vendor rather than switching to another product that might be better. Over time, vendors stop supporting old formats. As a result, organizational archives are filled with documents that are now difficult or impossible to read.

The OpenDocument specification was developed to create a vendor-neutral format that could support all the data formats common in office applications, including the following:

- Word processing documents (`.odt`)
- Spreadsheets (`.ods`)
- Presentations (`.odp`)
- Graphics (`.odg`)
- Mathematical formulas (`.odf`)

OpenDocument is built on top of the Extensible Markup Language (XML) specification, which is essentially a standardized way to build more specific data standards. Microsoft responded by creating its own "open" standard called Office Open XML (ooXML). The name "Office Open" here has nothing to do with OpenOffice.org, described previously. It refers to an open way of storing Microsoft Office files in XML format. The two standards have been approved by standards organizations, ISO for OpenDocument and ECMA for ooXML. Critics complain that ooXML is too cumbersome for companies other than Microsoft to fully implement. The ooXML specification is more than 6,000 pages long. Apple is a cosponsor of ooXML but also supports OpenDocument.

Although a single agreed-upon format for digital documents would be great, having two formats is a big improvement over having zillions of them, and it looks as though Mac users can work with both.

Finding Graphics, Design, and Personal Finance Programs

Okay, this is an odd grouping of programs. But they have two things in common: Many people use them, and the market leaders in each category have versions for both Windows and the Mac, with good compatibility between them. For the most part, all that is involved in switching is getting hold of a Mac version of the program in question. Check with each vendor to see whether switching to the Mac version entitles you to the upgrade price.

Graphics editing

Basic graphics editing capabilities are built into Apple's iLife suite (see Chapter 11), including the ability to crop images, adjust brightness and contrast, and remove the red-eye effect that sometimes appears when taking pictures of people using flash illumination. Apple's Aperture (see Chapter 11), a professional photographer's program, provides still more. Still, these programs don't match the capabilities of top-of-the-line graphics editors.

Photoshop

Adobe's Photoshop graphics editor has altered the meaning of photography from being a way to capture reality to a way to make an image of anything imaginable. My favorite example of the sophistication of this program is a wrinkle-removal feature that includes a slider so that you can adjust how many wrinkles to remove. It lets you make a portrait subject look just a bit younger — but not so much as to strain credulity. Photoshop is available in Mac and Windows editions that share underlying `.psd` file types. The new CS3 version of Photoshop has native support of both Intel Macs and PowerPC Macs. The CS2 version ran in emulation mode on the Intel-based Macs, resulting in sometimes sluggish performance.

Photoshop Elements

Photoshop's less expensive sibling, Photoshop Elements, also has file-compatible versions for both platforms, as do most of the members of the Adobe family. Although not as capable as Photoshop, it can meet the needs of many amateur photographers and is much less expensive than Photoshop. It is often included free with products such as scanners.

GIMP

The GNU Image Manipulation Program (GIMP) is a free, open source graphics-editing program with many, but not all, of the capabilities of Photoshop. As with OpenOffice.org, GIMP requires the X11 window manager. However, a version called Seashore (`seashore.sourceforge.net`), which uses the OS X Cocoa window manager, is being developed. As with OpenOffice.org, GIMP's user interface, shown in Figure 7-6, is more Windows-like than Mac-like. In particular, menus are associated with each window.

GIMP is one of the most mature open source programs, with a wide following and much Internet support. For example, visit `www.ghuj.com` for a large collection of GIMP tutorials. GIMP handles a wide variety of image formats and allows editing by layers and individual color channels. If your budget is limited and you need more image-manipulation capabilities than the iLife suite provides, GIMP is worth a try before you spend lots of money on brand P (that is, Photoshop). You can get more info at `www.gimp.org`. If you want to give it a try, follow the previous instructions for installing X11 given for OpenOffice.org. Then download the Mac application bundle for GIMP, which is available at `gimp-app.sourceforge.net`. Open the disk image for the application bundle and drag GIMP to your Applications folder. When you first start GIMP, it asks you a bunch of geeky questions concerning some folders it needs. Just let it do its thing by clicking the Continue button repeatedly.

Figure 7-6:
A photo of the family dog touched up using powerful image-editing tools.

GraphicConverter

GraphicConverter, found at `www.lemkesoft.com`, is an extremely handy shareware program that has long been a part of the Macintosh universe. It includes a number of image-editing tools, and even accepts many Photoshop-compatible plug-ins, allowing a variety of special effects. But its best attribute is its ability to import some 200 different file formats and save in 80 formats. It's well worth the $30 shareware fee.

Page-layout programs

Desktop publishing was born on the Macintosh, taking advantage of Apple's introduction to the industry of a high-resolution, what-you-see-is-what-you-get (WYSIWYG) display, a graphical interface, and laser printing. Even in corporations that have standardized on the Windows operating system, Macs are plentiful in the graphics design department. As mentioned previously, Apple's Pages program provides many tools for high-quality page layout and may be all you need if you're not a professional designer. But Pages is no threat to the top two programs industry uses, Adobe InDesign and QuarkXPress. Both programs have a long and strong association with the Mac platform. QuarkXPress started on the Mac, and InDesign traces its lineage to PageMaker, also a Mac-first program. Both are strongly supported on the Mac, and file transfer is generally straightforward. In fact, Quark uses the same application on both platforms.

Adobe also sells a document-processing program called FrameMaker that is often used for high-end technical documentation. However, the current version is not available for OS X, so if you need it, run it in Windows on your Mac.

Replacing Specialized Programs

Some software categories still exist for which the market leader doesn't offer an equivalent program that runs on Macs. Also, some companies expect their employees to use programs developed by that company's Information Technology (IT) department that run only in Microsoft Windows. The simple answer to such situations is to install Windows on your Mac, a process I discuss in detail in Chapter 13.

In some of these software categories, you find some quality Mac programs that are worth switching to. And more IT departments are replacing their internal applications with software that can be accessed from any Web browser.

Computer-aided design

In the early 1970s, when industry first began to use computer-aided design (CAD) systems to replace old-fashioned drafting boards, the software ran on 16-bit minicomputers with 1/1,000 the speed and 1/10,000 the memory of a low-end Mac. Those systems cost a couple hundred thousand dollars per seat, back when a single family home cost under $50,000. Modern CAD programs run on standard personal computers but are still pricey, often costing more than the computer they run on. The most popular CAD program on the market today is probably AutoCAD, from Autodesk. Autodesk does not sell a Mac version.

However, several CAD programs for the Mac are well reviewed and can exchange .dwg files with AutoCAD. Some players in this field include ArchiCAD, BOA, CADintosh, CADtools, DenebaCAD, MacDraft, PowerCADD, TurboCAD, VectorWorks, and Vellum Draft.

In addition, Google offers a Web-based application, Google SketchUp (sketchup.google.com), that can meet many design needs. The Web site www.architosh.com has reviews and other information for people, especially architects, who want to do CAD on the Mac.

Share the wealth

Many of the most creative ideas in personal computers come for individual developers who distribute their products as shareware. Most let you try their program for free, simply asking for a modest payment if you choose to keep using the program. Some distribute programs as freeware, possibly asking for a donation from those so motivated. So do the right thing and pay up when these programs save your butt!

Voice dictation

Take a letter. In days of old, an executive would utter those words and a secretary would come into the office with a notepad ready to take down the boss's words in shorthand, for later transcription on the new-fangled typewriter.

These days, good software is available for personal computers that converts your speech into text and that you can edit and use with a word processor. Currently, the product that has received the best reviews is Dragon Naturally Speaking. Unfortunately, it is not available for OS X. Fortunately, Nuance (`www.nuance.com`), the company that now markets NaturallySpeaking, also sells IBM's ViaVoice for OS X. Another OS X dictation product is iListen, from MacSpeech (`www.macspeech.com`). Neither product is currently as capable as NaturallySpeaking, however.

OS X does have built-in speech recognition that allows you to verbally order the operating system around. It also has the ability to go the other way, to turn text into speech. I talk more about these features in Chapter 14.

GPS navigation

The Global Positioning System (GPS) has revolutionized navigation. The U.S. Department of Defense began launching the constellation of satellites that make up the system in the late 1970s. Originally intended for military use, the system has long been open to civilian users. Anyone with a relatively inexpensive GPS receiver anywhere on the Earth's surface can determine his or her position to an accuracy of 50 feet or better.

Adding GPS to a laptop can enable any number of innovative applications, from vehicle navigation (cars, boats, planes, and even balloons) to collecting survey data. For a long time, GPS receiver manufacturers supported only the PC. In 2006, Garmin, one of the leading brands, announced plans to fully support Mac users. Mac GPS software is also available at `www.gpsy.com` and `www.macgpspro.com`.

You also need a GPS receiver. Many GPS units communicate using a serial protocol. This can often be accommodated using a serial-to-USB adapter, but it typically means keeping track of two cables. Newer GPS receivers use USB or even Bluetooth. Both are better for Mac use, and Bluetooth is ideal because no cable is required.

Adding Functionality as You Need It

Oodles of shareware and freeware programs are out there that you can download to add functionality to your Mac. I recommend that you take it easy at first and work with your Mac pretty much as it comes out of its box. Explore this rich world when you've grown more used to your Mac and have an easier time detecting when something isn't quite right after a program is installed.

Still, I do recommend making a few downloads sooner rather than later because they have particular relevance to easing the switching experience.

StuffIt Expander

OS X can open a variety of compressed files and archives and can do Zip compression (you right-click a file or folder and choose Create Archive). StuffIt Expander (www.stuffit.com), from Smith Micro Software, can open many more formats, including some older Mac formats such as .sit and .hqx. It comes free from the Web site, but you have to navigate past offers for more capable programs that are not free.

GraphicConverter

I describe GraphicConverter, the excellent Swiss Army knife for image formats by Lemkesoft, earlier in this chapter.

Flip4Mac

Quite a bit of content on the Internet is available only as Windows Media files (.wma and .wmv). With Windows Media Components for QuickTime, by Flip4Mac, you can play these files directly in QuickTime Player as long as they don't have digital rights management (DRM) restrictions. Flip4Mac also lets you view Windows Media content on the Internet from your Web browser. A

AppleWorks: RIP

For many years, Apple has had its own suite of productivity software called AppleWorks. It includes a word processor, spreadsheet, database, and a painting and drawing program. It is similar to Microsoft Works and even has a Windows version. Apple used to provide a copy with each Mac. Apple still sells AppleWorks, but it installs only on older Macs with the PowerPC processor.

---

free version is available from the Microsoft Mac site, www.microsoft.com/mac (click the Other Products link), or you can look for the link to the free version at flip4mac.com.

Adobe Flash Player and RealPlayer

Flash and Real are two other popular multimedia formats. Both have free players available for OS X. Adobe Flash used to be Macromedia Flash, and Real used to be RealAudio. Companies like to change their names because it cuts down on those nasty profits by confusing consumers, so they end up paying less in taxes. You can download the free players from www.adobe.com and www.real.com, respectively. Adobe has two versions, one for Intel Macs and the other for the older PowerPC Macs. RealPlayer can also play QuickTime files and will offer to take over for QuickTime Player if you let it.

Part III
Connecting Hither and Yon

The 5th Wave   By Rich Tennant

"Wow, I didn't know OS X could redirect an email message like that."

In this part . . .

Likely the first things you want to do once your Mac is set up are get online and check your email. Apple's software makes it easy to accomplish these tasks — most of the time. But connection scenarios vary and hiccups happen. In this part, I help you get on the air quickly. Then, I take a closer look at the various ways you can network a Mac. Finally, I deal with security. Hassle-free safe surfing is one of the great benefits of switching to a Mac, but there are simple things you can do to make Mac use even safer.

If you're browsing in the bookstore and have no intention of buying a Mac or this book, at least read what I have to say about security in Chapter 10. The advice there can reduce security problems with your Windows and Internet use, and that's in everyone's interest.

Chapter 8

Getting Your Mac Online

· ·

In This Chapter

▶ Using your current Internet service or maybe something better

▶ Selecting among Mac browsers

▶ Setting up your e-mail

▶ Using other online communications: Chat, voice, and video

· ·

*G*etting a Mac online is like teaching a duck to swim. It usually comes naturally. If you answered all the questions during the setup process outlined in Chapter 4, you're probably already online and working away. But if you have a problem, the solution may not be obvious.

Using Your Current Internet Account

If you have Internet service that you like, you can probably stick with it. Most Internet service providers (ISPs) support Macintosh users, and Macs can generally connect anyway with the few that say they don't. The first thing to try is to see whether your Internet connection works. If you have a high-speed modem — cable, DSL, or satellite — you should be all set.

If you do run into a glitch, the fixes depend on whether you're using an Ethernet or wireless connection for high-speed service. Also, if you're using dialup or a service at work or school, you have different items to check. The following sections have the details.

If you're looking to upgrade to cable, DSL, or satellite high-speed service, see the section "Upgrading Your Internet Service," later in this chapter.

Checking wires on an Ethernet connection

An Ethernet connection is one connected by an Ethernet networking cable. (Ethernet cables have plugs that look like the plugs used on telephones in North America, only fatter. But don't try to use a phone cable.) The following tips can help if you have this type of connection and you can't get online:

- ✓ **If your high-speed modem is connected to an Ethernet router or switch,** see whether it has an extra Ethernet port and run an Ethernet cable from it to the Ethernet port on your Mac.

  If you don't have a router or switch, you should get one — they're cheap enough — but in the meantime, you can unplug the Ethernet cable from your PC and plug it into your Mac.

- ✓ **If your PC is connected to your high-speed modem by a USB cable** — a rectangular metal plug — you may not be able to use that cable with your Mac, even though the Mac has USB ports. Check with the modem manufacturer to see whether it supports USB connections to OS X. If not, you must use an Ethernet cable.

  Most modems that support USB connections also have an Ethernet jack, but with many, you can only use one or the other, not both together. If you want to use the PC and your Mac, but your PC does not have an Ethernet port, you need a combined USB and Ethernet router.

Picking up WiFi signals at home

If you will be using wireless Internet with your computer, life is even easier. Most new Macs include built-in AirPort, the name Apple uses for WiFi. Another common name is 802.11, WiFi's very own IEEE standard number. The number 802.11 is followed by a letter that indicates the speed and frequency band supported.

All you need to use an existing WiFi service is a password, and not even that if security isn't enabled. See Chapter 9 for more about WiFi security, including what to do if you forget the password you initially set up.

If you don't already have WiFi and have or plan to get a MacBook or MacBook Pro laptop, consider getting a WiFi router. Having one lets you use your laptop anywhere you choose to work, as long as it's within range of the router. A WiFi router is also handy if your desktop installation is not near a phone or cable TV jack. You don't need to run cables everywhere. Apple sells its own brand of WiFi router called AirPort Extreme. While a tad pricey, it has many cool features that make it worth considering as your first WiFi base station. You can find out more about AirPort Extreme in Chapter 9, too.

Setting up dialup service

If you are connecting to the Internet using an old-fashioned dialup connection —
the kind that makes beep-boop-beeep-wahh-wahhh noises every time you
connect (I used to call them *whale songs*) — you need a USB dialup modem to
continue using that connection with your Mac. New Macs do not have built-in
modems. Apple sells a tiny USB dialup modem for about $50. Other USB
dialup modems may work. Again, check with the manufacturer.

To get your dialup service to work, make sure that you've followed these steps:

1. **Plug your modem into a USB port, and then plug the phone cable into
   the modem.**

2. **To set up your modem, select System Preferences from the
   Apple menu.**

3. **Double-click the Network icon.**

4. **Click the modem line to highlight it, and then click the Configure
   button.**

5. **Fill in the requested information.**

   You can likely find the information you need to set up your Mac's
   modem connection on your PC if you have been using it to access your
   dialup account:

   a. Choose Start⇨Control Panel, and double-click the Network
      Connections icon.

   b. Right-click your ISP's icon in the dialup area and select Properties
      from the context menu.

   c. Write down the setting info you see.

   d. Select System Preferences from your Mac's Apple menu.

   e. Click the Network icon.

   f. Select Modem from the Show popup menu, and write down those
      settings.

   g. Enter the settings from the PC in the appropriate boxes on
      your Mac.

   Alternatively, just give your ISP a call and ask the folks what settings you
   need. In any case, save the paper with the dialup setting info with your
   Mac's manuals.

6. **When you're done filling in the info, click the Apply Now button.**

Surfing the WiFi cloud

Many people who operate a WiFi access point or router do not turn on *any* security. Because the usable range of a WiFi signal can be a couple of hundred feet, someone outside the premises of the router owner can see the access point in his list of available connections and may be able to connect using it. Your computer may connect to an available access point without much warning if the access point you normally use is not available. In densely populated urban areas, several open signals can be available from many locations.

A WiFi connection is open because its owner didn't take the extra steps necessary to turn on one of the encryption features included in all WiFi access points. That can happen because the owner did not know how to turn on encryption, didn't want to be bothered, or deliberately chose to leave it off, thereby inviting others to use it. I go over the steps necessary to secure your WiFi connection in Chapter 9.

Open WiFi access points raise questions of security, ethics, and legality. Advocates of open access argue that turning on encryption is simple enough that any open access point is an implicit invitation for use. If your computer is well locked down, you have relatively little risk that an intruder will access your files through an open WiFi signal, though someone could use your connection for a nefarious purpose and you might have some explaining to do to the authorities. Sharing your WiFi connection with others may violate your ISP's terms of service, and many jurisdictions have laws against unauthorized access to someone else's computer.

Quite a few locales now offer free WiFi hotspots, and some municipalities are installing free WiFi in certain neighborhoods, or even citywide. OS X conveniently shows you which access points are open in the list that drops down when you click the WiFi icon in the menu bar. A quick check of your e-mail or being able to find directions to a restaurant from any street corner or coffeehouse is certainly handy, and it's neighborly to allow that. The use of open WiFi access should grow despite the many concerns raised.

Connecting at school, work, or elsewhere

If you plan to use your Mac at work or school, you will likely be connecting using that organization's Internet service:

- ✔ **If WiFi is available,** try selecting the school's or company's signal under the WiFi icon on your Mac's menu bar and open your Web browser. You will likely be taken to a page with instructions for logging in.

- ✔ **If you will be using wired Internet,** look for instructions on your organization's Web page or intranet from another computer, or visit your system administrator. Fresh-baked cookies are always welcome.

Upgrading Your Internet Service

When you get your new Mac, you may find this is a good time to upgrade your Internet service. If you're still using dialup, this might mean checking out DSL, cable, or satellite service. Or, maybe you just got a MacBook and want the ability to go online wherever you go. Whatever your reasons, the following sections help you get started with common Internet service upgrades.

Speeding up with DSL or cable service

If you are using dialup or you are not satisfied with the service you are presently using, this may be a good time to upgrade. If you live in an urban area, you probably have a choice of getting high-speed Internet service from your telephone company or from your cable television provider. The telephone company service is usually called DSL (digital subscriber line), but you may encounter the older term *asymmetric DSL* (ADSL). Both cable and DSL can work quite well, so it's worth checking what pricing plans and special features they each offer. Some things to remember are as follows:

- High-speed service can be more expensive than dialup, but you can share it with several computers and it doesn't tie up your landline voice service.

- The speeds quoted by service providers are best-case speeds. Things can run slower at peak times of the day or when some news event draws many people to the Net. Also, speeds for downloading data may be much faster than those for uploading, such as when you send messages with large attachments.

- Top cable speeds are generally higher than those for DSL, but cable prices are usually higher as well.

- You may not be able to get DSL service if you are too far from the telephone company's switching equipment.

- Some phone companies are installing fiber-optic lines to homes and businesses. These allow very high speed connections.

- You may have a choice of buying the high-speed modem you need or renting it from the service provider. Find out the difference in price, and figure out how long it will take to pay for the modem in higher fees. Also consider that rented modems usually include free service if the unit dies, which isn't uncommon.

✔ Check for package deals that bundle Internet access, television, and even phone service. These can be significantly cheaper than buying the services individually, but watch out for promotional prices that are only good for six months or a year. Ask what the rates will be after the promotion expires.

✔ Ask whether your service provider has a phone number you can call for dialup access when you are traveling.

✔ Ask your neighbors which Internet provider they're using, whether they like it, and what their customer service experiences have been.

✔ Back up your data before your installation appointment. The service provider's personnel are not necessarily computer experts and can cause unexpected problems.

Mobile Internet: Taking your connection with you

If you use your Mac when traveling, you can choose from a number of ways to access the Internet. Some involve little expense. Look for hotels that offer free Internet access when making travel reservations. Coffeehouses and public libraries often offer free WiFi connections. You can also take advantage of the WiFi cloud, described in the nearby sidebar, "Surfing the WiFi cloud." If you need something more dependable, you can try a wide-area network (WAN) or try using your cell phone as a modem.

Going first class

Many cell phone service providers offer wireless wide-area networking (WWAN) that communicates via radio signals using a special device that you plug into your laptop. Wide-area service is most often used by businesspeople. Although this service can by pricey, you typically get connect-anywhere service within the provider's coverage area. If you're considering this service, keep the following points in mind:

✔ Some WWAN radios are in ExpressCard/34 format. For these, you need the MacBook Pro, because it is currently the only model that accepts these cards.

✔ Other WWAN radios plug into a USB port; you should be able to use these on any new Mac.

✔ Do not get a WWAN card in PC card, PCMCIA, or ExpressCard/54 formats. These do not plug into in any Mac currently sold — though you may be able to find a clumsy adapter that works.

✔ Make sure that the coverage area covers the areas you cover.

The Mac road-warrior kit

If you're on the road a lot with your Mac portable, consider creating a travel kit that's always ready to go. Here are some items you should include:

✔ A short (3-foot) Ethernet cable

✔ A cheap three-way extension cord — to share power outlets at airports and lamp sockets in hotel rooms

✔ An airplane MagSafe power adapter (available at the Apple store)

✔ International power adapters (use Radio Shack Model 273-1405 or visit the Apple store)

✔ USB flash drive loaded with backup copies of files you'll need

✔ Apple modem and a telephone cable

✔ List of local modem access numbers — ask your ISP

✔ A couple of spare CD-Rs or DVD-Rs

✔ A checklist for other items you want to take, including your laptop and cell phone chargers and the serial number of your laptop

Cell phone as Bluetooth modem

Some cell phones can connect your Mac to the Internet. You don't even need a special cable — the cell phone talks to your Mac using Bluetooth wireless networking. You need a cell phone with this capability and a cellular service provider that allows such use — some don't.

These two different methods may be available:

✔ **Turn your cell phone into a dialup modem.** You need a dialup account to use this method, but some high-speed services allow dialup access, too.

✔ **Use the Internet data service that your cell phone provider offers.** This method is faster, but typically requires an extra monthly fee. Setting everything up can get complicated. Ask your service provider for instructions or do a Google search.

Upgrading your America Online service

If you connect to the Internet using AOL, you can continue to do so. AOL works fine with Macs. If you are planning to upgrade to high-speed service through another service provider, you can still take advantage of AOL's many other features by signing up for its free service:

1. **Go to** changeplan.aol.com.

   You can also enter the AOL keyword changeplan.

2. **Log on with your primary screen name, the one that is first on the drop-down list when you normally sign in.**

3. **Select the free service option.**

Instead of using Apple Mail, you send and receive e-mail through AOL's software, which you can download from `www.aol.com` or from an AOL CD. Or, you can access your e-mail and other AOL services using Safari or another Mac Web browser, also at AOL.com.

Internet from space — satellite service

If you live far from a cable or DSL Internet service and want something better than dialup, one option is available in most locations: getting Internet service via satellite. Compared to other high-speed services, satellite Internet service can have performance problems, particularly with online games and Voice over IP (VoIP) telephony, due to the relatively long time it takes for signals to get up to a satellite in a geosynchronous orbit and back down to Earth. Also, upload speeds are slower than download speeds. Despite the drawbacks, high-speed Internet service can make rural living feel a lot less isolated, and satellite service may well be worth the money if no other high-speed services are available.

Where am I on the Internet?

The Internet has two ways of referring to a computer hooked up to it: domain name and IP address. *Domain names* are snippets of text separated by dots, like `www.dummies.com`. The last snippet, `.com` in this case, is called the top level domain (TLD). Other common TLDs include `.edu` for schools; `.gov`, reserved for the U.S. government since they invented the Internet; and .org, usually not-for-profits. Two-letter TLDs are country codes: `.us` for the United States, `.uk` for the United Kingdom, `.bk` for Burkina Faso, and so on. You can find a complete list of TLDs at `www.iana.org/root-whois`.

To find a computer, the inner guts of the Internet use a bunch of numbers called the IP address. When you type a domain name into your browser's address bar, the name is sent to special computers on the Internet called domain name servers that look up the corresponding IP address in their database. The common form of IP address (IPv4) consists of four numbers separated by dots, such as 123.4.56.78. Each number is between 0 and 255. A computer with full status on the Internet has a permanently assigned IP address. Most individuals that connect through an Internet service provider are assigned one "leased" IP address for their entire home network. That number may change from time to time. Special blocks of IP addresses are reserved for private networks and are never transmitted on the public Internet. A newer form of IP addressing, known as IPv6, has lots more numbers so every computer, cell phone, and refrigerator can have its own IP address. Macs can handle IPv6, but the system has yet to be widely adopted.

The following tips can help you get started:

- ✔ A couple of variations exist, but you should look for two-way satellite service. It's relatively expensive, with a high initial cost for equipment and high monthly usage fees.

- ✔ Professional installation is generally required at an added cost. A small dish antenna is mounted outside your home.

- ✔ The installer needs to place the dish in a spot with an unobstructed view of the southern sky — that's assuming you live in the Northern Hemisphere.

- ✔ One satellite ISP that explicitly supports Macintosh customers is Skycasters.com. A Google search can find others.

Starting Up Your Web Browser

To surf the Internet, you need a program called a *browser*. Most people use Internet Explorer as their PC browser, but you may have switched to an alternate browser, such as Firefox. Here you find out what your browser options are and find a quick introduction to Safari, the browser included in Mac OS X.

Picking a browser

In addition to Apple's own browser, Safari, you can use Mac versions of several other popular browsers, including Firefox. You can download the following browsers for free and use with your Mac:

- ✔ **Firefox:** www.mozilla.com
- ✔ **Opera:** www.opera.com
- ✔ **Shiira:** www.shiira.jp
- ✔ **Camino:** www.caminobrowser.org

For the most part, the choice of browser is a matter of taste. Various Mac browsers interpret Internet standards in different ways. As a result, some Web sites don't work with Safari but work with Firefox, for example. Opera has strong support of accessibility — you can use it without a mouse. Camino boasts speed and elegance. Shiira has excellent Japanese support.

I suggest that you start off using Safari, unless you already use and like the PC version of one of the other browsers previously listed. But at least download and install Firefox. It's a chance to practice installing a Mac program, and you'll have it handy if you run into a Web site that doesn't work with Safari. The Firefox screen is shown in Figure 8-1.

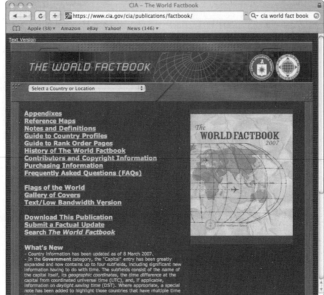

Some Web sites and corporate intranets require Internet Explorer for Windows. The most common reason is that they use *ActiveX controls,* which are only available in Windows. Microsoft once offered a version of Internet Explorer for Macs, but it has stopped development of this product. Even when it was offered, it did not support ActiveX controls. If you need to access a Web site that depends on ActiveX controls, you can run Windows on your Mac or use your old Windows machine.

Safari

Safari is a full-featured Web browser with good support for numerous Web standards. It includes the following features:

- Tabbed browsing
- Bookmarks set up to match the popular iTunes interface
- Built-in Google search box
- Password management using Keychain, a well-respected security system built into OS X
- Automatic form filler
- Pop-up ad blocker

Safari, which is shown in Figure 8-2 displaying the CIA World Factbook page, is built on WebKit, an open source Web-rendering engine. This engine is a computer program that knows how to display the various multimedia formats that the Web is built upon. Apple has added much functionality to WebKit, and it is being used by several other open source projects. Safari is built into the iPhone, and a free version is available for Windows, as well.

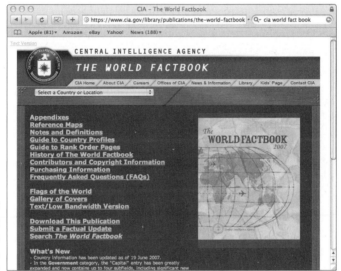

Figure 8-2:
Safari Web
browser.

Setting up Safari

Safari is ready to go out of the box. You might want to adjust the following settings to suit your needs:

1. **Select Preferences from the Safari window.**

2. **If you don't see the General preferences window shown in Figure 8-3, click the General icon in the upper-left corner and select the options you prefer.**

   The General window lets you specify your home page and control where downloaded files go and how long they are kept. You can also change your default browser here.

   Note that tabbed browsing is off by default. Click the Tabs icon and select the Enable Tabbed Browsing check box if you want to try this feature.

The Open Safe Files after Downloading check box is worth remembering. It is normally selected, allowing many types of multimedia to start up automatically when they are downloaded. If you hear about viruses affecting these types of files on a Mac, deselect this check box for the duration of the security scare.

Other Safari preference panes are reached by clicking the icons at the top of the window.

3. **When you're done, close the preferences window.**

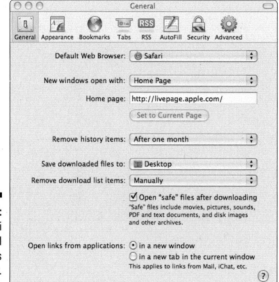

Figure 8-3:
Safari
General
preferences
window.

The Firefox Preferences settings are similar to Safari's.

Safari, Firefox, and most other browsers keep a history of the sites you've visited in the last few days. This can be handy when you want to go back to something interesting you saw, but it can compromise your privacy if others have access to your computer. The following items describe how to clear your history:

- ✔ In Safari, choose History⇨Clear History.

- ✔ In Firefox, choose Firefox⇨Preferences and click the Privacy icon. Then click the Clear button on the History line.

Switching Your E-Mail to Your Mac

Electronic mail was one of the first services on the Internet and only seems to get more popular. These days, just about everyone has an e-mail address. A large part of getting your Mac online is transferring all your e-mail accounts and addresses.

Moving to Apple Mail

OS X comes with a good e-mail program called, simply, *Mail.* While other mail readers are available for OS X, Apple's Mail has a couple of big advantages:

- ✔ It's free and already installed.
- ✔ Apple supports it, so there is no finger pointing if you have a problem and call AppleCare.
- ✔ It is well integrated with OS X and applications that come with it, including Address Book, iChat, and iPhoto. You can search individual mail messages using Spotlight, the OS X search tool, and it's easy to include photos, resizing and cropping them as needed without leaving Mail.

I've long been a fan of plain-text e-mail. It's what nature intended e-mail to be. But the world has gone for a more multimedia e-mail experience. Apple Mail leads the way with stationery templates that let you include photos, artwork, and fancy backgrounds in every message. You can (and should) have separate stationery for different purposes: personal messages, business correspondence, love letters, party invitations, marriage proposals, press releases, breakups, birth announcements, subpoenas, sympathy cards, classified documents, extortion notes, book proposals — the list is endless. Apple supplies a set of professionally designed templates to get you started. Figure 8-4 shows Apple Mail composing a templated message.

Another cute Mail feature lets you send messages to yourself. Called *notes,* these reminders are integrated with Apple's calendar program, iCal, so you can tack a note or to-do list onto an appointment or other event.

I discuss how to get the information you need to set up an e-mail account in Chapter 4. If you entered that information when you first turned your Mac on, you may already be good to go. Otherwise, Mail guides you through the process when you first start it up. And if that doesn't work, enter the information by selecting Preferences on the Mail menu and clicking the Accounts icon. See Figure 8-5.

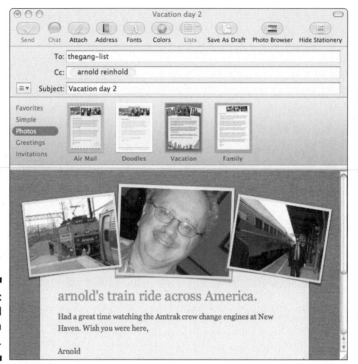

Figure 8-4:
Apple Mail
with a
template.

Figure 8-5:
Mail
preferences.

You can move your collection of e-mail messages from your PC. Mail can import mailboxes created by a number of other mail systems, including Outlook Express, Eudora, and Mozilla Netscape.

Choosing Entourage (from Microsoft)

A number of other mail readers work well in OS X. I have used Eudora for years and am happy with it. But if you are new to the Mac, you should stick with Apple's Mail. You might also consider Entourage, Microsoft's e-mail and personal organizer for the Mac. Entourage is included in Microsoft Office for the Mac and is the Mac equivalent of Outlook in Windows. If you really like Outlook or have to work with a Microsoft Exchange mail server at work, Entourage may be a better choice. Apple's Mail can work with Exchange server and is certainly worth a try, but the one-neck-to-wring philosophy works against Apple Mail here. Using a Microsoft product to connect to a Microsoft server may get you better support from Microsoft and your company's IT department.

Using Address Book and iSync

In OS X, Address Book is a separate application. Mail and other OS X applications, including iChat, make use of the Address Book database of contacts. You can search it with Spotlight. You can sync your address book with cell phones via Bluetooth and with other Macs you own via .Mac and the OS X iSync application. Apple's Address Book supports industry standards for contact information, including vCard and IMAP. You can even beam contacts from a Palm device to your Mac using its infrared port.

Some mobile devices require additional third-party software to sync with your Mac. For example, Pocketmac.com sells software that adds support for BlackBerrys and Windows Pocket PC devices. It can also link Entourage on your Mac with a wide variety of mobile devices. Markspace.com sells iSync software for Palm OS, Windows Mobile, and Sony PSP.

Transferring addresses from other mail services

You'll want to use the large collection of contact information you have accumulated over the years on your Mac. Different mail services often use proprietary formats for storing this information. Many tools are available on the Web that can assist you in moving your contacts.

Transferring your Outlook Express addresses

Fortunately, Outlook Express addresses are relatively easy to transfer. You start by grabbing your contacts from your PC:

1. **Plug a flash drive or external hard drive into your PC.**

2. **Create a new folder on that drive and name it, say,** `addresses to transfer.`

3. **From your PC's Start menu, open Outlook Express.**

4. **Choose Tools⇨Address Book, and then choose Edit⇨Select All.**

5. **Drag the selected addresses to the** `addresses to transfer` **folder.**

6. **Click the Remove Hardware icon in the Windows system tray.**

7. **Click the Safely Remove Mass Storage Device line that matches your flash drive in the window that appears. Count to ten, and then unplug the drive.**

On your Mac, you then follow these steps:

1. **Open the OS X Address Book application — it's in the Applications folder.**

2. **Plug the drive into your Mac.**

3. **Double-click the drive icon and then the** `addresses to transfer` **folder.**

4. **From the Finder menu, choose Edit⇨Select All.**

5. **Drag the selected contacts to the Address Book window.**

6. **Right-click the drive icon and select Eject.**

Transferring your AOL address book

Of course, you can use your AOL address book if you continue to use AOL's mail service. However, you may want to switch to Apple's Mail or another service, or you might want to consolidate all your contacts in Apple's Address Book. If this is the case, you have a couple of options:

- ✔ AOL has an arrangement with Plaxo.com that allows you to synchronize your AOL address book with Plaxo's service. Plaxo, in turn, offers a Mac OS X toolbar that lets you synchronize with Apple's Address Book. For more information, visit `aolsync.aol.com`.

- ✔ If you don't want a third party to see your address book, another option is the Windows program ePreserver from Connectedsw.com. It can transfer your AOL address book to Outlook Express, and you can transfer from there to the Mac as described in the previous section.

- ✔ Other possible approaches don't require a PC, but they typically involve transferring data through several e-mail programs.

Opting for online mail services

If you use your PC Web browser to access one of the online mail services, such as Google Gmail, MSN Hotmail, or Yahoo! Mail, you can continue to do so using any of the Mac browsers. Just enter the URL you normally use in the Mac browser's address bar.

Gmail and Yahoo! Mail also allow you to download and read your mail on your computer, using a mail program such as Apple's Mail. Both support the Post Office Protocol (POP). This feature is free in Gmail, but you must pay $20 per year to use it in Yahoo! Mail. It is not currently available for Hotmail. For Gmail instructions, go to the Gmail Web site's Help page and click the POP Access link. To sign up for the Yahoo! Mail POP service, click the Mail Upgrades link in your Yahoo! Mail window and then click the Upgrade to Yahoo! Mail Plus button.

Hushmail.com, a secure e-mail service, supports OS X and is worth considering if mail confidentiality is a concern. Read the part in Chapter 10 on picking cryptovariable passwords before signing up.

Handling common e-mail problems

E-mail's utility has diminished in recent years due to the rise of a number of antisocial uses. The first was junk e-mail advertising, known as *spam*. The name comes from a skit on Monty Python's Flying Circus, the BBC television comedy series. A Google search for `Monty Python spam video` is likely to find a clip of the original sketch. Watch it.

Unsolicited commercial e-mail or spam

One big problem with spam is that it can drown out your real messages, wasting your time and possibly causing you to miss something important. Most of the better e-mail services use special software that is intended to filter out spam. They are not completely effective, however. Apple's Mail program has its own spam filter that you train by indicating messages you think should have been caught as spam. It learns some of your criteria as you do this. For example, it might realize you are happy with the size of your body parts and suppress messages offering to enlarge them.

You can reduce the amount of spam you receive by selecting an unusual e-mail address, either random letters or some initials your friends might remember but spammers wouldn't come up with, such as `agrfromnyc`. Avoid e-mail addresses that end in numbers, such as `sampark456`. And don't post e-mails on Web sites and mailing lists without some disguise, such as `reinhold{you know what to type here}theworld.com`.

The mail order virus

Another concern is the use of e-mail for distributing viruses and other malware. This is less of an issue on Macs because few if any OS X viruses have been found in the wild so far.

Still, it's worth remembering the advice you have followed as a PC user: Don't open file attachments you were not expecting. The Mac has an added twist, because it asks for permission and a password when installing new software. If you get such a request after opening an e-mail or its attachment, just say no. And if you have other people with accounts on your Mac, particularly kids, don't give them administrative privileges. That way, they have to ask you before such an installation.

See Chapter 10 for more security tips.

419s and phishing

Most of us have been deluged by mail requesting assistance in handling a large sum of money, in return for which you get a nice cut of the proceeds. If you reply, you are eventually asked to advance a modest sum of money for necessary fees — an amount trivial compared to your eventual cut. After the criminals have you on the hook, you will see more requests for fees and perhaps an invitation to travel to some third-world country, where all sorts of mischief await. These e-mails are sometimes known as *419 scams.* Reportedly, they violate section 419 of the Nigerian penal code, Nigeria being one country where running these confidence games is a major industry. Never respond to one of these e-mails. Never. Ever. Period. The people who run them are experts at exploiting that tiny flicker of hope that, against all reason, the story is true. They can even make large sums of money appear in your bank account for a while. These disappear when the bank finds out that no funds are available to cover a transfer along the line. Don't respond. Ever.

Phishing is sending mail that pretends to be from one of your regular business contacts, a major bank, eBay, PayPal, and so on. You are asked to update your records, validate your credit card, or confirm a purchase you obviously did not make. These messages often appear very authentic, with corporate logos and valid links to the real company's Web site, such as links to the company's privacy policy or a Web page where you can report suspected fraud (always a nice touch). But they all contain an action link that takes you to a fake Web site that, again, looks like the real thing. There, you are asked to enter your password, credit card number, expiration date, date of birth, mother's maiden name, and so on — everything a hard-working identity thief could want. Dealing with these e-mails is tricky. The messages describe situations that *could* be true — unlike that e-mail from the heartbroken spouse of an executed African dictator with $35 million in a frozen bank account who found you through a mutual friend.

The most dangerous button

One button on your computer screen can get you into no end of trouble. It's the Send button in your e-mail program. When you click it, your message is on its way, unretrievable. It's all too easy to click the Send button when you think you've finished your message, particularly if you are replying to something that ticked you off. E-mail correspondence is different from speaking to someone in person or on the phone. No tone of voice exists to clue you in to the underlying emotions, and e-mail lacks the instant feedback of objections, grunts, and even pauses. And e-mails are written documents, easily preserved and searched for. Billion-dollar lawsuits and criminal trials have turned on a surfaced e-mail message.

E-mail may be the most powerful tool ever created for creating misunderstanding. Even if you think your message is level headed and couldn't possibly be taken the wrong way, it may contain typos and grammatical errors that can change its meaning, or just create an impression of carelessness.

Get in the habit of clicking the Save as Draft button instead of the Send button. Go have a cup of coffee, and give yourself some time to think it over. Then read the e-mail aloud — even to an empty office — before you send it.

One of my favorite *Mary Tyler Moore Show* moments was when Rhoda shows Mary a letter that Rhoda had written, professing undying love to a man she had just met. When asked for ways to improve the letter, Mary replied, "The important thing is that you don't send it." Sometimes the best use of mail is to get your thoughts on paper and then just leave them in the drafts folder.

If you think a message from eBay, PayPal, your bank, or some other source you're familiar with is not authentic, do not click any of its links, handy though that may seem. Instead, type the URL of the business directly into your Web browser's address bar. Then navigate to your personal account and log on to see whether any such requests are pending. If you are still not sure, call the company, using a phone number from a recent bill or bank statement, not from the suspect e-mail.

Instant Messaging

There used to be ads in the New York subway for a stenography school that read "if u cn rd ths u cn gt a gd job." Nowadays, the ability to read that ad just means that you use text instant messaging, or IM. The difference between IM and e-mail is that IM is live. You and the other person are both online at the same time. You type, the other person sees what you type, and he types something back. Systems like this, and the same abbreviated argot, go back to the dawn of electronic communication, with Morse code telegraphers chatting with each other over hundreds of miles of wire. The deaf community has been using this type of communication for decades, under the name TDD. The early Internet introduced a system called Internet Relay Chat (IRC) that was similar, but no permanently assigned names existed. It took commercial services, such as America Online, to add that important feature. Texting has since been added to cell phones, with the phone number serving as a unique identifier. Teens love it.

iChat

Unfortunately, the different commercial services rarely allow intercommunication among their systems. Apple's iChat program comes pretty close to being a universal communicator for instant messaging, and it can do a lot more than *how r u?* text messaging. With iChat, you have the following features at your disposal:

✔ You can chat on AOL's Instant Messenger (AIM), as well as Apple's own .Mac system. iChat also supports Jabber, a new open standard for IM. Jabber, in turn, lets you connect to ICQ, Yahoo! Messenger, and Google Talk. You can also chat directly with other OS X users on your local network using Bonjour.

✔ iChat can support voice and live video communications. The latter requires you to have a suitable video camera — iMacs and Apple laptops have them built in. You can invite up to nine other people for a voice conference or three other people for a videoconference. Video is transmitted using the ITU H.264 standard, which sends high-quality pictures over a limited bandwidth. You can videoconference with people on Windows computers as long as they have AOL Instant Messenger version 5.5 or later. It gets better.

✔ iChat Theater lets you share a slideshow or Keynote presentation with friends or business associates. They even see a live image of you as you give your presentation.

✔ iChat Screen Sharing lets you and another person control a single computer desktop, making it easy to collaborate on a project or help someone with a computer problem.

✔ Businesses can also set up private, secure iChat systems on their local network using OS X Server. The internal system can include non-Mac computers as well (see Chapter 15).

✔ Finally, iChat includes parental controls that let you limit what your kids can do and whom they can chat with.

All you need to set up iChat are the account names and passwords for each account you use. If your Mac does not have a built-in camera, iChatUSBCam, from `www.ecamm.com/mac/ichatusbcam`, can let you use an inexpensive USB camera.

Other IM systems

You can use your Mac to chat on other IM systems. Yahoo! Messenger and Windows Live (MSN) Messenger both have OS X clients you can download for free:

- Yahoo! Messenger: `messenger.yahoo.com/mac.php`
- Microsoft Messenger for Mac: `www.microsoft.com/mac/default.aspx?pid=msnmessenger`
- Mercury Messenger offers a Java-based MSN client that runs on OS X: `www.mercury.to`

The Windows Live client is also included in Microsoft Office.

Certain tricks let you access Windows Live and Yahoo! IM using iChat via Jabber servers. They're not for the fainthearted though. Here are a couple of links that can get you started:

```
www.jabber.org.au/ichat
www.allforces.com/2005/05/06/ichat-to-msn-through-jabber
```

Still another alternative is Adium, a popular open source messaging client for OS X that supports AIM, ICQ, Windows Live, Yahoo!, Jabber, and Google. You can download it for free at `trac.adiumx.com`.

Internet telephony via Skype

Apple's iChat has voice communications built in. Other systems allow voice communications over the Internet (VoIP), which are more like using a telephone. The Skype system, from `www.skype.com`, is an example and is free when you talk to other Skype-equipped computers. These can be Windows, Linux, and Pocket PC machines as well as Macs. Skype can also transfer files and do video, if you have a camera.

Skype offers a paid service that lets you call telephones all over the world for a small fee. Other paid services include inbound calls from telephones, voice mail, and SMS messages to and from cell phones.

Chapter 9

Networking the Mac Way

· ·

· ·

Computers without network connections are like fish without water, only they don't start to smell bad. And Macs are great network swimmers. They can connect to just about anything.

The earliest Macintosh came with built-in networking support using a proprietary system called AppleTalk. Apple has long since switched to widely accepted standards such as Ethernet and WiFi for digital communication between computers. These days, networking the Mac way is networking the computer industry way. Still, Apple leads by integrating multiple networking technologies into its products and by fielding innovative ways to make networking easier to use. One example is Bonjour, a set of software tools that let your computer find other services, such as printers, on a local-area network, without your having to type in magic incantations.

In this chapter, I cover the basics of Macintosh networking, including setting up wired and wireless networks. I also cover accessories such as keyboards, mice, and cell phones that network over short distances using a technology called Bluetooth. At the end of this chapter, you can also find out about unique ways of networking and about sharing files over your network.

Getting Wired with Ethernet

Important elements of the technology in Macintosh computers originated at Xerox's Palo Alto Research Center (PARC). The most famous example is the graphical user interface, but *Ethernet,* invented at PARC in the mid-1970s, was just as revolutionary. It let computers talk to each other without one being made a master of ceremonies that dictated which computer could talk when. The key idea in Ethernet was teaching computers manners so that they kept their messages short and did not interrupt another computer when it was talking. And, if by chance, two computers started talking at the same time, both would be silenced for a random few microseconds, making it less likely they would collide a second time.

All recent Macs have an Ethernet port, as do many PCs and quite a few printers and other devices, including the Apple TV. All you need to connect two such computers is an Ethernet cable. These are inexpensive, and you can find them in varying lengths at computer and electronics stores and many drugstores and supermarkets. With two devices connected via an Ethernet cable, you can create a local network that lets you transfer files easily.

Many offices have Ethernet jacks in the walls, allowing you to plug in to the corporate network. Check with your friendly IT staff before you do.

Strictly speaking, you find two types of Ethernet cable, straight thru and crossover. The first, as the name implies, connects each pin at one connector to the same pin at the other. The second swaps a pair of wires. You used to need a crossover cable to connect two computers or to connect a router to a high-speed modem, but modern routers and computers, including newer Macs, can automatically adapt themselves to either type of cable. You only need to know about this distinction if you are connecting two older computers.

Although connecting two devices with a cable is easy, you most likely want a network that's a little more capable. For example, your home network can enable two or more computers to share a printer and an Internet connection. To get that type of setup, you have a bit more work to do in order to set up an Ethernet network. The following sections walk you through the process.

Configuring Ethernet on your Mac

For the most part, Ethernet just works. If you need to configure its settings, follow these steps:

1. **Select System Preferences from the Apple menu, and click the Network icon.**

   You see the window shown in Figure 9-1.

2. **Select Built-in Ethernet from the sidebar.**

   The pane you see tells you your Mac's IP address and the IP address of your router, assuming that it sees it. Write down your router's IP address on a Post-It note or blank label and stick it on your router. You want it handy if you need to configure the router. You also see your address in the new, nobody-is-using-it-yet IPv6 addressing scheme.

Figure 9-1:
The System
Preferences
⇨Network
⇨Ethernet
pane.

3. **If you click the Advanced button, you see a pane, shown in Figure 9-2, with a row of buttons labeled TCP/IP, DNS, WINS, AppleTalk, 802.1X, Proxies, and Ethernet.**

If you are not a networking guru, don't mess with any of them unless someone instructs you to do so, such as a tech support person from your ISP or office IT department. Because many of these support people have limited Mac training, it's good to know where to find these settings. You may click the Ethernet button to see the unique address assigned to your Macintosh's Ethernet. It's called a MAC (Media Access Control) address, no relation to a Mac computer. You can also find it in the Hardware section of the About This Mac display on the Apple menu. This pane also shows the local IP address of this Mac and the IP address of your router.

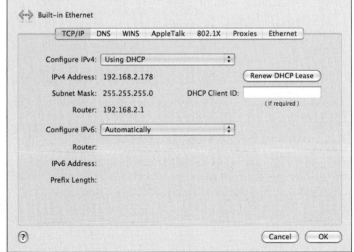

Figure 9-2:
The
Ethernet
Advanced
pane.

Understanding routers

If you want to connect more than two computers and hook them all up to the Internet, you need an Ethernet router. This is a small box with several Ethernet jacks so that you can plug in each computer. You use a special jack to connect the router to your high-speed Internet modem or to another router. Some routers also include a WiFi access point. I get to that in the next section.

Your router has a small computer inside that knows how to send the right messages to the right computer attached to it. Most routers have blinking lights in the front that give you some clue as to what is working and active. Other types of boxes, called *hubs* and *switches,* accomplish pretty much the same thing. Routers include a number of capabilities, such as firewalls for increased security and parental controls. You configure them using your Web browser — they look like a Web site with a special address.

Devices on your Ethernet are automatically assigned IP addresses in one of the special ranges that are reserved for private networks. These never go out on the public Internet, so you and your neighbors can be using the same addresses on your home networks without a problem. These numbers are usually assigned automatically. From the outside, your local network is known by the globally unique IP address assigned to it by your Internet service provider. Your computers — you can network more than one — use their internal addresses, and your router converts those to the external address automatically as needed, a process known as Network Address Translation (NAT).

Hooking up your router

You may already have a router as part of your PC installation. If so, you just need to run an Ethernet cable from your Mac to an empty port on your router. If not, and if you want to share your Internet connection with multiple computers, you should purchase a router. See Chapter 3 for suggestions.

The exact procedure for setting up a router can vary for different models, so look over the instructions that come with it and then save them with the other papers that came with your Mac. But the installation generally goes like this:

1. **Run an Ethernet cable from your high-speed modem to your router's WAN port.**

2. **Run an Ethernet cable from each computer you want to wire to the network to one of the router's LAN ports.**

   If you have a WiFi router, you don't need to run a cable to a WiFi-equipped computer, though you can if you want.

3. **Hook up power to your router.**

Typically, you plug the power unit that came with the router into an outlet on the wall or a power strip and then plug the power unit's wire into your router.

Configuring your router

Your router sits on your Network like any other computer. Most routers — Apple's AirPort Express is an exception I talk about later — put up their own Web site on your local network that you access with any Web browser, such as Safari. You configure the router through this Web site. Don't confuse this Web site with the router manufacturer's Web site, such as www.linksys.com. The one you use to change settings is literally inside your router and is only accessible from computers on your local network.

Your router keeps one of the internal IP addresses for itself, and you need to know that address to access the browser's Web site. The default address your browser uses is in its manual. In case you lost it, here are the IP addresses most often used by popular manufacturers, though the one used for your model may vary:

- D-Link:192.168.0.1
- Linksys: 192.168.1.1
- Netgear: 192.168.0.1
- SMC: 192.168.2.1
- USRobotics: 192.168.123.254

With the IP address in hand, you can set up your router as follows:

1. **Open your Web browser and type your router's IP address into the address bar.**

   So, for most SMC routers, you type **192.168.2.1** in your browser's address bar to access the router's Web page.

2. **When the router's logon screen appears asking for a password and, on many models, a username, enter the information that's requested.**

   If you assigned a password and forgot it, the simplest thing to do is to reset the router. However, you will lose any configuration information, such as game ports, you had previously set up. You might first try one of the common default passwords: admin, password, 1234, 12345, and none (that is, leave the password field blank).

   If all else fails, try resetting your router. This is often done by pressing a small button hidden behind a hole in the case. The standard method is to use a toothpick or straightened paper clip. After it is reset, your router will accept a default username and password. Again, check your manual. If you don't know your router's default password, try the ones listed previously or check the booklet that came with the router. If you can't find it, check the manufacturer's Web site. It helps to know the router's model number, too. Also, here is a Web site that compiles default usernames and passwords for routers: `www.phenoelit.de/dpl/dpl.html`.

3. **After you get past the router's logon screen, you see what looks like a mini Web site with many pages you can navigate through to change settings.**

   Figure 9-3 shows a typical router configuration page. Exactly what you can do varies by model, but common capabilities include the following:

   - Setting a new username and password.

   - Configuring how your router connects to your high-speed Internet modem.

   - Turning on or off a built-in firewall that helps protect computers on your local network from attacks via the Internet. This is done by blocking most ports, special code numbers your computer can respond to.

   - Allowing certain ports to be visible through the firewall, a capability needed for many online games.

   - Setting parental controls, such as limiting Internet use on certain computers to certain hours.

4. **When you're done, follow the prompts to save your settings, if needed, and exit your router's internal configuration page.**

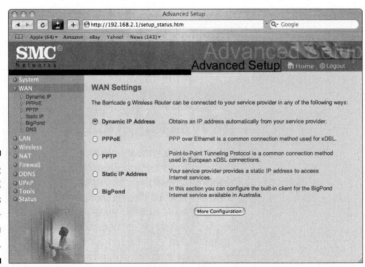

Figure 9-3: An SMC router's configuration screen.

Networking Wirelessly

Apple did not invent WiFi wireless networking, but it was the first company to popularize its use, under the brand name *AirPort*. A geekier name for the same thing is its Institute of Electrical and Electronics Engineers spec number, IEEE 802.11. Most new Macs, including all laptops, come with WiFi built in and ready to go. The models that don't come with AirPort just need to have an AirPort card installed to be on the air.

Ethernet has a geek name, too: IEEE 802.3. And, as the numbers suggest, WiFi is related to Ethernet. But instead of sending short messages over wires, WiFi sends them via radio signals. The WiFi protocol is more complicated than Ethernet's because radio signals can fade in and out as laptops move around, and you can move from one access point to another automatically.

Understanding access points

The heart of a WiFi network is an *access point* that supervises the communications. An access point may be built into your Ethernet router or it may be a stand-alone unit. Each access point has a limited range, up to about 300 feet, or 100 meters; however, you can have more than one access point, and they can talk to each other. To let WiFi computers within range access the Internet, at least one access point has to connect to your Internet modem, usually with an Ethernet cable.

WiFi comes in several flavors, denoted by lowercase letters attached to the geek name. They are 802.11a, 802.11b, 802.11g, and 802.11n. The 802.11b was the first version Apple introduced. It's also the slowest, nominally 11 Mbps (megabits per second). The 802.11g version came later and can operate at 54 Mbps. The *a* version is as fast as *g* but operates on a different frequency band. The latest version is 802.11n. It's up to five times as fast as *g* and can use both frequency bands. New Macs support all four standards. Recent PowerPC Macs support *b* and *g,* and older ones just support *b*.

The speeds you see for the various versions are maximum speeds. The speed you actually see depends on many factors, and it's usually no more than half the maximum. If you are connecting to the Internet using WiFi, you are also limited by the speed of your Internet connection, which, even with high-speed cable or DSL service, is usually slower than even 802.11b. Be aware that a WiFi network automatically throttles down to the speed of its slowest member, so if you have an older laptop that only knows how to speak 802.11b, you might want to turn it off or shut down WiFi on it when it's not in use. A big advantage of the faster speeds is the ability to stream media files between computers and to your home entertainment center's Apple TV.

WiFi security

Another issue WiFi has to deal with is security. Ethernet signals are pretty much confined to the wire, so unless a snoop enters your premises and taps in, your communications stay private. WiFi is radio and can go beyond your walls. A snoop could park on your street and pick up your WiFi signal with a laptop, or pick it up from miles away with a high-gain directional antenna — instructions are available on the Internet for making one out of a Pringles potato chip can. So the WiFi folks added an encryption option, which evolved into the following options:

- ✔ **WEP (Wired Equivalent Privacy):** The first form of encryption, WEP was meant to offer the same level of security you enjoy with wired Ethernet. Researchers soon found gaping holes in its design; using WEP is like posting a *Keep Out* sign on your property. Honest people respect it; determined crooks don't.

- ✔ **WPA (Wireless Protected Access) and WPA2:** These two newer security standards were added in response to the problems with WEP. The latter, WPA2, has the geek name of IEEE 802.11i. WPA and WPA2 provide protection more like a high chain-link fence (WPA2 adds barbed wire on top). But a fence is not worth much if the gate has a lock that's easy to pick. So to take full advantage of WPA and WPA2, you need to set a strong, cryptovariable-grade password when you set them up. I tell you how to pick strong passwords in the next chapter.

If you have to use WEP for some reason and you need to access corporate or other sensitive sites, see whether they support a Virtual Private Network (VPN). VPNs use "end-to-end" encryption, so data intercepted by a wireless snoop is meaningless to them. And be especially careful to check that Web sites are secure — look for the closed-lock icon — before entering passwords and other personal info.

Setting up your WiFi hardware

Most of the heavy lifting needed to set up a WiFi network takes place at the access point or base station. In the sections that follow, you find out how to set up WiFi connections in a number of different ways. I start by explaining Apple's access point and other access points. But this isn't your only option. Depending on your setup, you may want to make your Mac an access point or just network several computers wirelessly. Read on for details.

Apple's AirPort Extreme base station

If you already have a WiFi router or access point, you can use it with your Mac. (See the next section in this chapter.) But if you don't or want to move up to the faster 802.11n standard or just want more coverage in your home or office, consider getting Apple's WiFi base station, *AirPort Extreme*. Here's a quick overview of what it offers as I write this book:

- ✔ It supports all the WiFi transmission standards — *a, b, g,* and *n* — and the security standards WEP, WPA, and WPA2. See the section "Understanding access points," earlier in this chapter, for details about these standards.

- ✔ It has three Ethernet jacks for hooking up wired network connections to devices and a fourth Ethernet jack where you plug in your high-speed cable or DSL Internet modem. All operate at speeds up to 100 Mbps.

- ✔ It includes a USB jack, where you can plug in a printer or hard drive. They can then be shared by any Mac or PC on your network. Only one USB jack is available, so if you want both a hard drive and a printer, you need a USB hub. But these are cheap and let you connect more than one printer and more than one hard drive.

  Your Mac (or Macs) can use the shared hard drive for Time Machine backups. In the world of commercial networks, having disk volumes shared like this is called a *storage-area network,* or *SAN.* Commercial SAN systems go for big bucks.

- ✔ It can stream content, such as music, movies, and slideshows, to an Apple TV in your home entertainment center. The streamed content can come from your Mac or the shared disk. Everything plays together. Welcome to the future.

To set up your AirPort Extreme from OS X, you run the AirPort Setup Assistant program. It's in the Utilities folder that's inside your Applications folder. If you want to access the shared printer and hard drive from your PC, you load the Bonjour for Windows software that comes with the base station onto your PC. You need to be running at least Windows XP with Service Pack 2.

Configuring other base stations

Most non-Apple WiFi base stations are built into a router and are configured using your Web browser, as described in the section "Configuring your router," earlier in this chapter. When you enter the browser's IP address, username, and password, you see the usual router Web page, such as that shown earlier in Figure 9-3, with router configuration options plus additional ones for wireless, which include options for the following tasks:

- ✔ Turn on WiFi so that your hardware is enabled. This is also the place where you can turn off WiFi if the need arises.

- ✔ Set what WiFi modes are allowed — your old friends *a, b, g,* and *n.*

- ✔ Give your network a name, called a *service set identifier* (SSID). You should avoid using a name that reveals your identity, such as `therein holds`. Be creative.

✔ Decide whether to broadcast that name. Turning off SSID broadcast makes it a little harder for snoops to find you, but it's also harder for you to find your own network.

✔ Decide whether to turn on security and, if you do, decide what mode to use: WEP, WPA, or WPA2. If you know that all the computers and other WiFi devices you are using are relatively new and support WPA2, that's the security mode to use. Otherwise, I suggest WPA, which works with most stuff out there except some game controllers. WEP is a last resort, to be avoided if possible.

See the section "WiFi security," earlier in this chapter, for details.

✔ Decide what password to use for wireless security. The password you are asked to enter has nothing to do with your computer's logon password and should be different. WPA and WPA2 are both quite strong encryption schemes, as long as you use a WPA password that is hard to crack. WPA uses its password as a cryptographic key, and that key can be broken if the password is too simple. I discuss picking strong passwords in Chapter 10. But the bottom line is to use 16 or more random letters. Write them down and keep them somewhere safe. Yeah, I know, someone told you never to do that. I don't agree. You can read my reasons in the next chapter. If you forget your WiFi security password, reset the unit as described in the section "Configuring your router," earlier in this chapter, and create a new password.

Making your Mac a WiFi access point

If you have a WiFi-equipped Mac connected to the Internet by a wired Ethernet connection or even a dialup modem, you can turn that Mac into a WiFi access point and share the connection with other WiFi-equipped Macs and even PCs.

To do this, follow these steps on the computer that has the Internet connection:

1. **Select System Preferences from the Apple menu, and click the Sharing icon.**

2. **Click the Internet button.**

3. **From the Share Your Connection From popup menu, select the way this computer is connected to the Internet: typically Ethernet, Modem, or Bluetooth.**

4. **In the To Computers Using section, select the AirPort check box.**

5. **Click the AirPort Options button.**

6. **Assign your new network a name.**

7. **Turn on encryption if you like — yucky WEP is the only option — and enter a password.**

8. **Click the OK button.**

9. **Back in the Sharing pane, click the Start button in the Internet Sharing section.**

Your other computers should now see your new WiFi network. When you no longer want your Mac to serve as an access point, go back to the System Preferences Sharing pane and click the Stop button in the Internet Sharing section.

Creating a network with no base station

If you just want to network with a bunch of other WiFi-equipped computers, you don't need no stinkin' base station. Just follow these steps:

1. **Select Create Network from the Wireless icon list.**

2. **Give your network a name.**

3. **Turn on wimpy WEP encryption if you like — that's all Apple offers, so don't use this mode for sensitive information.**

   You're on the air.

Windows can do this trick, too, and you can join each other's networks. Computer-to-computer networks like this one show up in a separate section of the Wireless icon list.

A RADIUS you can ignore

When you set up an access point (other than AirPort), you may see configuration options for RADIUS or 802.11x. These are generally used by enterprise-scale installations that have computer servers set up to manage user authentication. WiFi access points can be set up to communicate with these Remote Authentication Dial-In User Service (RADIUS) servers to get their cryptographic keys and so on. Good stuff, but probably not something you need for a home or small office. If you work in a large enterprise that uses RADIUS, the IT staff can clue you in on what to do. If you *are* the IT staff, try reading a different book.

Connecting with WiFi

After you've set up your hardware, you're ready to connect to your network. Turn on AirPort — Apple's name for WiFi — by following these steps:

1. Click the Wireless icon at the top of your screen (see Figure 9-4).

Figure 9-4: Lots of WiFi networks to choose from, including one that is open.

2. Click the Wireless icon again, just once. Be patient. Count to five.

3. In a couple of seconds, a list of wireless networks that your Mac can hear will appear, such as the list shown in Figure 9-4.

Hopefully yours is on the list.

Beware of WiFi phishing! In public places, such as airports (the kind with runways) and computer trade shows, it's common to see computer-to-computer networks with names like "Open Hot Spot" or "Free Internet Access." The people who set these up usually don't have your best interests at heart. Windows users who log on to these sites often get a free virus sampler for their efforts. Mac viruses may show up one of these days, too. So stay away from computer-to-computer networks you don't know about and definitely don't give out personal information, such as a credit card number or even a home address — criminals will pay for information like "the Smith family is waiting to board a plane to Europe."

4. Select the network and enter your password when asked, assuming that you set one.

If you're joining a network that doesn't broadcast its name for the world to see, select Other from the Wireless icon list. You are then prompted for the name of the network (spelling counts), the type of security used, and the password, if any.

Figure 9-5 shows the AirPort pane of the System Preferences Network window. You usually have no business here besides checking status.

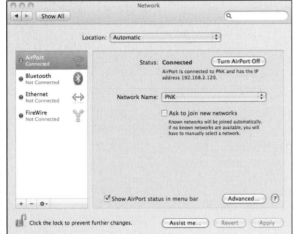

Figure 9-5:
The System
Preferences
⇨Network
⇨AirPort
pane.

Fixing interference problems

The performance you enjoy can also be reduced by interference from other radio signals. The *b* and *g* versions of WiFi operate on a radio band, 2.4 GHz, where licensed operation is permitted. This band is shared with other users, including Bluetooth hardware, cordless telephones, microwave ovens, and amateur radio, not to mention your neighbor's WiFi network. The *a* version operates at 5 GHz, also unlicensed, but a less-cluttered spot on your microwave dial. WiFi can use several different channels in each band — the number varies by country — so a fair amount of band sharing is possible.

Somewhere in the back of your computer's manual with all the other legal notices, you should see this notice:

> *This device complies with Part 15 of the FCC Rules. Operation is subject to the following two conditions: (1) This device may not cause harmful interference, and (2) this device must accept any interference received, including interference that may cause undesired operation.*

Of course, this legalese applies within the United States, but other countries have similar rules. If you do get interference, you are usually on your own.

You can take the following steps to combat interference and other signal problems:

- **Move your laptop.** Closer to the access point is usually better, but any change in position and orientation can help, even a few inches. (One-half wavelength at 2.4 GHz is about 5 inches, for those of you who know why this matters.)

- **Move the access point.** Put it in a more central location, hang it high on a wall, or move it away from a known source of interference, such as a cordless phone base station or a microwave oven. Experiment.

- **Adjust the access point's antenna.** Try small increments. If it has two antennas, have them point in different directions, at right angles to each other.

- **Turn off your cordless phone and unplug the base station.** If that reduces the interference, move your cordless phone and base station farther from the access point and from your laptop. Plug the base station into a different outlet. If those steps don't help, replace your cordless phone with a model that operates on a different frequency band (the band is usually marked on the package), or just go back to wired phones. (You carry a cell phone anyway.)

- **Get a new microwave oven.** You can easily tell whether your microwave oven causes network problems — the problems only happen when it's cooking. If the microwave is used infrequently, you might just live with the interference, but if it's used a lot, say in a small office at lunchtime, consider buying a newer model. They're cheap and you can return the new one if it's no better. Also, make sure that the microwave is on a different electrical circuit from your laptops and access points.

- **Buy a WiFi repeater.** These units plug into a wall outlet and retransmit WiFi signals from your access point for greater coverage. Having a second signal source may reduce interference problems.

Getting Personal with Bluetooth

Bluetooth is another wireless technology, but its mission differs from WiFi's. WiFi connects the computers and other devices within a home or place of business to create a local-area network. Bluetooth has a much shorter range, about 30 feet. It is designed to create a personal network around an individual. The most familiar example is the Bluetooth headset — a friend calls them *Borg implants,* after the evil *Star Trek* Cyborgs. These units fit over your ear and connect wirelessly to Bluetooth-equipped cell phones. They let the wearer talk hands-free. Bluetooth can also be used to connect a keyboard and mouse to your Mac without wires. Nintendo uses Bluetooth in its Wii game controllers. Bluetooth can link your Mac to your cell phone and PDA, allowing address book updates to be shared among all devices, a process called *synchronizing.*

Bluetooth was the nickname of a tenth-century Scandinavian king, Harold I, who unified many warring tribes. Like its namesake, Bluetooth networking can unify may disparate devices to create your own personal computing empire.

Pairing before sharing

Two Bluetooth devices can't talk with each other until they have been formally introduced, a process called *pairing*. You can easily understand why this is necessary. You don't want your Bluetooth cell phone chit-chatting with the cell phone of the person sitting next to you on the bus — unless he or she is cute. You might wonder how you get them to pair if they can't talk to each other. The answer is that you have to get one of them in a special state called *discoverable*. How this is done differs for each device. In some cases, you press a special button or hold down a regular button longer, or you must navigate through a cell phone menu maze. The details are in each device's manual. This leads me to state the following law:

King Harold's First Law of Bluetooth: *Never throw out the instruction booklet that comes with a Bluetooth device.* In Chapter 4, I suggest that you find a place to keep all the manuals and discs that come with your computer and accessories — one you won't forget about. You can keep cell phone and Bluetooth papers there, too. If you do lose the booklet, check the manufacturer's Web site. Most have instructions online for recent models.

Configuring Bluetooth

You configure Bluetooth by clicking the Bluetooth icon at the top of your Mac's screen. The list you see includes options to turn Bluetooth on and off, make your Mac discoverable by other Bluetooth devices, and browse for files on Bluetooth devices. You can also open the Bluetooth preferences screen shown in Figure 9-6, which is also available from System Preferences.

Figure 9-6:
Bluetooth preferences screen.

Networking in Other Ways

Ethernet, WiFi, and Bluetooth are the main ways to network Macs, but the following other tricks may come in handy:

- ✔ **FireWire:** You can connect a FireWire cable between two Macs, and OS X can use that cable as a network connection. FireWire shows up in the System Preferences Network pane's popup menu list, just like Ethernet or AirPort. You simply select it and configure it, if necessary, the same way you would configure Ethernet.

- ✔ **FireWire disk mode:** Another way to use FireWire to transfer data between two Macs is to reboot one of them (not both) while holding down the *T* key. That Mac will start up in what Apple calls FireWire disk mode. You see a large FireWire logo dancing around your computer's screen. If you then plug the other end of the FireWire cable into the Mac you did not reboot, the first Mac's hard drive will appear on the second Mac's desktop as just another hard drive. You can then move files to it or transfer files out of it, just like any external hard drive.

- ✔ **.Mac:** Apple's .Mac service lets subscribers share access to their iDisk. You can even synchronize files, contacts, and appointments between two Macs. Space is limited, however.

- ✔ **Sneakernet:** The ultimate fallback networking scheme is to use a USB flash drive to transfer data from one computer to another. A flash drive can easily fit in your pocket, and most incorporate a loop so that you can attach them to a key chain. Some people hang theirs around their neck on a lanyard. Wearing sneakers is optional.

Sharing Files over Your Network

Regardless of how you establish your network, you will probably want to use it to share files with other connected computers.

Sharing files from your Mac

You can also tell your Mac to make files available to other computers on your local network, or even over the Internet. From an administrator account, follow these steps:

1. **Select System Preferences from the Apple menu, and click the Sharing icon.**

   You see the Sharing pane shown in Figure 9-7.

Figure 9-7:
System
Preferences
Sharing
pane.

2. **Select the check boxes next to the sharing modes you wish to use.**

   Personal File Sharing allows other Macs to access files on this machine. To let your PC see your Mac files, click the Advance button and then select the Share Files and Folders Using SMB check box. You then have to specify which accounts on your Mac can use Windows sharing. Normally only the Public folder is shared, but you can specify other folders to be shared as well.

You can select more than one sharing mode, but each has some potential security risks, so don't select more modes than you plan to use.

Sharing files from your PC

I cover setting up PC file sharing from Windows XP in Chapter 6. (You right-click a folder you want to share, select Properties, and select the Share This Folder on the Network check box.) File sharing from Windows Vista is controlled from the Network and Sharing Center Control Panel. You select the check boxes next to the modes you want to enable. It works much like the process in OS X, except Vista only shares files in a Shared folder, and you have to promise Vista you won't share anything bad.

Seeing the files you shared

To see shared files from your Mac, follow these steps:

1. **Select Connect to Server from the Finder's Go menu, and then click the Browse button.**

   Or, you can click the Network icon in the sidebar of an open Finder window.

2. **Click the Servers line.**

   You see the Network browser shown in Figure 9-8.

3. **Click the server you want to access and log on.**

   You'll need a password for the other machine, if one has been set.

Figure 9-8:
The OS X
Network
browser.

The procedure from a PC is quite similar. Click the Network Neighborhood icon or select My Network Places from the Start menu.

Chapter 10

Staying Secure in a Connected World

As you most likely know, the convenience of hopping on the Internet has its downside: viruses, spyware, identity theft, and more. You're better equipped to avoid these hassles if you have at least a basic understanding of what they are and how to keep them at bay. One reason you may be switching to a Mac is precisely because you're looking for better security.

In this chapter, Mac security features are in the spotlight. You find out not only what Mac OS X does behind the scenes to keep the gunk away from your computer, but also how to take advantage of features and techniques that improve upon its already good defenses — namely strong passwords and file encryption tools. When the time comes to trade in your old Mac for a new one, this chapter also explains how to wipe data so that any valuable information it might contain is beyond a thief's reach.

What Makes a Mac More Secure?

Macs have a reputation for security on the Internet, and for the most part, it's well deserved. Critics say Macs have such a small share of the overall computer market that computer criminals and hacker hobbyists don't consider them worth the time to mount an attack. That may indeed be part of the story, but Mac users aren't complaining about being ignored. Popularity isn't always a good thing.

However, there is much more to Mac security. Apple built OS X on top of an operating system called UNIX that AT&T developed for its internal use, back when it was the telephone monopoly in the United States. UNIX had good security tools, and Apple added more.

Modern operating systems, such as OS X and Microsoft Windows, assign different levels of privilege to different programs. Operating systems are the gatekeepers of a computer, deciding what programs are allowed to run and what they are allowed to do. Intruders have two goals: to be able to run their evil programs on your computer and to get maximum privileges for their program. After they get that gold pass, the programs can install themselves in the innards of the operating system in ways that are hard to detect. The maximum permission level on many operating systems is the *root* level, and hacker tools that can penetrate to this level are called *rootkits.*

Windows XP lets many programs run at a maximum privilege level. If an attacker can subvert one of these programs — and he or she often can — the hacker is home free. OS X is more careful with the privileges it doles out. You can tell Windows to be more careful too, but doing so can cause problems for many programs that were designed to operate at a high privilege level. OS X has always restricted application program privileges, so all Mac apps are cool with those restrictions.

Just as in Windows, users can adjust security settings up or down in Mac OS X, but because OS X is shipped with security set at a high level to begin with, it is very hard for Mac viruses to spread. Epidemiologists have learned that they don't have to inoculate an entire population with a vaccine to stop an epidemic. As long as a large enough fraction of the population is immune, the disease stops spreading. It works the same for computers. Having most Macs set at a high security level makes it hard for any Mac virus to spread.

Protecting Yourself with Passwords

Never write down your password. Eat five servings of fruits and vegetables every day. Use a different password for every account. Get 30 minutes of aerobic exercise four times a week. Always select passwords with uppercase and lowercase letters, numbers, and special characters. Every time you're with that special someone, be sure to use a — well, you get the idea. We're constantly bombarded with good advice, advice we know we should listen to, but most of us fall short.

As computers and Internet technology have crept into more and more aspects of our daily lives, our use of passwords has exploded. E-mail, instant messaging, online banking, brokerage accounts, automated teller machines, computers, networking devices, multiplayer games, subscription Web sites — they all ask for passwords. And then we need a bunch more at work and school. The average computer user accesses dozens of different password-protected thingies. And the consequences of forgetting a password or having one fall into the wrong hands range from inconvenience to disaster.

Proper personal password policy

Your Mac is not an island, and no amount of fiddling with its security settings can protect you if you don't use passwords wisely. Increasingly, computer security experts are realizing that the standard password policy advice is unrealistic at best and counterproductive at worst. So, in the following sections, I present some suggestions for using passwords that you can actually follow and that can make you far more secure than the vast majority of other computer users.

Use a common password for unimportant accounts

If someone figures out the password for your newspaper subscriptions and other Web sites that demand registration for no good reason, it's not the end of the world. So it is reasonable to use one password for all such accounts. For extra credit, you might have two common passwords, one for stuff you *really* don't care about and a second for things like e-mail or instant messaging, where you have no big risk of financial loss, but you'd like to maintain some privacy.

Use separate, stronger passwords for important work accounts and for personal accounts, such as online banking, where real potential exists for misuse that can cost you money or enable identity theft.

Write down your passwords

Most people can't memorize as many passwords as they need for optimal security. It's too easy to forget the ones you don't use daily. Instead, they just keep recycling one or two easily remembered passwords. If software at work makes them pick a password with mixed cases and Japanese characters, they add the minimum needed to get past the password police.

You are more likely to pick strong passwords if you know they are written down some place, so you have no risk of forgetting them. The trick is to keep the list safe. The classic Post-it note stuck to your monitor is not what I have in mind. Good choices include the following places:

- **Your wallet:** You have other valuable information in there already, like your credit cards and driver's license. You are careful with it by habit. If you lose it, you quickly notice it's gone, and you can change the passwords on your computer accounts at the same time you are canceling your charge accounts.

- **A clever hiding place at home:** Use your ingenuity. A slip of paper doesn't take up much space. If you have a basement, you probably have lots of nooks and crannies. But be sure to pick a location you'll remember. The first place you think of is one you'll likely remember again.

✔ **A safe-deposit box:** Although awkward if you keep needing to add new accounts, this can be a good place for your master list. Keep recent changes in your wallet. For those who plan ahead, your next of kin will have a much easier time dealing with your estate if they acquire a list of your passwords after you're gone. If you want to take some secrets to the grave, use a separate password and leave it off this list.

✔ **A password manager program:** These applications keep all your passwords in an encrypted file. All you need to remember is one master password. And most of these programs offer to generate strong, random passwords for you when you open new accounts.

Mac OS X has a built-in password manager called *Keychain*. OS X automatically uses Keychain to store the passwords it needs, such as for WiFi, networks, and accessing various Web sites. You can see the passwords it stores, and add more entries if you wish, by opening Keychain Access in the Applications⇨ Utilities folder. You need to enter your logon password to see the stored passwords. Figure 10-1 shows the Keychain Access displaying a stored password. To add a new password, click the plus sign icon (+) at the bottom-left of the window.

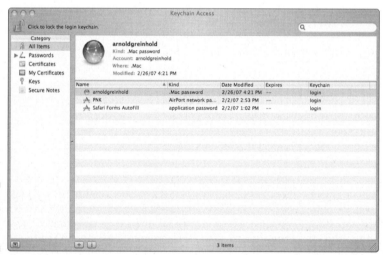

Figure 10-1:
Keychain
Access.

The following other good password managers, which are available for OS X and Palm OS, are free and open source:

✔ Mac programs include the Java version of Password Safe(`password safe.sourceforge.net`) and Password Gorilla (`www.fpx.de/fp/`

Software/Gorilla). Both are compatible with each other and with their Windows and Linux versions as well.

✔ For Palm OS, I suggest Keyring (gnukeyring.sourceforge.net). It's a handy program, but note that while you can back up your password file to your Mac during a Hotsync operation, you can only read the password file on a Palm OS device.

I expect a password manager will be available for iPhone in the near future, but I don't know of one yet. Check at www.ditchmypc.com for the latest info.

Don't change your passwords without a good reason

I know, the password police say to change passwords every few months. Some companies configure their software to require periodic changes. I find this advice dubious at best for most people. A miscreant who gets hold of your password is likely to use it promptly. And people forced to change passwords soon learn the minimum change they need to make to get by the password-change program. Attackers know those tricks, too. The time to really change passwords is when you think they may be compromised, such as when you have to give someone else a password — never a good thing to do, but it happens — or when a trusted employee quits or is fired. Using a sensitive password at a cybercafe is another occasion for a change.

Assessing risk

Security doesn't exist in a vacuum. You have to consider what risks you face. For computer security, risks fall into two major categories: outside risks and inside risks. Outside risks refer to things bad guys can do without entering your premises. This includes sniffing your WiFi signal from your parking lot, capturing your data as it makes its way through the Internet, or just stealing your laptop. Inside risks cover things that can be done by guests, family members, fellow employees, and the cleaning people.

In general, by using passwords, outside risks are easier to protect against than inside risks. There are too many ways a determined insider can capture your password, ranging from installing keystroke-capture software on your computer to placing a concealed video camera above your workstation. (With tiny, inexpensive wireless cameras, this is now alarmingly easy to do.)

Best practice for large organizations that demand strong internal security requires *two-factor authentication*. Users demonstrate who they are to the computer both by knowing a password or PIN and by having in their possession a small device called a token. Some tokens plug into the computer; others display a number that changes frequently. The user types the number into the computer along with the password during logon. At least one vendor, Cryptocard.com, supports two-factor authentication on Macs.

Picking powerful passwords

Passwords are like medicine. If all you have is a common cold, you might pick up whatever remedy catches your eye on the drugstore shelves. But if you have a serious condition, you want prescription drugs that are tested and known to work. Picking passwords is similar. If what you're protecting is stuff that doesn't matter all that much, most any password will do. But if your password is guarding information that could do real harm if the wrong people got hold of it — harm to yourself, to your family, to your business, or to your clients — you need a method of picking passwords whose quality is measurable.

You find lots of advice on how to create a password, and much of it is negative. Don't pick a single word in a dictionary. Don't use a password shorter than eight characters. Don't use passwords that people who know you might easily guess, such as the name of your kid, pet, or significant other. The positive advice mostly asks you to do something clever, like think of a famous quote, lyric, or title and then abbreviate it, for example, 2bornot2b, 0saycanuc, or S2Mac4D. The problem is that people who write password-cracking programs know all these tricks and have built them into their programs. And those password-cracking programs and dictionaries are widely available on the Internet.

The amazing power of random

Few silver bullets in life exist, but one is available for picking passwords. If you pick the letters or symbols of your password at random, and make it long enough, the odds of someone guessing it become astronomically low.

Most security experts don't push random passwords out of concern that most users won't accept them. They seem ugly and hard to remember. Because you've read this far into a computer-advice book, I think you are exceptional and might be willing to put in the little bit of effort needed to get the best security you can.

One reason I take a contrarian view on some standard password maxims is that they encourage less secure behavior. Asking people to have separate passwords for every account, telling them to never write passwords down, and forcing them to change passwords regularly absolutely guarantees that they will find ways to circumvent the process. And the ways most users do that are all too predictable. I think it's better to write down a random password than to memorize an easy one that won't stop an attacker anyway.

Another old saw asks people to include a mix of uppercase and lowercase letters, digits, and special characters in their passwords. The well-intentioned idea is to make their passwords more random. But most people simply add a digit or special character to their favorite password. And they typically do that in predictable ways as well. Security expert Bruce Schneier recently found that the most commonly used password on MySpace.com was `password1`.

Knowing the score

One nice thing about random passwords is that you can measure their strength. It's easy to assign a point score that says how hard they are to guess. Each additional point means that it's twice as hard to guess the password.

The way you figure the score is quite simple. Each character or symbol in the password gets a certain number of points, and you just add them up. The number of points per character depends on how many possibilities you choose from. If you pick a character at random from the 26 letters *a* to *z*, it gets 4.7 points. If the possibilities include the 26 letters and the 10 digits 0 to 9, you get 5.1 points per character. Pick at random from any of the 94 possible characters on a standard U.S. computer keyboard — lowercase and uppercase letters, digits, and special characters — and you score 6.5 points per character.

The thing to note is that the fancy passwords get more points per character, but not that many more. An 11-character password of single-case letters *a* through *z* has the same strength as an 8-character password made up of all 94 possible keyboard characters: about 52 points. Which style of password you choose is mostly a matter of taste. Both are equally secure. If you use your password a lot, saving three characters may be worth the trouble. On the other hand, if you travel to other countries and plan to use local computers there to log on to your accounts, you may have trouble. Some of the special characters in your password may not be on the keyboards you find there, and the ones that are present may be in unfamiliar locations on the local keyboards. And typing special characters on hand-held devices, such as the iPhone, can be a pain.

TECHNICAL STUFF

The true meaning of password points

You may be wondering what these points I keep talking about represent. Or not — in which case, feel free to skip this sidebar. The points I am using refer to a concept called *entropy,* and in the technical literature, the points are called *bits.* Entropy measures how random things are; the concept goes back to the nineteenth century, when scientists were trying to figure out how to make better steam engines. One bit or point is the amount of randomness introduced by flipping a fair coin. The formula I use to assign points to passwords was discovered by the great physicist Ludwig Boltzmann and is carved on his tombstone.

Making passwords memorable

Remembering passwords that contain special characters can be easier if you use short nicknames for the special characters. Table 10-1 offers some suggestions.

Table 10-1		Nicknaming Special Characters		
`	Ding		{	Sneer
~	Twiddle		}	Smirk
!	Bang		[	Uh
@	At		]	Duh
#	Hash		|	Pole
$	Bucks		\	Back
%	Ears		:	Eyes
^	Hat		;	Wink
&	And		"	Quote
*	Star		'	My
(	Frown		<	Mouth
)	Smile		>	Nose
_	Under		,	Tear
-	Dash		.	Dot
+	Plus		?	Huh?
=	Equals		/	Slash

Tell me a story

One way to memorize a random password is to make up a story that goes with the letters and symbols. For example, to remember the following password

```
1!30c;tF
```

you might make up a story about hearing one bang when your were 30 and seeing a winking tall fighter.

Permit Password Assistant to assist

The phrase "pick at random" is easier said than done. Computers are designed to do the same thing each time you run a program. Most computer programming languages include "random number generator" functions that aren't really random. Better operating systems, including OS X and Windows, have ways of making things truly random, measuring exactly how long it takes hard drive arms to move, for example. Unfortunately, many programs on the Internet that claim to make random passwords do not use these tools.

OS X includes its own password generator called Password Assistant. It's designed to help you pick passwords for your Mac OS X accounts, but you can use it for other purposes as well. Here is one way to do that:

1. **Open Keychain Access; it's in the Utilities folder, inside the Applications folder.**

2. **Click the plus sign near the bottom to create a new entry.**

   You don't have to save your new password in Keychain, but you can if you want. This is just one way to get at Password Assistant.

3. **Click the Key icon next to the Password field.**

   The Password Assistant window appears, as shown in Figure 10-2.

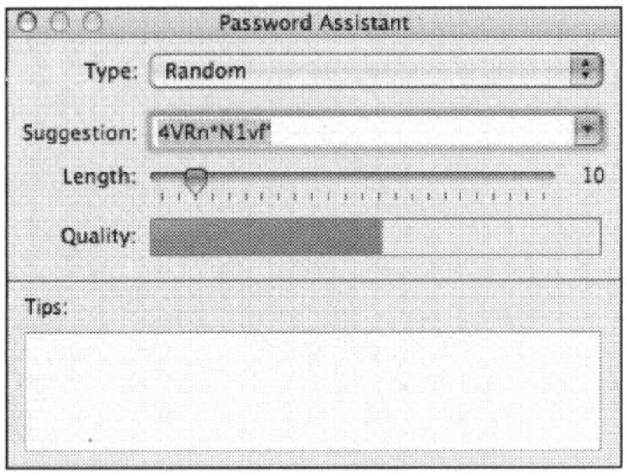

Figure 10-2:
OS X
Password
Assistant.

Type:	Random
Suggestion:	4VRn*N1vf
Length:	10
Quality:	
Tips:	

4. **From the Type popup menu, select Random to create a password.**

   For an explanation of the other options, see the nearby sidebar, "Ordering up passwords from Password Assistant."

5. **If you want your password to be a particular length, move the Length slider.**

   See the section "How long does it have to be?" later in this chapter, for details about how password length impacts security.

6. **After you have selected the password you want from the Suggestion field, write it down or save it in Keychain — or both.**

7. **To save your new password in Keychain, fill out the Keychain Item Name and Account Name fields and click the Add button. Otherwise click the Cancel button.**

If you use computers a lot, you'll be faced with the need to come up with a new password from time to time, often in situations when you are in a bit of a hurry. If you click the arrow next to the Suggestion field, Password Assistant shows you a list of candidate passwords. Write a bunch down on a slip of paper and carry it in your wallet so that you always have a few handy.

Other ways to pick random passwords

Be leery of password-picking programs you find perusing the Internet. Many are poorly written, and it's hard to tell which do an acceptable job. The password managers I mention earlier are pretty good. Here is a link to a password generator I wrote and trust: `www.theworld.com/~reinhold/passgen.html`.

Ordering up passwords from Password Assistant

Password Assistant truly excels when you need a secure random password, but if you've just plain had it thinking up your own passwords, Assistant offers many more options:

✔ **Memorable** offers passwords made up of two dictionary words separated by a number and a special character, for example, `rig25{laden`. They're good for medium security with a strength in the 40- to 45-point range. Longer passwords of this type are not much stronger, so pick one around 12 characters long.

✔ **Letters & Numbers** mixes uppercase and lowercase letters and digits, for example, `io5ItCqm8N`. Used that way, the passwords are worth almost 6 points per letter. If you don't want to mess with the Shift key, make all the letters the same case, in which case their worth drops to 5.2 points per letter. This is not much of a loss, but remember to type in your single-case version: `io5itcqm8n`. Don't cut and paste from Password Assistant.

✔ **Numbers only** is handy for picking new personal identification numbers (PINs) for credit cards and so on, but you need a long number for a strong password. Digits are worth 3.3 points each.

✔ **Random** uses all the characters on the keyboard and produces passwords that look like `G!0chN6-j2`. Score 6.5 points per character.

✔ **FIPS-181 compliant** makes up letter-only passwords that are relatively easy to pronounce, like `voofyaidia`. The method used is specified in a U.S. government Federal Information Processing Specification, hence the name. FIPS-181 passwords are worth 4 points per letter.

One way to guarantee that your password is random is to select the letters one at a time, using ordinary, six-sided dice:

1. **Throw the pair of dice.**

2. **Use the two numbers you get to pick a character from Table 10-2.**

   Use the die that lands to the left to pick the row and the other die to pick the column. (Yes, *die* is the singular of dice.) So, rolling a 3, 5 would add the letter q to your password.

3. **Keep rolling and picking letters or numbers from the table until the password is the length that you're looking for. See the next section in this chapter for details.**

Table 10-2		Generating Passwords with Dice				
	1	**2**	**3**	**4**	**5**	**6**
1	a	b	c	d	e	f
2	g	h	i	j	k	l
3	m	n	o	p	q	r
4	s	t	u	v	w	x
5	y	z	0	1	2	3
6	4	5	6	7	8	9

How long does it have to be?

Your password, that is. As with other size questions, this one generates much controversy. Here are some guidelines I think are reasonable for most users:

- ✔ **Low security** doesn't require much to achieve. An 8-character Password Assistant "Memorable" password will do fine. Or, you can recycle an old, inactive password you remember well, as long as you haven't used it in a while and it isn't similar to others you use.

- ✔ **Medium security** won't stop a determined and skilled attacker, but the attacker will probably go pick on someone else who is an easier mark. I suggest at least 46 points, a 7 character Password Assistant "Random" password, 10 random letters, or a 12-character FIPS-181 pronounceable password — breaking it into two words may make it easier to remember. (If you're unsure what the points mean, see the section "Knowing the score," earlier in this chapter.)

✔ **High security** is a pretty open-ended concept, but I suggest at least 56 points, a 9-character Password Assistant "Random" password, or 11 random letters and numbers.

✔ **Cryptovariable passwords** are for programs that turn your password into an encryption key. Most applications that employ passwords use them as a gatekeeper. Know the password and you are allowed access to the computer or program in question. But some passwords work harder. They are used as the key or cryptovariable in an encryption algorithm. Examples of passwords that need cryptovariable strength include the following:

• WPA and WPA2 wireless network passwords

• Your OS X master password

• FileVault passwords

• Passwords for encrypted e-mail

• Passwords of other disk-encryption schemes

For cryptovariable applications, people often use a *passphrase* instead of a password. Passphrases are longer and often made up of words selected at random on the theory that a sequence of words is easier to memorize than a long sequence of letters. See `www.diceware.com` for suggestions on picking a strong but memorable passphrase using dice.

Cryptovariable passwords should have at least 65 points. This requirement can be met with a 10-character Password Assistant "Random" password, 13 random letters and numbers, or a 5-word Diceware passphrase.

✔ **Windows passwords:** If you continue to use your Windows computer along with your Mac, know that a longstanding security flaw exists in Windows XP and earlier versions of windows, having to do with support for an old network standard called LanManager. You can turn LanManager off, and it's a good idea to do this, but you can avoid the problem entirely by using passwords that are at least 15 characters long.

Hardening OS X

Out of the box, OS X offers good security. But you can do a number of things — besides picking good passwords — to make it even stronger. Read on for details about using FileVault, making encrypted volumes, and using other security tricks and tips.

Locking up your data with FileVault

With FileVault, OS X can encrypt each user account. All the data associated with that user is scrambled using the widely accepted AES-128 cipher.

Using FileVault is an excellent idea if you store sensitive data and you travel with a laptop, or if many people have access to your computer. Microsoft has a similar feature called BitLocker, but it is only available in the more expensive versions of Vista.

Encryption slows hard drive access somewhat and may affect tasks that involve a lot of data, such as movie editing or Photoshop work. One compromise is to have two user accounts, one with FileVault for sensitive work and the other without FileVault protection for work where processing speed matters.

To turn on FileVault for a user, follow these steps:

1. **Log on as that user.**

   If you like, you can turn on FileVault while creating a new account — you'll see a check box to select.

2. **Select System Preferences from the Apple menu and click the Security icon.**

3. **Click the FileVault tab at the top, if it isn't already highlighted.**

   You see the FileVault setup window shown in Figure 10-3.

Figure 10-3:
The FileVault setup window.

4. **If you have not already done so, set a master password for your Mac by clicking the Set Master Password button.**

   This allows you to recover data from any FileVault user that has forgotten his password. Knowing the master password also lets you reset any user's logon password.

5. **Choose a cryptovariable-level password as described in the section "How long does it have to be?" earlier in this chapter, and write down that password.**

   You can call up Password Assistant to help you choose this password by clicking the Key icon next to the password entry field.

6. **Because FileVault encrypts your home directory using your logon password, your account should have a high-security-level password. If you need to change your logon password, select System Preferences from the Apple menu and click the Accounts icon.**

7. **Change your logon password. Log out and log back on to make sure that everything is working.**

8. **After you have a master password set and you are okay with your logon password, return to the System Preferences Security screen and click the Turn On FileVault button.**

   Depending on how much data is in your home directory, the initial encryption process could take a while. If you are working on your laptop, plug in the charger. If you already have sensitive info stored in your account, select the Secure Erase check box to ensure that OS X thoroughly obliterates the unencrypted data when it's done encrypting.

When you log out of a FileVault account, OS X often asks your permission to tidy up and recover some unused space. Only say yes if you have time and battery power for the operation to complete. Otherwise, tell OS X to wait.

Making an encrypted volume

If you have some data you want to protect, but don't want to go to the bother of encrypting your entire user directory, you have another option. You can create an encrypted disk image. This is a file that looks like a disk volume when you open it. It looks very much like the volumes typically created when you download an application program. It even has the same .dmg extension, but you will need a password to open it.

To create an encrypted volume, follow these steps:

1. **Go to the Utilities folder in your Applications folder and open Disk Utility.**

Advanced Encryption Standard (AES)

The security features in OS X use an algorithm, called the Advanced Encryption Standard (AES), for scrambling data. AES was selected by the U.S. National Institute of Standards and Technology (NIST) in 2001 after a lengthy public competition. The winning design was submitted by two Belgian researchers, Vincent Rijmen and Joan Daemen. AES is something called a *block cipher*. It takes data in 128-bit chunks and scrambles it into another 128 bits. The exact way it scrambles the data is determined by another block of digital data called a *key* or *cryptovariable*. AES comes in three flavors,

with 128-, 192-, or 256-bit keys. Apple uses the 128-bit version. While it did not participate in the original design and selection, the U.S. National Security Agency has stated that the AES cipher can be used to protect classified information; the 128-bit version, which Apple uses, is approved for information at the Secret level. That does not mean that you can use Macs to take home classified documents. The NSA has a stringent approval process for devices used to store and transmit such data — you must consider a lot more than the strength of the codes. But it is a strong vote of confidence in AES.

2. **Choose File➪New➪New Blank Image.**

3. **Pick a size for your volume that's large enough for everything you plan to store in it, with room to spare.**

   If you keep it below 700MB, the encrypted volume will fit on a CD-R should you choose to back it up that way.

4. **Give the volume a name, like** `Super Secret War Plans` **or** `Recipes`.

5. **Select AES-128 Encryption.**

6. **Click the Create button.**

7. **When prompted, enter a password.**

   If you click the small Key icon, Password Assistant appears to offer suggestions. See the sidebar "Ordering up passwords from Password Assistant," elsewhere in this chapter, for more on using this feature and for password selection in general.

8. **If you don't want OS X to store the password in Keychain, deselect the Remember Password check box.**

Enhancing your Mac's security

Besides choosing good passwords, you can do a number of things to make your Mac even more secure.

Setting safer settings

Select System Preferences from the Apple menu. Click the Security icon, and then click the System tab. You see the window shown in Figure 10-4. You can select several check boxes to enhance your Mac's security, usually at the price of some minor added inconvenience in operation. Here is a rundown of the check boxes and what they mean for your security:

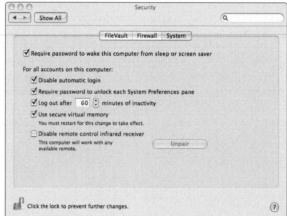

Figure 10-4:
The OS X
Security
settings
window.

✔ **Require Password to Wake This Computer from Sleep or Screen Saver:**
A common security problem is the unattended machine. You go get a cup of cappuccino, and someone sits down at your computer and does as she pleases. Selecting this check box and, perhaps, the Log Out after *xx* Minutes of Inactivity check box can help prevent this, but you will be typing your password *a lot.*

✔ **Disable Automatic Login:** Select this check box if you care about security. If you don't select it, the computer will automatically log on to the primary account every time you restart it.

✔ **Require Password to Unlock Each System Preferences Pane:** If many people share your computer (your kids in particular) and you want to retain strict control, select this check box. Otherwise, don't bother.

✔ **Use Secure Virtual Memory:** If you plan to use FileVault, select this check box. Your Mac sometimes writes temporary information to disk to free more of its main memory. Because this temporary information can contain sensitive information, you want it encrypted, too.

✔ **Disable Remote Control Infrared Receiver:** Someone with a remote could get your computer to display images you'd rather not share. If this prospect frightens you, select this check box.

Keeping up to date with Software Update

Computer security is a moving target. Researchers and hackers are constantly finding holes in software. And new revisions of software intended to add features can also inadvertently introduce new security bugs. Apple works hard to correct problems and periodically distributes corrections via the Internet. Out of the box, your Mac checks for available updates weekly. To check now, select Software Update from the Apple menu. You can change how often automatic checking occurs by selecting System Preferences from the Apple menu and clicking the Software Update icon. This is also the place to check which updates have already been installed, if you care.

Securing your e-mail

If you use programs like Pretty Good Privacy (PGP, from www.pgp.com), Gnu Privacy Guard (GnuPG from macgpg.sourceforge.net), or Hushmail.com to encrypt and electronically sign e-mail, you'll be glad to know that Mac versions of these programs are available.

Remember to transfer your PGP keyrings with the rest of your files. Make sure that everything is working properly before disposing of your PC.

Watching out for phishing

As a PC user, you've undoubtedly encountered phishing, e-mail messages that look like legitimate requests from upstanding organizations. The message includes a link that takes you to what seems like the Web site of that organization, where you're asked to enter your account number, password, and any other personal info they think you can be conned into surrendering. If you have any doubt that the message is phony, do not click the link in the e-mail. Go to the organization's Web site by typing their URL in you browser's address field and navigate to your account.

Locking it up

Computer security is almost meaningless without physical security. If a sophisticated attacker gets to spend quality time alone with your Mac, all the fancy technology may be of no avail. Laptops are easier to steal than desktop machines, but they are also easier to lock in a desk or safe. All Mac laptops have a hole in the side designed to accept a mechanical locking device, such as those made by Kensington.com.

Another cheap thing to do is to record your computer's serial number. Select About This Mac from the Apple menu. The serial number is listed in the hardware Overview section. It is also a good idea to mark your computer with your name and address. You can place an address label inside your laptop's battery compartment. A colored sticker on the outside of your laptop makes it harder for a thief at the airport to hide in a crowd.

Removing Data from an Old Mac

When the time comes to get a new Mac and you want to sell the old one or give it to a friend or charity, it's wise to erase all your data files. I discuss how to do this for old PCs in Chapter 6. Of course, you should first transfer the files to your new machine; see the previous chapter for networking tips. You also should deauthorize your Mac from the iTunes Store if you have been using it. See the next chapter for instructions on how to do this and what to do if you forgot. And it's always a good idea to make a backup of your most important files on a DVD-R or an external hard drive. But then what?

Deleting user accounts

If you have the original discs that came with your Mac, your can use them to restore it to its original state. Here's a different approach that lets you give away your Mac in a more updated state:

1. **Select System Preferences from the Apple menu and click the Accounts icon.**

2. **Click the Lock icon and enter your password.**

3. **Create a new account, maybe with the name of the person who is going to get the machine. Be sure to select the check box that says Allow User to Administer This Computer.**

   You can use your name as the password and say that you're doing this as the password hint.

4. **Select Logout from the Apple menu.**

   After you see the logon screen, click the new account name and enter the password you just created.

5. **Again, select System Preferences from the Apple menu and click the Accounts icon. Click the Lock icon.**

6. **Go to your new computer and triple-check that all the files for all accounts on the old machine have been transferred.**

   Go have a cup of coffee and check again when you come back.

   This is your last chance to copy these files to your new computer.

7. **Back on the old machine, delete each account, except the one you just created, by clicking the old account's icon and then clicking the minus (–) button.**

   Confirm that you really want to erase everything, with no extra copy. Let it cook; this process can take a while.

8. **If you have applications you don't want to transfer, delete them from the Applications folder.**

9. **Double-click your hard drive icon and see whether any of your files have leaked into this top-level directory. If so, drag them to the Trash.**

10. **Select Empty Trash from the Finder menu.**

   Regardless of whether you rebuilt OS X from scratch or deleted accounts as I suggested, your sensitive files are not necessarily gone yet. To obliterate them permanently, erase the free space on your hard drive. In the next section, you find out how.

Securing empty trash and erasing free space

If you store sensitive data on your computer, particularly on a laptop, get in the habit of selecting Secure Empty Trash from the Finder menu whenever you want to empty the Trash — the Mac equivalent of the Windows Recycle Bin, the place files get moved to when you delete them. Otherwise, your data remains in unassigned areas of your hard drive until such time as the operating system needs that space to store something else. With today's large hard drives, that may be never.

Secure Empty Trash can take a while if you are deleting large files, and even if you are careful to use it all the time, it's a good idea to write over all the free space on your hard drive every so often. Apple supplies a tool for doing this, which works as follows:

1. **Open Disk Utility.**

   It's in the Utilities folder inside the Applications folder.

2. **Select your hard drive and click/select the Erase Free Space button.**

3. **Choose one of the three options.**

   The default option, which overwrites all free disk space with 0s just once, can take an hour or more. The more secure 7-pass method can take overnight, and the 35-pass method for the paranoid can take a couple of days.

   I suggest using the 7-pass method, unless your friend is coming over in an hour to pick up the machine. At least do the 1-pass erase. You can stall her that long.

Virus protection?

Coming from the Windows world, you may feel naked without a virus-protection program. As of this writing, no reported OS X viruses are in circulation — the buzz phrase is *in the wild*. However, while Apple has done a good job with OS X security, no one claims it is perfect, and Apple's market share is increasing, making it an ever-more-tempting target for virus writers. Several PC antivirus companies offer programs for OS X and, of course, if you install Windows XP on your Mac and plan to connect it to the Internet, you should install a PC antivirus program for Windows in that partition. Based on the current situation, I think you can hold off buying a Mac antivirus program as long as you check Software Update regularly, keep an eye

on at least one independent Mac information Web site, and hang on to your PC-user caution about installing strange software.

One exception is if you regularly exchange files created in Microsoft Office. One class of virus uses the Office macro feature, and a few of those viruses can infect Macs. More likely, you can spread a virus you got from one user to others in your office. The major antivirus vendors sell versions for the Mac. There's also a free antivirus program for the Mac called ClamXav, available from www.clamxav.com. It's based on a open source antivirus project called Calmav.

Checking checksums

Security-related programs are often distributed with a checksum or hash that lets you verify that the program you received has not been modified — a good practice. Two types of checksums are widely used: md5 and sha1. OS X can compute either type by using the UNIX command line in the Terminal window. (See Chapter 17.) The command for md5 is just md5, followed by a space, followed by the file path. For sha1, type the command openssl sha1, followed by a space, followed by the file path.

Drag the file's icon to the Terminal window, and the file path is filled in automatically.

Part IV
More Software, More Choices

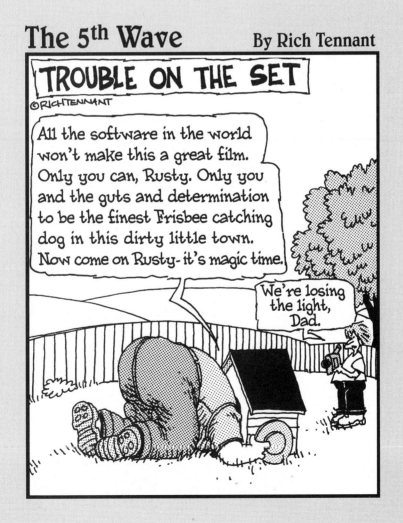

In this part . . .

Macs come with a ton of software. I introduce Apple's iLife digital lifestyle suite and discuss other software that comes with your Mac. These programs are simple, but powerful and fun to use. And because they all come from Apple, they play well together. But if you're a long-time Windows user, there's likely to be some application on Windows you miss. You have several options for running Windows on you Mac. I discuss them in the last chapter of this part.

Chapter 11

The Sweet iLife Suite

Apple's Mac OS X comes with an amazing collection of software to help you create and enjoy what Apple refers to as your digital life: music, photos, home movies, and Web content. The programs in the iLife suite are as follows:

- ✔ **iTunes:** Manages your music and videos, syncs with your iPod, and talks to the online iTunes Store.

- ✔ **iPhoto:** Takes care of everything associated with digital photography, including getting images from your digital camera, performing basic editing, organizing images into slideshows and albums, and printing the albums.

- ✔ **iMovie:** Lets you import and edit all those home movies you took of your vacations and kids (but never watch) and turn them into professional-looking mini-biopics that won't bore your guests. They might even garner 15 minutes of fame on YouTube. In your work life, you can produce video clips that compellingly present your ideas.

- ✔ **iDVD:** Takes those edited iMovie shorts and epics and burns them to DVDs that you can play on almost any DVD player or computer with a DVD reader. Makes the grandparents very happy.

- ✔ **GarageBand:** Helps you put together the original score for the home video epic, or just fan those long-suppressed creative musical talents of yours.

- ✔ **iWeb:** Takes all this creative output and builds it into spectacular Web pages.

Because all these programs are built by Apple, using the OS X toolbox, they all work well together. You can use an iTunes playlist as a background for your iPhoto slideshow. You can integrate iPhoto images into your iMovie, animating the images using cinematographic techniques pioneered by Ken Burns. Your creations can also extend beyond your Mac. You can carry your digital works on your iPod and iPhone or show them on your home entertainment center using Apple TV.

Although Apple emphasizes the personal use of these products, they have obvious business uses as well: slideshows for presentations, sales and training videos, and creating less-boring Web sites.

You don't need to worry about installing iLife. It's on your Mac already, in your Applications folder, with shortcuts on the Dock. There's nothing to do. Sorry.

Easy Listening with iTunes

If you have an iPod, you already know about iTunes. It's the one program from the collection that's available for Windows PCs, and it's absolutely necessary to use an iPod. Many Windows users who don't own iPods use iTunes as their music player. The short story is that iTunes on the Mac is pretty much the same as iTunes in Windows.

To move over to the Mac, you just need to transfer your iTunes library from the PC. When you're ready to ditch the PC, you'll want to go through the procedure needed to disassociate your PC from your iTunes library. Your iTunes library can only have up to five computers "associated" with it at any time. That means only those computers can have the keys necessary to play restricted music you have purchased from the iTunes Store. I go over this procedure in the section "Managing authorizations in iTunes," later in this chapter.

---

iTunes plus

Traditionally, music sold over the Internet has been protected by Digital Rights Management (DRM) technology, which encrypts the music data and allows play only on authorized devices. Apple's iTunes Store now sells some music without DRM restrictions. Only a few record labels have allowed DRM-free sales so far. But such files have the advantage that they aren't subject to the five-computer limit, and they can be played on any music player, not just iPods.

The magical iPod

If you don't own an iPod and have any love of music, find something to use as a bookmark here while you go to the store and buy one. It's the greatest improvement in recorded music since the introduction of high fidelity in the 1950s. Owning an iPod welds music to your personal space. It becomes something you always have with you. William Congreve got it right in *The Mourning Bride,* back in 1697 (reportedly while attending an early Vista planning meeting):

> *Musick has Charms to sooth a savage Breast,*
> *To soften Rocks, or bend a knotted Oak.*
> *I've read, that things inanimate have mov'd,*
> *And, as with living Souls, have been inform'd,*
> *By Magick Numbers and persuasive Sound.*

The iPod is not just a digital accessory; it informs our living souls.

Yes, iPods can do other things. They can serve as a utilitarian portable hard drive, older siblings to flash drives. And the spiffy video models can store and play movies, TV programs, music videos, and your photograph collection. They are also great for listening to podcasts and recorded books. But the ability to add one's favorite music to the unavoidable humdrum of the day — that's life changing.

Getting started with iTunes

When you first get your Mac, you need to follow a fairly simple setup process to organize all your music. Follow these steps:

1. **Double-click iTunes, either on the Dock or in the Applications folder.**

2. **Go through the Setup Assistant that offers to have iTunes handle audio content from the Internet, making it your audio-helper application.**

   Unless you've downloaded other audio software, the alternative is to use Apple's QuickTime.

iTunes then offers to search your home folder for MP3 and AAC music files. If you have transferred a bunch over from your PC, this is an opportunity to get them all organized by iTunes. Always double-check that you have backed up all the files. You can easily add them later if you prefer. See the section "Importing your iTunes collection," later in this chapter, for details.

iTunes then offers to take you to the iTunes Store. The next section introduces you to the store.

Shopping the iTunes Store

When you first start iTunes, it takes you to the front window of the iTunes Store (ITS). If iPod has revolutionized the way we listen to music, ITS has revolutionized the way it is sold.

Notice that I said sold, not distributed. Only a small fraction of the songs on most iPods have been purchased through ITS. Much of it comes from compact discs that people already own and simply transfer to their iPods. The rest comes from file-sharing programs such as BitTorrent and the former incarnation of Napster.

It seems that the recording industry didn't think through all the implications when it switched to CDs from the older vinyl LP records, the kind with a wiggly spiral groove that made a needle vibrate to reproduce sound. After computers and the Internet became fast enough, the digital data on CDs was too easily copied and shared.

Apple figured that many people would do the right thing and buy their music, instead of downloading it for free, if the price was right and the process was convenient enough. Users have downloaded more than 2 billion songs from ITS, and it ranks among the top five music retailers in the United States.

In the iTunes Store, you see a screen similar to that shown in Figure 11-1, with ads for various offerings and a list on the left of different types of content that are for sale. The following steps walk you through the store:

Figure 11-1:
The iTunes Store front window.

1. **Click the Sign In button in the upper-right corner.**

2. **If you already have an Apple account (for example, if you use iTunes on your PC), enter your account name and password. You can also use an AOL account if you have one. Otherwise, click the Create New Account button and have your credit card handy.**

   ITS has a huge selection of recorded music, but Apple makes it easy to find what you want.

3. **Browse by genre or use the search box in the upper-right corner of the iTunes window.**

   Search results appear in the lower half of the iTunes window, and you can sort by genre, title, artist, album, popularity, price, or running length. Just click the headings of the listing.

   If you double-click a song's entry in the list, you hear a 30-second selection from the song.

4. **To purchase a song or other item, click the Buy button, and you are asked for your password.**

   The song, album, or other item is automatically downloaded to your Mac and then to your iPod the next time you plug it in.

Apple has tried to make shopping simple at ITS by having an easy-to-understand price structure. As I write this book, songs cost 99 cents each, TV shows are $1.99, and most music albums and feature movies are $9.99. You can even buy games for your video iPod for $4.99. ITS even has PacMan and Ms. PacMan, with the original artwork from 1980. I dropped more than 20 quarters into the arcade versions of these games, back when you could actually buy something with a quarter. Get Ms. PacMan if you're buying only one.

Importing your iTunes collection

If you already have a collection of music and videos on your PC, copy the iTunes library from your PC to the Mac. (See Chapter 6.) Did that already? Then you may need to follow these steps:

1. **On your Mac, open iTunes and choose File⇨Add to Library.**

2. **Find the folder that contains all the music and video files you copied to your Mac.**

3. **Click the Choose button.**

   iTunes on the Mac adds the PC files to its library, all neatly organized the way you had them.

If your PC is so hosed that you can't recover your iTunes library and you don't have a backup, you still have hope. Apple allows you to transfer music you previously purchased from the iTunes Store from your iPod to another computer. In iTunes, choose File⟹Transfer Purchases from iPod.

Two freeware programs, Ollie's iPod Extractor and Senuti are also available to copy any songs from your iPod to your Mac, without duplicating the ones that are already there. A Google search can find them, or you can try your favorite download site.

Managing authorizations in iTunes

As I mentioned earlier in this chapter, Apple's digital rights management scheme lets you have media you purchased on iTunes playable on up to five computers at any one time. If you are planning to keep your PC for a while and you are not close to the five-computer limit, you can leave the PC authorized.

To authorize your Mac, just try to play one of your purchased songs. iTunes will ask for your Apple ID and password. Be sure to enter the ones you used to purchase the song. You only have to do this for one purchased song.

When you're ready to get rid of your Windows PC, be sure to deauthorize it first by following these steps:

1. **Open iTunes on your PC.**

2. **Choose Store⟹Deauthorize Computer.**

3. **Select Deauthorize Computer for Apple Account.**

4. **Enter your Apple ID and password and confirm your intentions.**

Apple determines a Windows computer's identity by looking at a number of factors, including the amount of RAM and the hard drive size, so don't mess with these before you deauthorize your PC. (Macs have a hardware serial number, so changing the hard drive, adding RAM, and so on don't affect things.)

If your PC is so messed up that you can't run iTunes to deauthorize, or if you just forgot to do it before you ditched the PC, it stays on the list of machines that count against your five-computer limit. However, you have an escape valve. When you get to the point where you have used up all five slots, you can blow them *all* away and reauthorize the computers you still want by playing a purchased song on each of them. However, Apple limits you to resetting the authorized computer list only once a year. To reset the list, follow these steps:

1. **Choose View My Account from the iTunes Store menu.**

2. **Enter your password.**

   If you are at the five-computer limit and you have not exercised this option in the last 12 months, you should see a Deauthorize All button on the Account Information screen.

3. **Click the Deauthorize All button.**

4. **Play a song on each computer that you want to authorize.**

Copying CDs to iTunes

If you've never used iTunes before, you'll want to add some music. If you own music CDs, you can add them to the iTunes library by simply sliding them into your Mac's CD/DVD slot. iTunes will copy the files from the CD to its library while it plays the CD for you. The CD won't take as long to copy as it does to play, however, so you can stop the music when iTunes says the transfer is done.

Apple's AAC compression scheme is used by default when iTunes imports CDs. You can change to another format, such as MP3, by selecting Preferences from the iTunes menu. Click the Advanced icon and then the Importing button. You can change many other options here as well, such as whether iTunes plays tracks while it's importing a CD.

Adding video to iTunes (and an iPod)

Transferring video is another matter. You can't simply put a movie DVD into your Mac and transfer the movie to view on your iPod. Movie DVDs have copy protection, whereas music CDs generally do not. You have to do two things to make such a transfer possible:

- ✔ Extract the movie from the DVD in an unencrypted format.
- ✔ Convert the file to one of the video formats that the iPod can understand.

Software is available that can perform each step. A Google search on "DVD to iPod" should find several resources. The first step involves getting past the copy protection on the DVD. The movie industry says that's illegal, though others say you should have the right to view DVDs you own any way you wish.

Video that is not copy protected, such as your home movies, must still be converted to an iPod-friendly format. One way to do this is to use iMovie, which is already installed on your Mac. Select iPod from the iMovie Share menu. I tell you more about iMovie in the section "Directing Your Own Epic with iMovie," later in this chapter.

Playing with iTunes

After you transfer your library to the Mac, it's time to enjoy your music and other media files in their new home. You won't find things much different from iTunes on your PC. If you're new to iTunes, here are a few popular tasks to help you get started:

- ✔ Syncing your iPod. To sync your iPod to your iTunes library, you just plug its cable in a USB port on the Mac that has the library stored on it. You can sync to only one iTunes library.

- ✔ To create a new play list, click the plus icon (+) at the bottom of the iTunes sidebar.

- ✔ To add a tune to your playlist, simply drag it from the music list to the play list entry in the sidebar.

- ✔ To create a mixed disc, insert a blank writable CD and choose File➪Burn Playlist to Disc.

Picturing iPhoto

Once upon a time, taking photographs involved buying a roll of film, loading it in a camera, shooting 24 or 36 pictures, taking the film out of the camera (don't forget to rewind first!), bringing the exposed film to a camera store or drugstore, waiting a day or so, picking up the pictures, selecting a few negatives to be copied or enlarged, sticking the rest in a shoe box pending some day when you have more free time to organize them (which birthday party was that and who's the guy next to Aunt Harriet?), and pasting them into a photo album. For the more serious photographers, there was an interlude in a dark room with red lights and temperature-controlled trays of smelly chemicals.

Except for those who truly love the film process — and there's a lot to love — digital cameras have taken over photography. Good-quality ones are inexpensive, while the top-of-the-line models are becoming more affordable. And try to buy a cell phone that doesn't have a camera. The one in the iPhone is a respectable 2-megapixel camera. You have no more film to buy — just AA batteries and maybe a memory card or two. And that shoebox is now a hard drive. But we are still waiting for the free time we need to organize our photos.

Wouldn't it be great to have a program that could suck photos down from any camera as soon as you plugged it in, keep the shots organized by when you took them and which batch you downloaded, let you see a large swath of your collection spread out on the screen like a light table, and let you annotate and organize them into albums and slideshows? Shouldn't it also display your slideshow on your screen or on a television, maybe adding music from your iTunes collection? And why not allow you to ship those photos off for printing on your color printer or at a professional shop — and maybe even print bound books of your photos so that you can have paste-free albums?

That's iPhoto in a nutshell. If you've used Google's Picasa on your PC, you are familiar with the concept. But with iPhoto, you have nothing to download. It's waiting for you in the Applications folder.

If you own a digital camera, you most likely can use it with iPhoto. iPhoto supports most brands and models. You can check to see whether your model is supported by visiting the iPhoto Web site, `www.apple.com/ilife/iphoto`, or just shoot a few pictures and plug it into a USB or FireWire port.

When iPhoto first starts up, it asks whether you want it to take over every time you plug in your camera. iPhoto knows about almost every digital camera out there. You could go to your camera manufacturer's Web page to download their software, but why bother? Just say Yes.

Transferring your image collection to iPhoto

You likely have many valuable images stored on your PC. You can move your collection from your PC to your Mac through iPhoto by importing photos. What this means is that iTunes adds your photos to its database and creates thumbnail versions for fast display. iPhoto can read a wide variety of file types, including the following:

- ✔ BMP
- ✔ GIF
- ✔ JPEG/JFIF
- ✔ MacPaint
- ✔ PICT
- ✔ PNG
- ✔ Photoshop (with layers)
- ✔ SGI
- ✔ Targa
- ✔ FlashPix
- ✔ TIFF

Edited files are stored in their original file type, except for GIF images, which are saved in the JPEG (.jpg) format. Also, you can import RAW files from a number of high-end camera models, but RAW is also converted to JPEG in iPhoto. See the section "Moving up to Aperture," later in this chapter, for details about this higher-end photo software, which offers more robust support for RAW and advanced photography in general.

iPhoto lets you export files in JPEG, TIFF, or PNG format.

iPhoto can store up to 250,000 photos. That's about 250 shoe boxes. But iPhoto has its own idea of how to store them in its library. If you already have a large collection of digital photos, all organized in folders, you might want them kept that way. You can order iPhoto to do just that, as follows:

1. **Select Preferences from the iPhoto menu.**
2. **Click the Advanced button.**
3. **Deselect the Copy Files to iPhoto Library Folder When Adding to Library check box.**
4. **Close the Preferences window.**

Now when you import your photos, iTunes will leave them organized the way you had them in the folders you set up, instead of using the normal method of filing the photos by date. However, if you edit one of those photos, iTunes will save the edited version in its library, leaving the original where it was.

Before importing, check the names of your photos. iPhoto may have trouble with text added to the end of an automatic camera name, for example, "DSCF0123.JPG Our Hotel." Just reverse the order, and it will import properly.

To import your photos to iPhoto, follow these steps:

1. **Copy your PC photos to the Pictures folder.**
2. **Choose File➪Import to Library.**
3. **Find the folder or folders with the photos you want to import and select them.**
4. **Click the Import button.**

You may want to experiment with bringing folders in one at a time to find a way of organizing the photos in iPhoto that works best for you. You might try the iPhoto folder import script at scriptbuilders.net/files/iphoto folderimport1.0.html. Drag a folder that contains photos to this script's icon, and it will import all the files in the folder and create an appropriate folder and albums in iPhoto.

After you move all your photos from your PC into iPhoto, you should back up your OS X Pictures folder. If you've enabled Time Machine, it will do the backup for you. If not, or if you like the added security of having a backup in a separate place, copy your Pictures folder to a DVD-ROM or an external hard drive. I cover various was to back up data in Chapter 6. Having all your photos organized and safely backed up is a great feeling.

Organizing the iPhoto way

iPhoto has its own way of storing and organizing photos. Here are the options:

- ✔ **Events:** iPhoto groups all the photos you take on a single day as an event. You can split one event into two or merge events together. You can move individual photos from one event to another. As you slide your mouse pointer across an event image, you see all the photos in the event, an effect Apple calls skimming.

- ✔ **Albums:** An *album* is a named set of photos. A photo can be in more than one album. The photo is only stored once, however, so having photos in more than one album does not waste space. Albums work a lot like playlists in iTunes. To create a new album, choose File➪New Album or click the plus icon (+) in the lower-left corner. You add photos to an album by selecting and dragging them from the main display.

- ✔ **Smart albums:** A *smart album* contains photos based on search criteria you select. It works a lot like Spotlight. To make a smart album, choose File➪New Smart Album.

- ✔ **Folders:** *Folders* in iPhoto are a way to add organization to your collection. You create a new folder from the File menu. Folders can contain albums and other folders. They can also contain slideshows, books, calendars, and other iPhoto projects. Again, you can drag things into and out of a folder and move them around as you wish. Items can be in only one folder, however.

Viewing and sorting your photos

The main iPhoto display area, shown in Figure 11-2, shows small versions of your photos arranged on a dark background, much like a slide sorter from the film era. How small? The slider on the lower-right border of the iPhoto window lets you adjust the thumbnail size to suit your needs.

iPhoto offers a number of ways to see just what you want:

- ✔ Choose Photos in the sidebar, and all your photos are displayed.
- ✔ Click a folder or album, and just those photos are shown.

✔ Choose View⇨Sort Photos and then select one of the following options:

- **By Event:** This is the default view.

- **By Date:** The date is stored with the file when you import your photo.

- **By Keyword:** Keywords are tags you add to a photo by clicking the key icon at the bottom right of the window or pressing ⌘+I. iPhoto comes with a simple set of keywords, but you can invent your own in iPhoto Preferences by clicking the Keyword tab.

- **By Title:** A photo's title is the name or number given to it by your camera, but you can change the name by clicking the small I icon at the bottom right of the window.

- **By Rating:** The By Rating sort does not refer to how professional-looking iPhoto thinks your photos are. You assign your own rating to photos, from one to five stars. It's worth remembering the keyboard shortcuts. Select the photo or photos you want to rate and press ⌘+1 for one star, ⌘+2 for two stars — up to ⌘+5 for five stars. Pressing ⌘+0 means no rating. If you forget, choose Photos⇨My Rating. This menu choice has all the options and can remind you of the shortcuts.

- **Manual:** Manual lets you move photos around by dragging them. It's ideal for slideshows.

You can also select Ascending or Descending sort order.

Editing your iPhotos

When you select a photo in the main display, iPhoto presents you with several editing icons at the bottom of its window, as shown in Figure 11-3. Unlike higher-end editing programs, you are not given a bewildering array of tools and options. iPhoto gets right to the point. You have the following options:

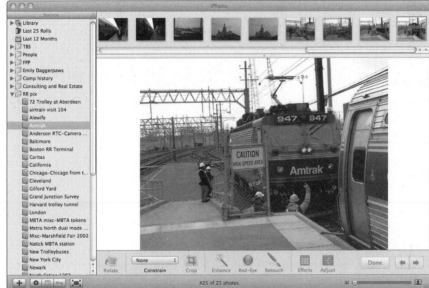

Figure 11-3:
Editing
options in
iPhoto.

- ✔ **Rotate** turns photos in 90-degree increments. The default is clockwise. You can select counterclockwise in the iTunes➪Preferences dialog box, or press the Option key while clicking to get the opposite rotation.

- ✔ **Constrain** picks an ultimate size you are aiming for and makes it happen.

- ✔ **Crop** selects the area of the photo you want to see using a gray overlay that you can move or adjust to size.

- ✔ **Enhance** applies filters that Apple thinks will generally do the right thing. It usually does.

- ✔ **Red eye** just asks you to click the center of each eye in a portrait. iPhoto does the rest. This doesn't work on photos of cats.

- ✔ **Retouch** gets rid of scratches, dust marks, and the so on. Just rub over them with the cursor.

✔ **Effects** displays a matrix of image treatments, such as Black & White, Sepia, Antique, Fade Color, Boost Color, Matte, Vignette, and Edge Blur, with your original in the center. Pick one you like.

✔ **Adjust** shows a pane with sliders to control individual attributes such as brightness, contrast, saturation, temperature, and exposure. You can also rotate the image plus or minus ten degrees using the straighten control.

No matter what you do to your photo, you can always undo it all. Choose Photo➪Revert to Original to do this.

Sharing photos in slideshows and prints

Okay, so what to do with all those photos? Why, show them to someone else, of course. iPhoto excels in tools to share your images, including slideshows and easy ways to make prints.

You can upload selected photos to your Web Gallery on .Mac, if you are a subscriber, letting the world see your photos or protecting them with a password.

At its simplest level, creating a slideshow involves selecting a bunch of pictures and putting them in order to tell a story. In iPhoto, that is just the beginning. Here's how to create a slideshow:

1. **In iPhoto, select and arrange your photos in the main display.**

2. **Click the Slideshow icon at the bottom of the window.**

   An icon for your new slideshow appears in the sidebar — you can rename it — and Slideshow view appears in the main display.

3. **Rearrange the thumbnails of the images that appear at the top if you like.**

   At the bottom are icons that allow you to add excitement to your show. You can select from a variety of ways to change from one slide to the next, called *transitions.* The default is an automatic Ken Burns effect.

4. **If you like, select background music for your show from your iTunes library, GarageBand, or the sample selections that come with iPhoto by clicking the Music icon at the bottom-right of the window.**

When you're done, you can display your show on-screen, burn it to DVD, upload it to .Mac, or use it in other ways such as podcasts or online presentations. See the Share menu for options.

An easy way to share your photos with friends is via e-mail. Just click the Email icon at the bottom of the window. iPhoto asks you to select what size photo to send.

Although slideshows and e-mail are handy, many people still appreciate photos they can hold in their hand. Until everyone carries a video iPod or iPhone, paper prints still have a role. To create prints, iPhoto offers the following options:

- ✔ You can print photos on your color printer by choosing File➪Print.

- ✔ You can order professional prints for a fee over the Internet. Click the Order Prints icon at the lower-right corner.

- ✔ You can use iPhoto tools to let you make custom greeting cards, calendars, and album books from your photos. You can drag photos one at a time or ask iPhoto to flow a bunch of them into the template you select. Click the appropriate icon at the bottom of the iPhoto window to get started (refer to Figure 11-2).

Moving up to Aperture

AApple sells a more advanced photo-management software package, called Aperture, that is aimed at professional photographers. It has more support for RAW images and can work with a much bigger photo library. It has more image-editing capabilities, but it can also integrate with Adobe Photoshop. You find tools to help you manage projects, including the ability to work with several versions of the same photo at once. A handy image loupe, shown in Figure 11-4, magnifies a small area of the photo as you slide the loupe over the screen.

Figure 11-4: Apple's Aperture photo software with loupe tool.

If you're serious about photography and have invested big bucks in camera iron and glass, Aperture's $300 price tag should not be an obstacle to moving up.

Directing Your Own Epic with iMovie

Great movies aren't created in a studio or on location. They're created in the editing room. The pioneering Russian filmmaker Lev Kuleshov proved the point by splicing a shot of a famous Russian actor between shots of a plate of soup, a girl at play, and an old woman in a coffin. It appeared like he was looking at each. Audiences that were shown the short admired the different emotions the actor displayed as he viewed each scene. But Kuleshov had used the same shot of the actor in each setting. The juxtaposition or montage created the strong emotion in the minds of the viewers.

For most of the twentieth century, films were edited by cutting strips of film apart with a blade, arranging them artfully, and splicing them together to form the master image. Many specialized machines were invented to help in the cutting room. But no filmmaker in the first eight decades of motion pictures imagined the powerful editing capabilities that come free with your Macintosh, in the form of iMovie. Professional filmmakers today use still more capable software products. Apple makes one of the best, Final Cut, which I talk about later. But if you haven't done film editing before, the limitations of iMovie are not going to hold you back for some time. As Walter Murch, who won three Oscars for editing and sound mixing, put it:

> "Film editing is now something almost everyone can do at a simple level and enjoy it, but to take it to a higher level requires the same dedication and persistence that any art form does."

By the way, Murch was honored with a fourth Oscar nomination for *Cold Mountain,* which he edited using Final Cut Pro on a Macintosh G4, a wimpy machine compared to Macs on sale today.

Importing and editing video in iMovie

First things first. Make sure that you have enough hard drive space. Moving images uses lots of bits. Fifteen minutes of film can take up 3.2GB of space. Remember that you need space for all the raw footage you plan to edit, not just the final product. I suggest getting a large external FireWire drive for any large film-editing project you undertake. Add the word *terabyte* to your vocabulary.

If you have some digital camcorder footage that you'd like to edit, follow these steps to import it into iMovie and begin editing:

1. **Connect your video camera to your Mac with the camera's cable and put the camera in the proper mode.**

   You should see iMovie's Import window, and newer cameras present a list of clips.

2. **Select the clips you want to import in Manual mode, or select Automatic in the Import window to import them all.**

3. **When you are ready, click the Import button.**

   iMovie automatically divides your video into separate clips by looking at the time codes recorded on the tape. Stills from the beginning of each clip, and every 5 seconds thereafter, appear in the Clips pane in the bottom of the iMovie window, as shown in Figure 11-5. You adjust the interval between stills with the slider in the lower-right. As you move your mouse pointer over each clip, you see it play, and iMovie stores video clips in a common library, by event, as in iPhoto. You see a list of events stored in your library in a list at lower-left.

Figure 11-5: The beginning stages of an iMovie project.

Ken Burns and his effect

The documentary films of Ken Burns have brought to life, for millions of viewers, whole eras of American history — the building of the Brooklyn Bridge, the rise of jazz and baseball, and the development of radio. For his most acclaimed series, *The Civil War,* Burns faced an opportunity and a problem. The Civil War was fought after the invention of photography, and archives were filled with black-and-white images, some by great early photographers like Mathew Brady. These archives presented an opportunity to visually tell the story of this horrific war. The problem was how to keep from boring an audience that was used to movie footage of war. Burns solved the problem by panning the camera across the still images and slowly zooming in or out to create a sense of motion. *The Civil War* won numerous awards, including two Emmys, for its ability to convey not just the facts of history but also its emotional impact.

Apple has incorporated into its iLife suite the technique that Ken Burns made such masterful use of. They even call it "the Ken Burns effect." It operates by default in iPhoto slideshows and even in the OS X screen saver. But you can customize it by selecting a starting and ending version of the image. The same feature is available in iMovie and allows you to incorporate iPhoto stills as dynamic images in your cinematic projects.

4. **Edit each clip to show just what you want to include in your movie and then drag it to the project window at upper left.**

Drag your mouse with the left button down over a clip and a yellow box appears, showing the segment you selected. You can then drag each selected segment to the project window at the top left, placing them in the order you like. You can use different segments from the same cut. If you just click on a clip, iMovie selects a 4-second segment.

You can also add sound, photos, titles, and transitions using the four icons to the right of the central toolbar. Click an icon to see the options and drag the ones you want to your project window, placing them where you want them, even between clips. You can rearrange elements of your movie by dragging. Click an element to edit it and press Delete to remove it from the movie. iMovie saves your project as you work on it. Choose File⇨Duplicate Project to save a checkpoint.

Sound sources include iTunes and a set of prerecorded effects. To record narration, click the microphone icon. When your movie is ready, use the Share menu to transfer it to iTunes, an iPod, the Web, and more.

Importing video from your PC

If you have video that you transferred from your PC, you can incorporate it into your iMovie project with the File⇨Import command. iMovie can accept any format that QuickTime understands. As its name implies, it can work with high-definition video sources, including HDTV in 720p and 1080i formats.

One thing that vanilla QuickTime can't understand is Microsoft Windows Media (`.wmv`) files. Plug-ins from `flip4mac.com` can usually solve this problem.

Finding other sources for video

You can use the following other sources to get video into your iMovie:

- ✔ **Built-in camera:** Want to try out iMovie but you don't own a digital camcorder? If you have a recent Apple laptop or iMac, your already have a built-in iSight camera, which you can use as an input source for iMovie. Just click the Camera icon on the central toobar. iMovie will show you sitting in front of your keyboard, with a button that lets you start and stop recording from iSight. Lights, camera, *action!*

- ✔ **iPhoto:** Still photographs can be added to your iMovie project and animated using the Ken Burns effect (see the nearby sidebar, "Ken Burns and his effect"). If your camera takes videos, you can grab those from iTunes as well.

- ✔ **Internet video:** A vast amount of video is available on the World Wide Web. Anything you download in a QuickTime-compatible format can be imported to iMovie. But be careful of copyright issues. (When I first typed the previous sentence, the fifth word read *copyfight.* That typo pretty much sums up what you want to avoid.)

Moving up to Final Cut

You can accomplish a lot with iMovie, but it has its limits. When you are ready for the training wheels to come off, Apple has excellent industrial-strength solutions waiting for you, some at consumer-strength prices.

Apple's top-of-the-line video-editing suite is Final Cut Studio. It includes the following:

- ✔ **Final Cut Pro:** Not many computer programs win Emmys. It has also been used to edit over two dozen feature-length films. It supports most high-definition formats, DV, SD, HDV, XDCAM HD, DVCPRO HD, and uncompressed HD. Figure 11-6 shows Final Cut Pro's rich interface.

- ✔ **Soundtrack Pro:** As Apple puts it, the soundtrack is half the picture. Soundtrack Pro includes more than 50 professional-effect plug-ins.

Figure 11-6:
Final Cut
Pro.

✔ **Motion:** An animation package that creates motion graphics in real time.

✔ **DVD Studio Pro:** Transfers HD content to optical disc formats.

✔ **Compressor:** An audio and video compression application that auto-mates encoding and format conversions.

Apple separately sells Shake, a video-compositing tool for professional special effects.

Still waiting to be green-lighted for that full-length epic? Apple has a scaled-down version of Final Cut called Final Cut Express in the under-$300 class. It has the same interface as Final Cut Pro, but not all the tools and formats. It also comes with a scaled-back, but still powerful, version of Soundtrack.

Burning Movies with iDVD

Apple's iDVD is something of a one-trick pony. It takes content that you created with other iLife applications — your iMovie films and iPhoto slideshows — and transfers them to DVD-R so that they can be shown on an ordinary DVD player.

You need a Mac that can burn DVDs, such as one with what Apple calls a SuperDrive. Low-end Macs with only "combo" drives can play DVDs, but they can't burn them on the internal drive. You can, however, add a USB or FireWire DVD burner to one of these Macs.

If you only want to back up your media files to a DVD, you don't need iDVD. OS X Finder lets you do that. Just don't try to play your backup DVD on your home entertainment center.

Most of what iDVD does is kind of boring: converting stuff to the right video formats and putting the bits in the place on the DVD where consumer players expect them. But Apple can add some pizzazz in one place: themes for the main DVD menu. Here's how it works:

1. **The main screen of iDVD shows a collection of Apple-created themes on the right hand side. Select one you like by clicking it.**

   In Figure 11-7, you can see the travel theme.

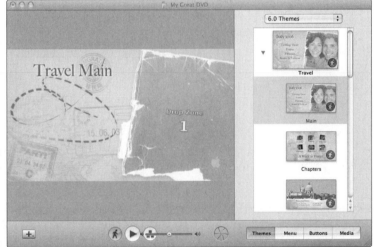

Figure 11-7: iDVD's theme selection screen.

2. **Drag movies and photos from the Finder or any iLife application to designated image areas within the themes.**

   iDVD can even animate the images so that your menu is even more inviting.

   If you'd like a scene selection menu, iDVD can add one based on your iMovie chapter divisions.

3. **Choose File⇨Burn DVD.**

If you need to create a DVD quickly, use the OneStep DVD function that burns the entire contents of the tape in an attached DV camcorder. Just select OneStep DVD from the iDVD File menu.

Composing Using GarageBand

There's an old joke about someone asking a police officer in Manhattan how to get to Carnegie Hall. "Practice six hours every day" comes the reply. Making music has traditionally required both talent and manual skills that take years to master. People who don't start young and keep working at their instrument are consigned to taking guitar or piano lessons at adult ed, where they might progress to plunking out a few tunes at a party.

Computers have leveled the playing field somewhat. Programs like Apple's GarageBand, shown in Figure 11-8, come with prerecorded loops that you can transform and combine to get a sound you want. You can add your own tracks by connecting a keyboard or other instrument that has a MIDI interface, or just use the on-screen keyboard. If your performance isn't quite up to snuff, you can try again or edit out the imperfections. You can also add tracks that were performed live and recorded with a microphone.

Figure 11-8:
Apple's GarageBand laying down tracks.

Apple offers add-ins to GarageBand in the form of Jam Packs. These include the following:

- World Music Jam Pack
- Rhythm Section Jam Pack
- Symphony Orchestra Jam Pack
- Remix Tools Jam Pack

You can export your composition to iTunes or use it as part of the sound-track for your slideshow or iMovie. The latter use may be one of the most valuable aspects of GarageBand.

If you plan to distribute your iLife compositions beyond your circle of family and friends, you can't just dub in selections from your favorite group's album, even if you purchased it fair and square from the iTunes Store. What you bought entitles you to listen to, not incorporate into your own work, the copyrighted music. Original music and sound effects you create on Garage-Band, even those that use Apple's prerecorded loops, are yours to use as you see fit.

For an in-depth look at recording music with GarageBand, check out *GarageBand For Dummies,* by Bob LeVitus (published by Wiley).

Podcasting with GarageBand

If you'd like to try your hand at podcasting (creating audio or video essays that are distributed over the Net and often played on iPods), GarageBand has the tools you need.

You can use the built-in microphone in your Mac. GarageBand can enhance the sound and reduce background noise. If you use a musical soundtrack, GarageBand can automatically "duck" the soundtrack under your voice when you are speaking. Add sound effects as well, if you like — GarageBand comes with over 200. You can also have a video track with a title screen and other photos you might want to add. If you have a .Mac account, you can publish your podcast online with a single click.

Because programs like GarageBand make podcasting so easy, everyone can do it, and it seems like everyone *is* doing it. If you want your podcasts to stand out, pick topics you know about, take the time to develop an outline or script, pick one point and make it, well, lose the *umm*s and *uh*s and *likes,* and keep it short.

Moving up from GarageBand

Just as with iPhoto and iMovie, Apple has better music-creation tools ready whenever you are: Logic and Logic Pro. One of the classic rites of passage for a new musical group was coming up with the thousands of dollars needed to rent a sound studio for a few hours so that they could cut a demo tape. Groups have found that for a lot less money, they can build a sound studio in their basement that can keep up with the pros. A Mac is often at its heart of this process. You need additional equipment, including good microphones, preamps, and a multi-input audio interface with a USB or, preferably, a

FireWire interface. Sites like www.tweakheadz.com have lots of resources to help you get started.

Homing In on iWeb

Apple brings its template approach to building personal Web pages with iWeb. The program comes with a dozen themes. Each theme has coordinated templates for the Welcome page, narratives, photos, movies, blogs, and podcasts. See Figure 11-9. You can modify or customize the templates if you wish, and automated tools help to simplify blogging. iWeb relieves you from coding or other Web page internals. If you have .Mac, you can publish your page and update it with a single click.

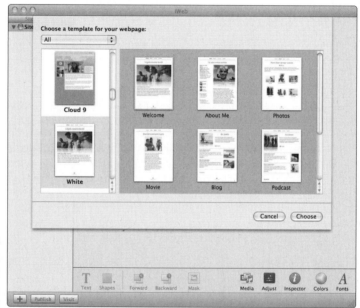

Figure 11-9:
An iWeb template.

Moving up from iWeb

iWeb is narrowly focused on personal Web pages. You might be able to adapt its templates to a simple business, but that is about it. Apple lacks a high-end program for Web-page design, unlike its great software for photos, movies, and music. Many word processing and page-layout programs can output in

Web-ready HTML format, including TextEdit and Microsoft Word. Adobe. com's Dreamweaver is probably the most-often-used tool by professionals on Macs and in Windows. A good free, visual Web-page editor can be found at www.nvu.com. You can find a complete rundown of Mac Web-creation programs at www.pure-mac.com/webed.html.

Making Web sites that work

With tools like iWeb, creating a Web page is easy. Making ones that accomplish their goals is another matter. Here are some tips for making your Web site effective:

- ✔ **Make sure that you are providing information that someone else cares about.** You don't need a large audience, but you must address the needs of your niche. Content counts.

- ✔ **Say what you most need to say on the first screen a visitor sees.** Keep it simple. You have at most ten seconds to convince the visitor to go further into your site. Be sure to include any keywords that you want Google to index in the initial paragraphs.

- ✔ **Get an easy-to-remember Web address,** preferably in the .com top-level domain. No, they aren't all taken. If a name you like isn't taken, register it immediately. One-year registrations are cheap. Mark the renewal date a month ahead on your calendar so you won't forget to renew. When you've settled on a name, don't change it. Links to your site are priceless.

- ✔ **On the garish World Wide Web, restraint stands out.** Use color and graphics to enhance your messages. Avoid clichés like animated .gif files and Under Construction signs. If a page isn't ready, don't link to it.

- ✔ **Put up what you have now and improve it later.** The visitors you missed today won't be back tomorrow.

- ✔ **Test your site with different browsers,** including Internet Explorer in Windows and Firefox. Test it on a dialup connection, too. Ask someone who doesn't know your site to find it and check it out while you watch. Keep your mouth shut while the person does this — it won't be easy — and videotape the session or take notes.

- ✔ **Keep your site current.** Out-of-date information destroys your whole site's credibility. Regularly purge references to "upcoming" events that have already happened and to dead external links. Don't include high-maintenance items like events if you are not prepared to keep them updated. Less is more.

- ✔ **Give visitors a compelling reason to return to your site.** What that reason is depends on the goals of your site, but it must have a clear benefit for them, not just for you.

Chapter 12

Enjoying Other OS X Goodies

Mac OS X is filled with programs and features that make time spent in front of your computer more productive, more interesting, and more fun. In this chapter, I introduce some of my favorites.

Adding Handy Widgets to the Dashboard

Dashboard provides an easy way to see and use widgets, mini-applications that grab specific information from the Internet or help with narrow but useful tasks. Figure 12-1 shows a typical Dashboard arrangement, including a calendar, a clock, a translator, a flight tracker, weather, and more. Of course, you can move widgets around, add new ones, and drop stale ones. You're in charge. Some widgets are silly, some are fun, and some seem indispensable after you are used to having them around.

To work with widgets, you just need to know a few tips:

✔ To make your widgets appear, press F12. The desktop you've been working on grays into the background, and a layer with colorful widgets appears.

✔ To add more widgets, click the plus sign in the lower-left corner. A scrolling list appears at the bottom of your screen. Click icons for widgets you want to add.

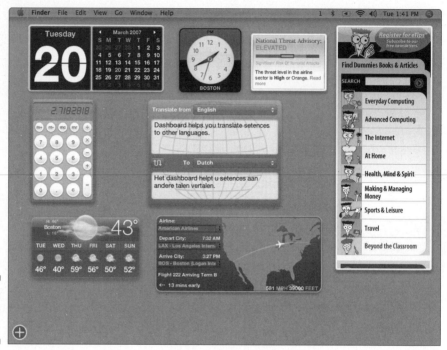

Figure 12-1:
The
Dashboard.

✔ You also click the plus sign when you want to delete widgets. When you do, all the current ones show up with an *X* in the upper-left corner. Click the *X,* and they're gone.

✔ Many widgets have a lowercase *i* in the lower-right corner. Click it and the widget flips over and shows you what settings you can adjust to customize it.

Apple includes a collection of widgets with OS X, but many more are available from `apple.com/downloads/dashboard`. Many are freeware, but some ask for a fee.

You can have multiple instances of a widget running simultaneously with different customizations, such as a clock with different time zones or weather reports from different locales. Some widgets that come with OS X include the following:

✔ **Stocks:** Watch your favorite securities and funds fluctuate.

✔ **Weather:** Temperature, highs, lows, and a six-day forecast.

✔ **Movies:** Find what's playing where, see previews, and buy tickets from Fandango.

- ✔ **Dictionary and thesaurus:** Don't guess; look it up.

- ✔ **World time:** Is it too early to call Tokyo?

- ✔ **Calendar:** What day is the 23rd of next month?

- ✔ **Phone book:** Let your mouse do the walking.

- ✔ **Address book:** Easy access to your contact list.

- ✔ **Stickies:** These won't fall off your monitor.

- ✔ **Tile game:** A classic.

- ✔ **Unit converter:** Metric to English, sure. But it also knows currency exchange rates.

- ✔ **Flight tracker:** Where are they now? When will they get here?

- ✔ **Ski report:** Packed ice or fresh powder?

- ✔ **Language translator:** Translates a sentence or two between Chinese, Dutch, English, French, German, Greek, Italian, Korean, Russian, and Spanish.

You even have a Widget widget to help you manage all your widgets.

Download more

You can find many more widgets to play with. Here are some examples, and all are freeware:

- ✔ **Starry Night Widget:** See the planets and constellations as they appear right now at any location on Earth.

- ✔ **iStat Pro:** Display the status of the CPU, memory, hard drives, internal and external IP address, bandwidth, battery, uptime, and fans.

- ✔ **Sudoku Widget:** A wildly popular number game. Get your rivals at work hooked on Sudoku and career success is assured.

- ✔ **Mirror:** See yourself on-screen and touch up your hair. Uses your iSight camera.

- ✔ **Corporate Ipsum:** Generate nonsense text whenever you need it, such as the following: interactively orchestrate superior portals without team-driven platforms, collaboratively actualize plug-and-play outsourcing and maintainable applications, distinctively simplify front-end platforms before backward-compatible relationships.

- ✔ **Countdown Dashboard Widget:** Make a countdown timer to any event you choose: graduation, vacation, dentist appointments, book deadlines, and so on.

✔ **Fans:** Your Mac has cooling fans inside that spin at different rates depending on how hard your CPU is working. Seriously. The first time my normally quiet MacBook started to sound like an airplane taking off was a tad alarming. The Fans Widget shows animated fans spinning to match the current speed of your real fans.

✔ **Kennedy Space Center Video:** Watch what's happening at everyone's favorite spaceport. Over a dozen Webcams to choose from.

✔ **I Love Lamp:** You've heard of the infamous lava lamp from the 1960s?

Hundreds more widgets are available, and more keep popping up.

Roll your own

You can select a portion of a Web page and create a widget that shows the latest version of just that piece, a feature Apple calls WebClips. Follow these steps:

1. **Open Safari and go to the Web site you want to wigitize.**

2. **Choose File⇨Open in Dashboard or click the Dashboard icon.**

3. **Select the section of the page that you want to capture.**

   In the upper-right corner of Figure 12-1, you see two Web clips I made. One is from the U.S. Department of Homeland Security (dhs.gov), showing the current terrorist threat level; the other, from Dummies.com, shows a search box for finding the latest *For Dummies* titles.

Apple even provides a program, called Dashcode, to help you build your own widget. Make a widget to track your favorite blog. The possibilities are endless. Dashcode is in the Xcode folder on your OS X install DVD.

Controlling Windows Fast with Exposé

The more useful computers become, the more cluttered the screen gets. At any given time, you may be working with half a dozen applications at once, each with multiple windows open. Exposé provides the following shortcuts to help you find the window you are looking for:

✔ Press F9 and all your open windows shrink and arrange themselves on your screen so that none of them overlap. You get an overview of everything. Click the window you want and it comes to the front, or press F9 again and your screen returns to its previous mess.

✔ F10 works like F9, but pressing F10 rearranges only the windows from the application you are currently working on.

✔ Press F11 to make all the windows go away so that you can see your desktop. (They don't completely go away — you can see the edges of the windows along the border of your screen. Clicking one of those windows' edges brings you out of Exposé with that window in front.)

✔ Press F12 to bring up the Dashboard.

You can pick different keys to perform these functions and also make the corner of your screen a hot spot for the same actions. Follow these steps:

1. **Open System Preferences under the Apple menu.**

2. **Select Exposé & Spaces.**

   You see a pane similar to Figure 12-2.

3. **Select which keys or corners you want to perform the desired action on your screen.**

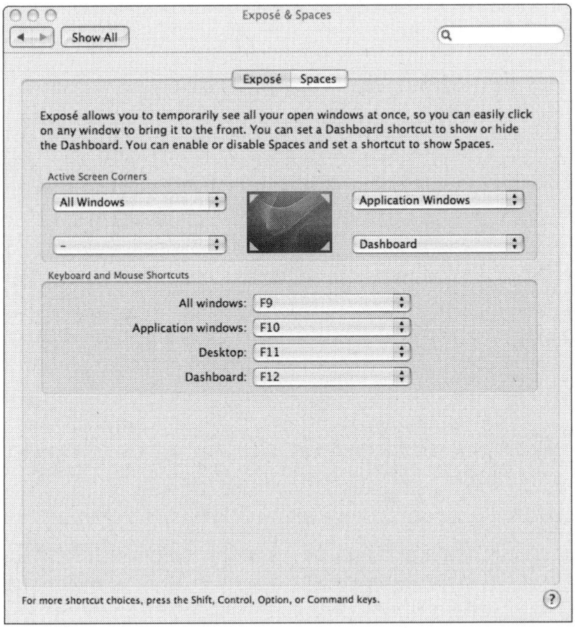

Figure 12-2:
The Exposé preferences pane.

Organizing Work Areas with Spaces

I'm one of those people who always has several projects going on at once. My fantasy is a studio where I can have a table or workbench for each project, so I can walk up to it whenever I want and pick up where I left off. Apple hasn't offered me a studio, but OS X provides the next-best thing — a bunch of virtual work tables called Spaces. You can have up to 16 of them. Specific applications can be assigned to specific spaces, or an app can be available to all spaces. You set up Spaces as follows:

1. **Open System Preferences under the Apple menu.**

2. **Select Exposé & Spaces, and then click the Spaces tab.**

   You see a window like Figure 12-3.

3. **Add the applications you want and assign them a space or set them to be available to all spaces.**

   Figure 12-3 shows Spaces with three spaces populated (see the Application Bindings area of the dialog box).

   When you're done with the setup, activate Spaces by pressing F8 and selecting the space you want. Or, switch spaces by holding down Ctrl and pressing either the arrow key or the number key that corresponds to the space you want.

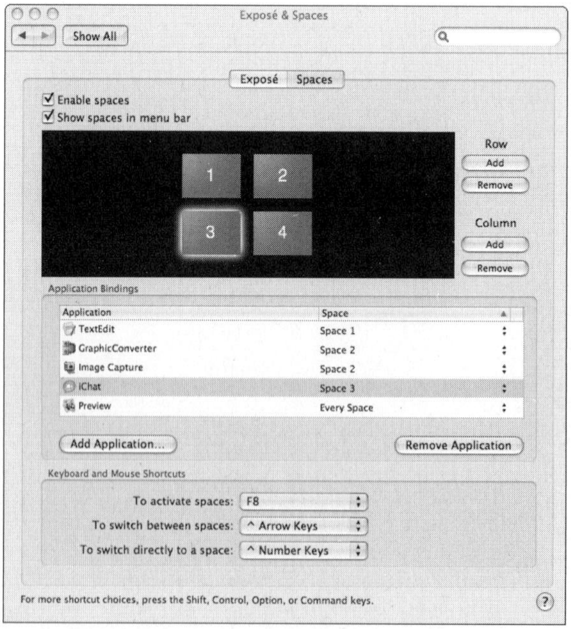

Figure 12-3: Preferences for Spaces.

Searching for Files with Spotlight

After you've been using computers for a while, sooner or later you encounter difficulty finding a file. You know it's in there somewhere. Spotlight is a search tool that helps you find that file by typing words that the file likely contains and other characteristics, such as its name, the date you created it, what kind of file it is, and so on. Searching through gigabytes of hard-drive space can take some time, even on a fast computer, so Spotlight keeps an index of every word you use in documents, e-mail messages, and so on. It does this in the background, so you hardly notice. But these indexes make searching very fast.

A Spotlight icon is located on the menu bar at the upper-right corner of your screen. Click it to open a search box. You also see search boxes in each Finder window. You can also press ⌘+F when you are in the Finder.

Customizing searches

You can tell Spotlight your search preferences and how you want to see results by clicking the Spotlight icon in System Preferences. You see a pane similar to Figure 12-4. Deselect the items that you don't want to search. You can drag individual lines up and down to reorder the way items appear in a search.

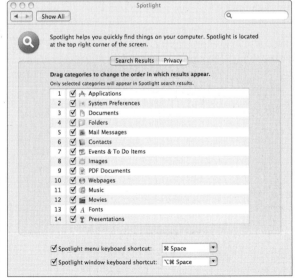

Figure 12-4:
Customizing Spotlight's search order.

Of course, you may have things you'd rather not have found in a search. Click the Privacy tab in the Spotlight preferences pane and drag into the window those files and folders you don't want to have searched. Spotlight won't return matches from those files and folders.

Spotlight normally tries to match all the words you type in its search box. If you want to search for dogs *or* cats, type **dogs | cats**. If you want to search for pets but no dogs, type **pets -dogs**.

See www.apple.com/macosx/features/spotlight for more clever Spotlight tricks.

Searching with Smart Folders

Wouldn't it be convenient to find all the files associated with the Zorchcastle Project without having to do a search each time? Spotlight offers a tool to do this called Smart Folders. Here's how it works:

1. **In the Finder, create a folder by choosing Finder⇨New Smart Folder.**

   Of course, if your project isn't named Zorchcastle, you're out of luck. Smart Folders only works with "Zorchcastle." Just kidding.

2. **Enter the words or other criteria you want into the Smart Folder's search area.**

   You add more criteria by clicking the little plus buttons (+).

3. **To keep your handy new Smart Folder around, click the Save button and give it a name.**

   Keep the Smart Folder around, and it will always show the files that match the criteria you set, including new files you've saved after you set up the Smart Folder. The Smart Folder stays wherever you put it, such as on the desktop or in your Documents folder. You can find it the same way you find any other folder.

   Figure 12-5 shows a Smart Folder looking for files created in the last month whose name starts with "Ch."

Figure 12-5:
A Smart
Folder.

Automator and AppleScript

Every now and then you are faced with a task that is highly repetitious. A bunch of photos have to be sized to fit a catalog, or some illustrations have to be numbered a certain way to work with a publishing system. Apple provides a couple of techniques for doing this.

If you're comfortable with computer programming, OS X comes with a scripting language called AppleScript. Most OS X applications can be called from AppleScript programs, so you can use them as tools in your program.

Most of us are not up for writing programs every time a tedious chore presents itself, so Apple has a simple way to automate your life, called, interestingly, the Automator. OS X includes a library with hundreds of Automator actions you can choose from. See Figure 12-6. You can even ask Automator to watch what you are doing as you go through the routine once and record your actions. You can then play them back or edit the actions.

Apple has a nice tutorial on using Automator at
www.apple.com/macosx/features/automator.

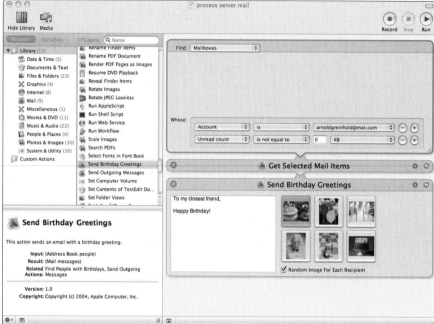

Figure 12-6:
An
Automator
workflow to
send
birthday
greetings.

Chapter 13

Oops, It's a PC: Running Windows on Your Mac

● ●

In This Chapter

▶ The day the Earth moved

▶ The many ways to dance together

▶ The four solutions

● ●

The Earth moved on June 6, 2005. Pigs flew. All flights to Hades were canceled because it had frozen over. On that day, Apple CEO Steve Jobs announced that Apple would begin using microprocessors from Intel in all its new products.

Since the beginning of the rivalry between Apple and Microsoft, one constant point of contention was the underlying hardware. Microsoft designed its products to run on Intel's *x*86 series microprocessors. Apple used Motorola 680x0 micros, later switching to the PowerPC, which was jointly developed by Motorola and IBM. Apple ran ads showing Army tanks guarding a G3 Mac, briefly subject to U.S. arms export regulation, while stating that Windows PCs were harmless.

Jobs concluded that Intel had a better plan for developing the kind of microprocessors Apple needed and did the unthinkable. The transition went surprisingly smoothly. Today, all Macs sold not only have Intel microprocessors inside, but they also closely adhere to industry standards for PC design. They really are PCs. If you take a fancy to Apple's elegant hardware but only have eyes for Vista, you can get the Mac you like and just run Vista on it. You do have to buy a Vista license separately — an added expense — but otherwise you have just another Vista machine.

The real win for Mac owners in this sea of change is the ability to run both Mac OS X and Windows on the same Mac. And you can, quite easily. The tricky part is choosing which of several methods exist for doing this. You have three main candidates. Here's a quick rundown. I explain each in more detail in this chapter:

- ✔ **Dual-booting:** You pick your poison when you boot up your computer: OS X or Windows. Dual-booting capability is built into OS X 10.5 (Leopard), but again you need to obtain a Windows license. Apple calls this technology *BootCamp.*

- ✔ **Virtualization:** Run both operating systems at the same time and switch between apps effortlessly. OS X and Windows play nicely together. Currently, two vendors offer this solution: Parallels.com and VMware.com.

- ✔ **API translation:** Run Windows applications on your Mac without installing Windows. This does not yet work for all applications, but if you only need to run a few applications that are on the "okay" list, you save money and aggravation by not buying and installing Windows.

Pulling the Rabbit Out of the Hat

Magic starts with understanding the obvious. How can you run both OS X and Windows? Well, if you've bought a Mac and still have your old PC, it's easy — just turn them both on. You have the situation shown in Figure 13-1. I labeled one computer a Mac and one a Dell, but the second could be any Windows PC. Indeed, as just mentioned, because your new Mac is really a PC, the computer on the right could be another Mac.

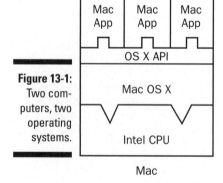
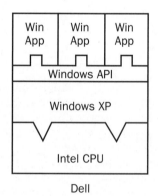

Figure 13-1: Two computers, two operating systems.

If you don't care about spending money, you could buy two Macs, leave OS X on one, and replace OS X with Windows on the other. You'd be in the same situation as shown in Figure 13-2, which is not really different than Figure 13-1.

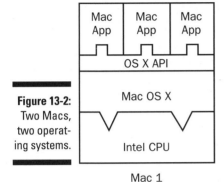

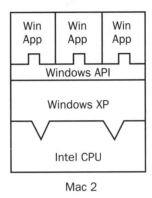

Mac 1   Mac 2

Figure 13-2: Two Macs, two operating systems.

When you install an operating system on a computer, it is stored on your hard drive. Well, you can have two (or more) hard drives and install a different OS on each. You can then tell your Mac (and your PC) from which hard drive you want to *boot* — start up.

You don't even need two physical drives. You can use Disk Utility to split or *partition* your hard drive into two (or more) sections called *volumes*. From then on, the computer considers each volume as a separate hard drive, and you can install different operating systems on each. This situation is depicted in Figure 13-3.

Why can't I run OS X on a Dell?

If you've been following all this, you may be wondering: If Macs are just like any other PC, why can't I run OS X on a Dell or HP or any other Windows box that doesn't come from Apple? It's a good question. There are two answers. First, some components in the Windows PC probably require drivers that are not available for OS X. Windows drivers don't work in OS X. Apple only makes drivers for the components it uses in making Macs. This reason only prevents cross-use up to a point. You find overlap in components, and some people are skilled enough to make the necessary drivers, at least for the more popular configurations of Windows PCs, and make them available.

The other reason is that Apple doesn't want you to run OS X on a Windows box — at least for now. Apple makes money selling the complete package: hardware and software. At the moment, it isn't ready to license OS X for other computers — it may never be — and it certainly doesn't want people to pirate OS X. So Apple has built tests into OS X that can detect a non-Apple PC. Exactly how is a closely guarded secret. The company has even applied for patents on some techniques for concealing the methods they use.

One benefit of having OS X only run on Apple hardware is that Apple does not require registration for each new OS X installation. Microsoft, by contrast, requires such registration in its Windows Genuine Advantage program, and changes to a PC's configuration can trigger a request to reregister.

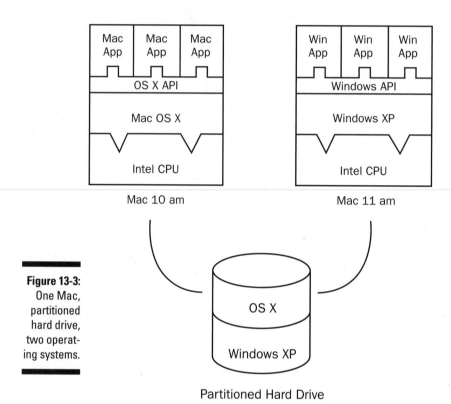

Figure 13-3:
One Mac,
partitioned
hard drive,
two operat-
ing systems.

Partitioned Hard Drive

At 10:00 a.m., you boot your Mac in OS X to check your mail and search the Web for information you need for a presentation you're working on. At 11:00 a.m., you reboot into Windows to run some corporate applications that require Internet Explorer. At 11:30, you reboot to OS X to finish that presentation in Keynote. It's a tad tedious, but it all works.

Getting Started with BootCamp

BootCamp is included with Mac OS X 10.5 (Leopard), and to use it, you need the following:

✔ An Intel Mac with at least 10GB of free hard drive space.

✔ A bona fide installation disc for Microsoft Windows XP, Service Pack 2, Home or Professional, or Microsoft Windows Vista.

After you install Windows by using BootCamp, you select which operating system you want, Windows or OS X, by holding down the Option key (the Alt key if you are using a Windows keyboard) while starting up. I would include a screen shot of BootCamp in action, but you know what Windows looks like.

Virtualize Me

Dual-booting is great if you only need to use Windows every so often. It can get old fast if you need to switch several times a day. Wouldn't it be wonderful if you could run both operating systems at the same time and switch between them as easily as you switch between applications in OS X? The technology that makes such a switch possible has been around since the 1960s, but it has taken off in the last few years and has become one of the hottest topics in computing: *virtualization*.

With virtualization, an extra layer, called a *hypervisor*, is inserted between the operating system and the computer. Operating systems include software called a *supervisor*, so the term *hypervisor* was invented to connote something with even more authority than a supervisor. The hypervisor's role is to divide the CPU's attention between two or more virtual machines, each with its own operating system. This is shown schematically in Figure 13-4. Each virtual machine looks to its operating system as though it had a complete, unvarnished CPU all to itself. The hypervisor makes sure that each virtual machine gets a fair share of the real CPU's resources, and decides which operating system gets to appear on the real computer's display and where to direct mouse and keyboard actions.

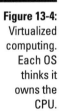

Figure 13-4:
Virtualized computing. Each OS thinks it owns the CPU.

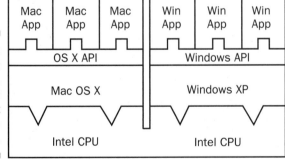

In the following sections, you find out about the pros and cons of virtualization as well as about programs you can use to add this hypervisor to your system. The two vendors that offer a virtualization solution for OS X are Parallels.com and VMware Fusion from VMware.com, which is owned by EMC Corporation.

Advantages and disadvantages of virtualization

Virtualization is the most convenient solution to running Windows on a Mac. You get both operating systems running at the same time, and you can quickly switch back and forth, with no rebooting. Virtualization also supports a wide variety of operating systems. You want MS-DOS or OS/2 on your Mac? No problem.

Virtualization has the following disadvantages:

- ✔ It's the most expensive solution to running Windows on a Mac, because you must buy the virtualization package and obtain a Windows license.

- ✔ Microsoft's current Vista license only allows use in a virtual machine for the more expensive, higher-end versions of Vista, not the Home editions.

- ✔ The hypervisor layer causes a small performance penalty, though special hardware in the Intel Core processors used in Macs, called Intel Virtualization Technology (VT-x), is designed to speed virtualization.

- ✔ You have to deal with two different operating systems.

- ✔ Peripheral support may be less than ideal.

- ✔ It discourages you from making the leap to OS X, because the more-familiar Windows programs are always easily available.

- ✔ The virtualized version of OS X may not take full advantage of the multi-core Mac processors.

Parallels

Parallels was the first company to sell virtualization for OS X. Its product, Parallels Desktop, runs on any Intel Mac, though Parallels recommends having 1GB of RAM or more and 15GB of free hard drive space. It supports a wide range of guest operating systems, including the following:

- ✔ Most versions of Microsoft Windows, starting with 3.11, 98, Me, NT, 2000, XP, 2003, and Vista

- ✔ Many popular Linux distributions, including Debian, Fedora Core, Mandriva, Red Hat, SUSE, Ubuntu, and Xandrox

- ✔ FreeBSD 4 and 5

- ✔ IBM's legendary OS/2 Warp 3, 4, and 4.5

✔ Sun's Solaris 9 and 10

✔ MS-DOS 6.22

Parallels has a feature called Parallels Transporter that migrates your existing PC to the Mac, which greatly simplifies the process of getting on the Mac. It can also use a BootCamp partition if you have previously created one.

Perhaps the sweetest feature of Parallels Desktop is Coherence, which lets you run Windows applications from the Mac desktop as though they were Mac apps. You don't have to look at Windows at all. You can even drag and drop files between the two operating systems. Windows apps show up on the OS X Dock with a *W* symbol, indicating their Windows origin.

Parallels offers a separate tool, called Compressor, that the company claims reduces the size of a virtual machine stored on your hard drive by 50 percent or more, saving disk space and improving performance.

Parallels has limited support for USB 2.0. It does not currently support certain classes of devices, such as cameras and microphones.

VMware Fusion

VMware largely started the *x*86 virtualization business in 1998. The company is a leading supplier of virtualization products, such as its VMware Workstation, in the Windows and Linux enterprise markets. Its virtualization product for the Mac, VMware Fusion, is based on the same proven technology. So, even though VMware entered the OS X market a little later than Parallels, it brings along considerable depth of experience. Virtual machines created with other VMware products can run on the Mac, and similarly, virtual machines created with VMware Fusion on the Mac can run on other systems. VMware has a Virtual Appliance Marketplace, where you can try one of hundreds of preconfigured virtual solutions on your Mac.

One neat feature allows you to take a snapshot of your VMware virtual machine when you have it set up the way you like it. You can then roll back to that configuration with a single click anytime you wish. You can copy and paste text between Windows and Mac applications and drag and drop files from one to the other. It also offers full USB 2.0 support and can run some games that depend on DirectX 8.1. VMware has similar installation requirements as Parallels Desktop.

Choosing between Parallels and VMware is tough. They are both good products. If you work in an organization that uses other VMware products, that might tip the decision in VMware's favor.

Imitation, the Sincerest Form of Flattery

One problem exists with both the dual-boot and the virtualization approaches: You need a copy of Windows. That is an added expense, and it means you have one more operating system to maintain, update, defrag, and so on. You probably just want to run some Windows-only applications. Suppose that you could sneak them onto your Mac without having to install the whole Windows boat? You can do that, too — sort of. I say sort of, because it only works with some Windows apps, though the list is growing.

Why running Windows applications will (or won't) work

To understand how this approach works, it helps to consider why it is a problem. Windows programs run on the same Intel microprocessors as newer Macs. Why can't I just insert a Windows program disc in my Mac and start it up? The reason is that all applications have to talk to the operating system to get basic services, like opening files or getting told when the user clicks a mouse button or presses a key. For the programmers who create applications, an operating system is nothing but a giant catalog of services they can call. Hundreds of services exist. The geek phrase for the collection of services an OS provides is *application program interfaces,* or APIs. Unfortunately, the APIs that Mac OS X provides are set up very differently than the ones Windows provides. They speak different languages, in effect.

But while the languages are different, the underlying concepts are the same. So some people came up with the idea of building a layer of software that would sit on top of one operating system and provide the APIs that a program for a second operating system would expect. This approach is illustrated in Figure 13-5, showing a compatibility layer known as Wine. On a case-by-case basis, translating each operating system service is not so hard. Intercept a request address to the second operating system to open a file, and convert it to the open-file request in the host system. What is hard is getting it all exactly right for the thousands of services involved.

The Wine project, www.winehq.org, was originally aimed at running Windows programs, particularly Microsoft Office, on Intel-based Linux computers. Microsoft does not offer Office for Linux. The Wine project started in 1993, and people have been working on it ever since. One problem is that every time Microsoft comes out with a new version of Windows, dozens of new APIs must be added, and others may have changed in subtle ways. And Microsoft does not always document its APIs as thoroughly as Wine developers might desire, so a certain amount of trial and error exists in the Wine development process.

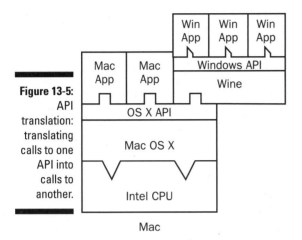

Figure 13-5:
API
translation:
translating
calls to one
API into
calls to
another.

CodeWeavers — Wine on a Mac

Mac OS X shares a common UNIX heritage with Linux. So when Apple announced it was switching to Intel microprocessors, it created the possibility of running Wine on Macs. It was such an attractive idea that a company, CodeWeavers.com, decided to make a business of creating the OS X version of Wine. The company's product is called CrossOver Mac. The good news is that it costs a lot less than a Windows license. The bad news, which CodeWeavers freely admits, is that it only works with a few Windows programs, though the list is expanding. You can check the status of the program or programs you are interested in by visiting the CodeWeavers compatibility center. The company even has a process where you can influence its priorities in getting applications to work. See www.codeweavers.com/compatibility/browse/votes.

As of this writing, CodeWeavers officially supports the following applications:

✔ Microsoft Outlook

✔ Microsoft Project

✔ Microsoft Visio

✔ Half-Life 2

✔ Quicken

Most features in some older versions of Microsoft Office work. Hopefully, the list will grow.

One other important use for CrossOver exists. If your organization has some Windows applications and you would like them to work on Macs, CodeWeavers can test the application to see whether it works on CrossOver, and if not, CodeWeavers can attempt to get it to work by fixing problems the way developers fix any bug. CodeWeavers even has tools to help you. Because a free trial period is available, you have little to lose in giving it a try.

Emulation — the Other White Meat

A fourth approach is available to get one operating system to run on top of another. Called *emulation,* it's used when different CPU types are involved. The idea is to write a program in the language of the host CPU that examines each machine-language instruction in the program for the second CPU and does what that instruction calls for. Figure 13-6 suggests how this works. This approach is not relevant to running Windows on Intel Macs because Windows uses instructions that execute properly on the Intel microprocessor.

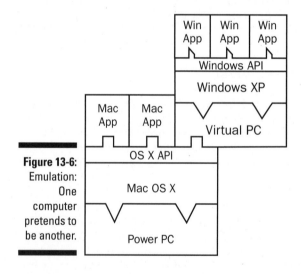

Figure 13-6:
Emulation:
One
computer
pretends to
be another.

Virtual PC

Emulation was used with older PowerPC Macs to run Windows. It was used in a product called Virtual PC. But, as you might imagine, emulation is slower than the other solutions mentioned earlier in this chapter, solutions that let most instructions be executed by the CPU hardware at high speed. The company that made VirtualPC was eventually bought out by Microsoft, which still offers the emulator for non-Intel Macs as Virtual PC for Macs. See `www.microsoft.com/mac/products/virtualpc/virtualpc.aspx`. Microsoft also sells a Windows virtualization tool under the Virtual PC 2007 brand.

Security issues

It's neat to have Windows at your disposal on your Mac, but do remember it's still Windows. That means you should follow all the security and antivirus guidelines recommended for Windows on a PC, including enabling Windows Update and having up-to-date antivirus software installed. As a former Windows user, you know the drill.

It might be wise to get your mail and do your Web surfing in OS X, and restrict Internet access on the Windows side to situations where it's needed, such as accessing sites that you already know about and trust and that require Internet Explorer or ActiveX. You should

also not use the same password for Windows that you use on the Mac. See Chapter 10 for more password suggestions.

One advantage of running Windows on a Mac is that you can keep important files on the Mac side, using shared folders. Then, if your Windows machine gets infected by some nasty malware, you can simply delete the Windows virtual disk and restore a copy that you saved when you were sure it was in a clean state, or simply reinstall Windows from the original disc. Virus hunters use virtualization for this very reason.

Rosetta at your service

Emulation does have a role in your Intel Mac. It's how OS X can run programs that are only available for the PowerPC version of OS X. Apple calls this technology *Rosetta,* after the famous stone whose multilanguage inscriptions allowed Egyptian hieroglyphics to be decoded. Rosetta goes beyond simple translation and converts key parts of the PowerPC software into Intel instructions for greater speed.

Rosetta is built into OS X on Intel machines and just does its thing when it encounters a PowerPC-only program. You don't have to install it or configure it — you never know it's there. Still, applications that demand high performance, such as image editing in Photoshop, are not good candidates for Rosetta. This book was written on a PowerPC version of Microsoft Word, at times on a PowerPC G4 iMac, and at other times, on my Intel MacBook laptop via Rosetta. I never noticed any difference.

Rosetta works only on programs that run in OS X. It does not support applications that only ran in Mac OS 9 and older versions of Mac OS, including applications written for the Motorola 68000. Other emulators are available for them, but they are far from seamless. See Chapter 16.

Most applications for OS X are now available as Universal Binaries. This means that the application disc contains a version of the program for Intel processors and a version for PowerPC processors. The installation process automatically puts the right version on your hard drive. Though it is cool technology, Rosetta's role is diminishing.

Part V
Specialty Switching Scenarios

"Don't be silly - of course my passwords are safe. I keep them written on my window, but then I pull the shade if anyone walks in the room."

In this part . . .

We're all different and the problems and opportunities we encounter when we switch computer systems depends on our situation and needs. In this part, I deal with topics that may not interest everyone who switches. The first chapter of this part covers kids, seniors, and people with disabilities. Then, I discuss using Macs in business settings, the heartland of Windows dominance. Chapter 16 is for folks who are switching from computer operating systems other than Windows XP. In particular, users of older Mac operating systems can find upgrading to OS X challenging. The last chapter in this part dives a bit deeper into OS X and introduces the UNIX layer underneath all the graphical glitz.

Chapter 14

Switching with the Whole Family in Mind

*B*uying a computer for home use involves a special set of challenges. In a work environment, personal computing may just mean that each employee has his own machine. But in a family setting, *personal* means much more. Computers become part of us, woven into our daily routine and even our psyches. The choices we make in which computers we give our children and how we set them up can affect their development. For an elderly person or someone with a disability, the right computer can improve their quality of life.

In this chapter, you find out about features and software on your Mac that help kids, parents, and the whole family enjoy their home computer that much more.

Macs for Kids

Kids take to computers like raccoons to suburbia. It may not be the environment nature intended, but kids quickly become comfortable in front of a screen — perhaps too comfortable.

Check out these positives about computers for kids:

- ✔ They provide an outlet for artistic expression and creativity.
- ✔ They offer information about every topic imaginable, much of it true.
- ✔ They let kids chat with friends and be at home at the same time, without running up minutes on their cell phones.

✔ They offer opportunities for personal contact with new people and cultures.

✔ They can help develop and improve reading, writing, and language skills.

✔ They can support kids with special needs and their parents.

But you find some big negatives as well:

✔ Video games can be unbelievably addictive, especially for boys.

✔ Time spent in front of a computer is time not spent doing chores, homework, and ordinary play.

✔ Our kids are getting fat from lack of physical activity. TV is the main culprit, but computers are catching up.

✔ It's hard for kids to resist the temptation to download music and videos without paying for them.

✔ It's also too tempting to copy material off the Web and pass it off as their own schoolwork.

✔ Like suburbia must seem to raccoons, the Internet is littered with garbage cans.

Establishing parental control

If you're switching your kids to a Mac, you have a unique opportunity to regain some control over their computer usage. You'll have to act fast though. Your kids probably know more about computers than you do, so it's best to get things set up correctly from the beginning. I go over the steps in more detail here than for other topics because establishing control over your kids' computer use is vital and because I know how harassed and time-constrained most parents are.

Computers and young children

I'm not convinced that really young kids need to have computer access. I'm talking about kids in the fourth grade or younger. Young kids need to relate to the real world and, especially, other people. They do that by playing with toys, kids, and adults. Computers are mostly a distraction from the task of being children. Perhaps you can make an argument that computers are less passive babysitters than television. But neither is particularly desirable, and kid computer use should really be supervised anyway.

Think long and hard before introducing your kids to computers, and make careful choices about what kind of programs and Web sites they are exposed to.

The first thing you must do is make yourself the administrator for your kids' Mac. That means you should be the one to go through the startup sequence described in Chapter 4 and become the first user of the computer. If you are giving your kids accounts on the that Mac you use, you've in effect already done this.

Next, you should set up a separate account for each child who will be using the computer. If you have more than one child and are giving each one his or her own Mac — what good parents you are — it's still a good idea to give each kid an account on each machine. That way, if one child borrows an older sibling's Mac, she still has the restrictions you impose.

Setting up accounts is easy. Follow these steps:

1. **Select System Preferences from the Apple menu and click the Accounts icon.**

   It's the one with a silhouette of two heads. You see the pane shown in Figure 14-1.

Figure 14-1: The Accounts system preferences pane.

2. **Click the plus sign in the lower-left corner to add a new account.**

   You may have to click the Lock icon first and enter your password.

3. **When you see a pane that asks for the name and password of the new account, as shown in Figure 14-2, fill in the name and password you want your child to have.**

   Here are some tips for choosing names and passwords specifically for kids:

   • Because the account name and short name are used in OS X for many purposes and may show up during Internet use, *do not include your kids' last name on the account.* Billy or Billy R should do fine.

- In Chapter 10, I emphasize the security value of using random passwords. If anything, security is more important for kids on the Internet. You can ask OS X to suggest a short, 7- to 9-character, random password of letters and numbers by clicking the Key icon next to the password field.

- An alternative for kids who are very young is to combine a name and number from two different parts of their lives, such as a character from a favorite story and their room number in school.

- Tape your child's password to his or her monitor until the child learns it. It won't take long.

- While you're at it, help your child make up a separate password for all the junk Internet sites that require registration. Who knows what some of those sites do with the passwords they accumulate?

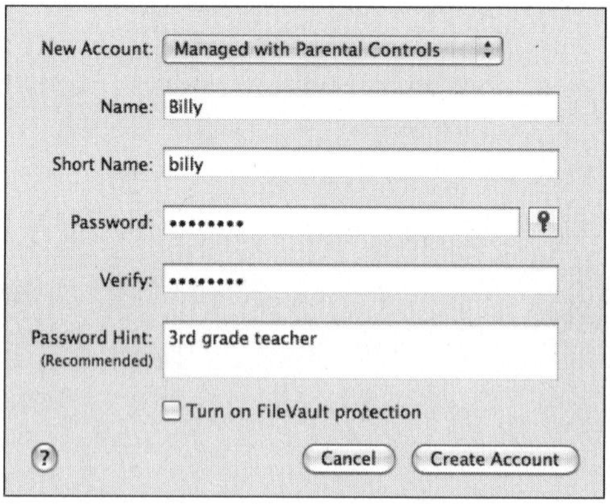

Figure 14-2:
The New
Account
pane.

4. **Because this is an account for a child, select Managed with Parental Controls from the New Account drop-down list.**

   Other account options include Standard and Administrator. Don't give your kids administrative privileges. This does mean they will pester you from time to time to enter your password so that they can do something that requires these privileges, such as installing some downloaded software. Trust me: You want to know about these things. Ask questions like what the software is for, and ask to visit the Web site from which it came. Don't be afraid to veto the installation.

5. **Click the Create Account button.**

   When you are done, you see the Accounts system preferences pane again, as shown in Figure 14-3, this time with the new account highlighted.

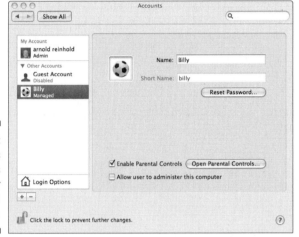

Figure 14-3:
Billy's
account is
ready for
parental
controls.

6. **Select the account you just created, if it's not already selected, and select the Enable Parental Controls check box.**

7. **Click the Open Parental Controls button.**

   The Parental Controls System pane appears, as shown in Figure 14-4. You see tabs for several other panes:

   - System
   - Content
   - Mail & iChat
   - Time Limits
   - Logs

8. **Each pane has settings that let you sculpt your child's computer and Internet usage. Using the information in the sections that follow, set up the controls for the account.**

   By logging on as the administrator under your own account, you can return to the Parental Controls settings to adjust them if needed. Just open System Preferences from the Apple menu.

The System pane

The first item in the Parental Controls System pane (refer to Figure 14-4) lets you require Simple Finder for this account. Simple Finder replaces the usual OS X desktop with a screen that contains big, square buttons. Each button launches an application from the list of those you permit. Many applications provide reduced menus when Simple Finder is in use. Simple Finder removes much of the complexity of the OS X interface and makes the computer more of an appliance.

Figure 14-4:
The
Parental
Controls
System
pane.

Below that choice is an area where you can limit the applications this user can launch to only those you specify. Simply deselect those you don't want to allow access to. At the bottom of the pane are a series of check boxes that let you give this user specific privileges:

- ✔ **Can Administer Printers:** This might be a good idea for kids who are a little older. They might learn enough to help you with printer problems.

- ✔ **Can Burn CDs and DVDs:** You might want to wait on this until you set clear guidelines on what they can and cannot share with their friends.

- ✔ **Can Change Password:** Knowing your kid's password makes it easier to check what's on the computer, but you have other ways to do this.

- ✔ **Can Modify the Dock:** Let young kids mess with the Dock, and they will keep pestering you to find the stuff they dragged off of it (to watch it go poof). Don't select this check box.

The Content pane

OS X offers a number of options to limit what content your kids can see, using the Content pane depicted in Figure 14-5. One example is the Hide Profanity in Dictionary check box. However, there comes a stage in your child's development where it might be better for him or her to find out what words mean from a dictionary instead of on the street. You can also ask OS X to try to limit access to adult sites automatically. If you then click the Customize button, you can list sites you want added or specifically banned. The third option restricts your kids to only those sites you specifically choose.

Figure 14-5:
The
Parental
Controls
Content
pane.

The rest of the Content pane offers you some choices on what kind of content your kids gets to see online:

✔ **Allow Unrestricted Access to Websites:** Select this check box for older kids only. You can still check the logs to see where they are going.

✔ **Try to Limit Access to Adult Websites Automatically:** This option uses filters that attempt to determine what is and is not kid appropriate. They are not foolproof, occasionally letting bad stuff through and, at the same time, limiting access to sites that are harmless. And, you find a third class of sites to consider: those that provide sound information on health, sex, and what's happening to kids' bodies as they mature. If you select this check box, a Customize button appears. Click it and you see a pane with two text areas. In the top one, you specify sites that are always allowed, perhaps a health information for kids site that you've reviewed. The bottom one lists sites that are never allowed, a trickier proposition because so many exist.

✔ **Allow Access to Only These Websites:** This may be the sanest option for the younger set. You can surf sites first and add ones that you deem appropriate. You can even add Safari bookmarks and folders to this list.

The Mail & iChat pane

As I mention in Chapter 8, your Mac is a great communication tool. Your kids will figure this out faster than you. The Mail & iChat pane, shown in Figure 14-6, lets you decide to whom they can talk via e-mail or instant messaging (IM). Note that the controls here only apply to Apple's Mail and iChat. If your kids can download another mail or IM program, such as AOL's AIM, all bets are off. Some mail programs, such as Yahoo! Mail and Gmail, only require a Web browser. So, if you want your "white list" restrictions enforced, you must also limit the programs your children can download and block access to e-mail sites.

Figure 14-6:
The
Parental
Controls
Mail & iChat
pane.

This pane also lets you specify an e-mail address — yours presumably — where notifications are sent when someone not on the white list attempts to contact your kid in Mail or iChat.

The Time Limits pane

I love this feature. Other programs for limiting kids' use are often too complex for mere parents to understand, much less set up and explain to their kids. This one is easy. You have two types of control, as shown in Figure 14-7. One limits the amount of time a child can use the computer each day. The other blocks any usage after bedtime. And you find two sets of controls for each limit: one for weekdays and the other for the weekends. It's simple, and it works.

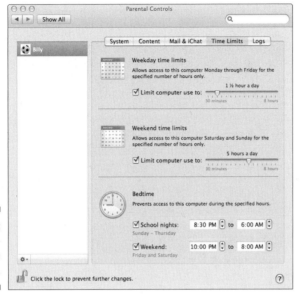

Figure 14-7:
The easy-to-
use Time
Limits pane.

The Logs pane

OS X keeps track of what your kids are up to online. You can see the logs by periodically visiting this pane, as shown in Figure 14-8.

Figure 14-8:
The
Parental
Controls
Logs pane.

You can choose to see logged activity for Web sites your child visited, Web sites he attempted to visit but where access was blocked, applications he used, and iChat conversations he engaged in.

Setting limits

Having all these tools at a parent's disposal is great, but setting limits can be hard. It's usually easier to start with more restricted access and add additional time and privileges as the child matures and demonstrates responsibility. For very young children, not having computer access may be the easiest starting point.

Discuss reasonable computer limits with other parents in your circle. A group consensus can be easier to enforce. And pay attention to your own computer usage. Kids learn by example.

Keeping kids safe online

Incidents in which kids get hurt and that have some connection to the Internet always get great play in the press. Incidents in which kids get hurt on the street or at the playground often don't. Still, your kids need to develop some online smarts about online conduct. Here are some tips you can share with them. Avoid heavy-handed lectures with threats of draconian punishment, though. You want your child to feel safe coming to you if she encounters anything that feels creepy.

Here are some basic rules:

- Don't tell people you meet online your last name, address, or phone number. Be careful if the online person asks a lot of questions about you, like where you go to school or what your parents do for a living.

- Don't tell anyone your password. No one should ever need it.

- Sometimes people on the Internet pretend to be very different from who they really are. They may pretend to be an adult when they are really a child, or pretend to be a kid when they are really an adult. They may pretend to be a teacher or doctor or policeman when they are not. They may even pretend to be a girl when they are a boy or vice versa.

- Never agree to see someone in person that you first met online without asking your parents first.

- Remember that people can find out a lot about your family on the Internet. If someone you don't know says he is a friend of your family and asks you to go with him, don't go just because he seems to know a lot about you and your parents.

✔ If someone is making you feel uncomfortable or scaring you, tell your parents. Especially be sure to tell them if the person asks you not to.

Social networking sites

Social networking Web sites, such as MySpace.com and Facebook.com, have integrated themselves into the social lives of teenagers. MySpace has over 100 million accounts. Facebook, which is aimed at high school and college students, has over 16 million. Both sites encourage members to build profiles with personal information, including accounts and photographs of recent activities. Members designate other members as "friends" who then gain additional access to their page. Both sites have privacy options that members can select. These can limit what information nonfriends can see and what information will be revealed about them in a search. Members use the site to send messages to other users.

MySpace requires members to be at least 14 years old and sets privacy restrictions on those 16 and under. Restrictions are also in place for members over 18 connecting with the youngest members. However, kids and adults can always lie about their age. Potential employers and colleges might also be looking at candidates' profiles on these sites.

Young people start using these social networking sites about the same time as they stop listening to what their parents say. Still, it's worth having a conversation with your teen about the short-term and long-term privacy concerns and the dangers of meeting, in person, people you know only online. At some point, they won't bring you along, but you can still implore them to at least bring a friend along for the first meeting.

Downloading music

Another aspect of kid culture on the Internet — downloading music without paying for it — continues to generate controversy. The recording industry blames the practice for a slowdown in sales. Others question this and point to high prices for CDs and a lack of compelling product as the cause.

The Recording Industry Association of America (RIAA) has managed to shut down free file-sharing sites like Napster and Grokster early, through legal action, but other peer-to-peer systems, such as BitTorrent.com, which have no central indexing service — and which are used for other purposes as well — have proven more difficult to stop. So the RIAA has started taking legal action against individual downloaders and their parents. While some have fought these suits, most are forced to accept expensive settlement terms.

Whatever you think of the RIAA's tactics and their justification, there is a lot to be said for staying out of their gun sights. And most people agree that performers deserve to be compensated for their work. Giving your kid an iPod and a computer without giving him the means to pay for songs is asking for trouble. You might give a monthly allowance at the iTunes Store, perhaps based on chores or schoolwork. Go to the iTunes Store, and click the iTunes Gifts link in the Quick Links section.

Finding software for kids

Kids have lots to do just with the iLife suite that comes with all Macs. You can buy or download many other titles for free. However, adult supervision is required whenever software is downloaded from the Internet. One source for children's software that runs on Macs is Apple's Macintosh Products Guide, at `guide.apple.com/uscategories/kids.lasso`. You can also check out the education page at `guide.apple.com/uscategories/education.lasso`. Many major Web sites have special sections for kids. And a Google search for "kid-safe Web sites" will turn up several guides to such sites. But no substitute exists for checking out new sites yourself before letting your kids visit.

Macs for Seniors

The extraterrestrials who monitor our television signals must be certain that no one over 40 buys Apple products because no one older is ever seen in its TV commercials. The truth is that people over 40 are *more* likely to buy Macs. One reason may be that older consumers seek quality over price. They remember how difficult it was to use computers, and they know who made it easy.

If I give them a Mac, won't my kids be unprepared for a Windows world?

I've heard this objection more than once. For now and the foreseeable future, the working world is dominated by Windows. Many colleges require entering students to have a Windows laptop — though some prefer Macs. One answer, of course, is that Macs can run Windows (see Chapter 13). So, if your child takes his MacBook to school, he can use whatever software is required. But you have a better response. For years, Microsoft has followed Apple's lead in new interfaces and features. Several reviewers have remarked on the similarities between Windows Vista and OS X Tiger. So giving your kids a Mac may be the *best* way to prepare them for the Windows of the future.

A still-older generation, comprising the parents of the 40s and 50s set, in many cases has never used computers. Personal computers offer many ways to improve the lives of these seniors, and Macs are the ideal choice for them. While some seniors start riding motorcycles and take up scuba diving, most have a harder time picking up new skills.

If you are buying a Mac for your parents, consider that you may end up as their main source of tech support. Getting them a computer that is easier to set up, easier to show them how to use, and less likely to require help with problems like viruses and malware will save you time and money in the long run.

More importantly, giving your folks a computer that's easy to use and less trouble-prone makes them more likely to actually use it and derive benefit from it. Seniors can use a Mac in these ways:

- ✔ E-mail and instant messaging are great ways to stay in touch with friends and family, particularly grandchildren who are away at school.
- ✔ Video iChat can enable them to be part of family events, even if they can no longer travel easily.
- ✔ Voice over IP services can keep their phone bills down.
- ✔ The Internet is a great resource for information on health maintenance and medical conditions.
- ✔ Internet shopping can empower seniors who have limited mobility.
- ✔ The Mac's clean interface can make it easier for seniors with disabilities to use. I talk more about Macs and people with disabilities in the next section of this chapter.

A great way to preserve family history is to digitize old family photos using a scanner or commercial service and ask your parents to annotate them in iPhoto. If typing is a problem, you can put the photos in a slideshow and have them record their comments in GarageBand as they step through the photos.

Simple Finder, which I mention earlier in this chapter as a way to make Macs easier for young children to operate, can perform the same function for seniors who may be unfamiliar with computers.

What model to get

For seniors who travel regularly, a basic MacBook is an inexpensive do-everything companion. By seeking hotel accommodations that include Internet access, seniors can stay in touch anywhere in the world. Using their digital camera and iSight, iPhoto, and iWeb, they can share their travel experiences with family and friends almost as these events happen.

For those who mostly stay at home, the iMac is hard to beat. It's a single unit, so no wires are going to get accidentally disconnected, resulting in panicked service calls to you. The low-end model has most everything they need.

If seniors enjoy sharing photos of their grandkids, an iPhone is another great gift, allowing them to always carry a whole library of photos with them.

Speeding photos to the grandparents' Mac

Perhaps the best application for grandparents is iPhoto's photocasting capability. You put the latest photos of the kids into an iPhoto album and click the Photocast This Album button. The album is uploaded to your .Mac account, where it's "published" for authorized subscribers.

Assuming that the grandparents' computer subscribes to your family photo feed, a simple one-time setup, the photos are automatically downloaded to their iPhoto library, where they can be watched immediately. They can even display the photos as their screen saver. As you add new photos to the photocast album, they are automatically uploaded and then downloaded.

To subscribe to a photocast, in iPhoto, choose File⇨Subscribe to Photocast. Fill in the address of the photocast when prompted. Alternately, you can click a link to the photocast on your Web page or in an e-mail message.

You make a photocast display as the screen saver by following these steps:

1. **Select System Preferences from the Apple menu.**
2. **Click the Desktop & Screen Saver icon in System Preferences.**
3. **Click the Screen Saver tab.**
4. **In the list that appears on the left of the Screen Saver pane, shown in Figure 14-9, scroll down to Pictures and then click .Mac and RSS.**
5. **Click the Options button.**
6. **In the pane that appears, select the feeds you want to display in the screen saver. You can reorder the feeds shown by dragging them to the new order.**

   Your latest photos of the kids will now appear on the grandparents' Mac as soon as you add them to your photocast album in iPhoto.

Setting Up Your Mac for Specific Needs

OS X provides an array of accessibility features that enable people to use the Mac in ways that are different from — or more comfortable than — the standard setup of reading on-screen at the default sizes and using the keyboard and mouse to give computer commands. You control most of these features from the Universal Access window in System Preferences. (The one exception is VoiceOver, Apple's screen reader, which has its own setup utility in the Utilities folder, but that utility can also be easily accessed from the Universal Access Seeing pane. See Figure 14-10.) The following sections introduce the available options and describe how they work.

Figure 14-9:
The Screen
Saver pane.

Setting up the screen when you have limited vision

When you click on the Universal Access icon, you see the Seeing pane shown in Figure 14-10, where you can control features that aid people with vision difficulties. Note that the pane appears in large type to avoid the Catch 22 problem where someone with limited vision can't use the tool to increase the type size because the tool's type size is too small.

Here's a quick introduction to the available features:

- ✔ **VoiceOver:** This pane turns VoiceOver on or off and can send you to the VoiceOver setup utility. I explain VoiceOver in more detail in the next section.

- ✔ **Zoom:** When you enable the handy Zoom feature, you can magnify the screen by pressing ⌘+Option+=. Pressing ⌘+Option+- (⌘+Option+hyphen) reverses the magnification.

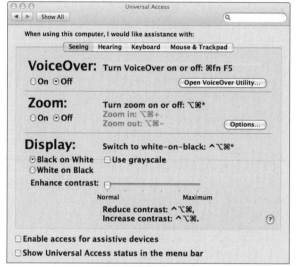

Figure 14-10:
The
Universal
Access
Seeing
pane.

✔ **Display:** In this section, you can change the screen from black on white to white on black, if this helps. Move the slider to adjust the contrast, if you like.

✔ **Enable Access for Assistive Devices check box:** Selecting this check box enables your Mac to work with a variety of assistive technologies and software packages that are designed to help users with special computer-use needs. For more information, see the Macintosh Product Guide at guide.apple.com/uscategories/assisttech.lasso.

Listening instead of reading with VoiceOver

Apple's VoiceOver is a screen reader that's designed to make using a Mac easier by speaking the contents of the screen. Although that may seem a simple and obvious idea, for someone trying to use a computer in this way, a poorly designed screen reader is almost useless. A user wants the screen reader to speak the text of interest at the moment and as little else as possible. The user also wants to be able to speed up the reading as much as possible without losing intelligibility. Otherwise, work becomes painfully slow.

Therefore, it is not surprising that VoiceOver comes with a plethora of customizable options. It also offers several different voices, including Alex, a voice that's engineered to work well when sped up. Figure 14-11 shows the VoiceOver Utility Verbosity screen. You find eight options in the sidebar, each with many options:

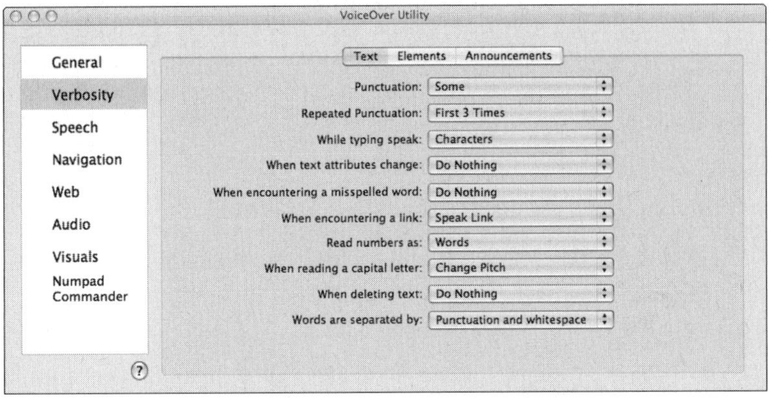

Figure 14-11:
The
VoiceOver
Utility
Verbosity
screen.

✔ **General** lets you control portable preferences.

✔ **Verbosity** controls how much VoiceOver says in various situations, such as when it encounters a misspelled word. For example, a user might want a different behavior when reading a memo she received versus proofreading her own writing.

✔ **Speech** lets you choose among some two dozen virtual speakers and adjust their settings. Most are more fun than productive. Voices with real names, like Alex or Kathy, tend to be more suited for serious use than nicknames like Bubbles. But you can find exceptions. Princess isn't bad, but Albert is. The Pronunciation tab lets you customize how special characters, initialisms, abbreviations, and so on are spoken.

✔ **Navigation** determines what VoiceOver does as you move around the screen and change focus.

✔ **Web** controls how you hear the content of Web pages.

✔ **Audio** Controls sound output.

✔ **Visuals** controls how VoiceOver elements, such as its cursor, are shown on-screen.

✔ **Numpad Commander** lets you assign special functions to the numeric keypad keys.

Adjusting settings in the Hearing pane

Compared to the Seeing pane, there's not much to the Hearing pane. A personal computer is primarily controlled by visual cues anyway. Here you can tell OS X to flash the screen when it issues an alert, a handy feature for those of us with full hearing. You also find a button that takes you to the Sound system preferences pane, where you can adjust the volume of your Mac's audio. You can generally do that using your keyboard as well.

Changing how the keyboard works

The Keyboard pane, shown in Figure 14-12, offers settings that can make using a keyboard easier:

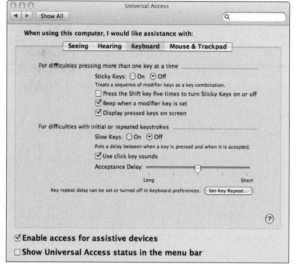

Figure 14-12:
The
Universal
Access
Keyboard
pane.

✔ If you have difficulty doing complex key presses, like the ⌘+Option+= combination for Zoom mentioned earlier in this chapter, try turning on Sticky Keys. The Sticky Keys option, which is controlled from this pane, lets you press the keys one at a time to effect the desired combination. For example, you would first press ⌘, then Option, and then the equal sign (=). You can also control what feedback OS X gives you when you do this.

✔ Another problem some people have is unsteady hands; they may accidentally press a desired key more than once. Another option on this pane lets you set a time delay between key presses to reduce this problem.

✔ Note that you can find additional settings related to the keyboard in the Keyboard & Mouse window of System Preferences.

Speaking of keyboards, a number of specialized keyboards are available to assist with various problems, ranging from repetitive stress injuries to users who can use only one hand. As long as a specialized keyboard uses a USB interface, the keyboard should work on a Mac.

Mousing the way you like

Some people have a hard time using a computer mouse. If the default mouse setup doesn't work well for you or someone in your household, give the following options a try:

✔ **Turn on Mouse Keys:** For people who have trouble using a mouse, Apple provides an alternative, where you move the cursor around the screen using the numeric keypad. After Mouse Keys is turned on, pressing any digit but 5 and 0 moves the cursor a short distance in the direction of that key (relative to 5). The 5 key acts like a mouse click. The 0 key acts like press and hold — say, if you want to drag a file to a folder. When you have the file where you want to drop it, press 5 to release the hold.

Mouse Keys work best with a keyboard that has a separate numeric keypad. If you have a laptop and want to make extensive use of this feature, consider getting an external keyboard or numeric keypad. Be sure to get a USB model.

Mouse Keys is a feature worth knowing about if your mouse or touchpad is ever unusable and you're in a rush to finish something.

✔ **Increase the mouse cursor size:** Another feature that's located on the Universal Access Mouse & Trackpad pane and that's valuable for all users is the ability to make the mouse cursor arrow bigger. Particularly at high-resolution display settings, it's easy to lose that sucker in the desktop clutter.

✔ **Tab to access menus:** You can also eliminate the need for mouse use to access menus. Instead, you press Tab to move between control items and the arrow keys to select within menus. This option is turned on using the Keyboard & Mouse window in System Preferences, on the Keyboard Shortcuts tab. The Full Keyboard Access option is down at the bottom.

If mice don't work for you, other options besides Mouse Keys are available for Macs:

✔ **Trackballs:** These have a smooth, round ball on top that you roll in various directions to control the cursor.

✔ **Touchpads:** These allow you to control the cursor by sliding your finger on a sensitive surface. Apple's laptops have touchpads built-in, but you can buy third-party units to use with your desktop setup if you want.

✔ **Graphics tablets:** These have a flat surface with a position sensing pen. If you use one, you can take advantage of Apple's Inkwell technology, which can turn handwriting into text that you can use in any application.

Again, you should buy one of these with a USB interface. More than one pointing device can be attached and active at the same time. Even if you like using a mouse, having an alternative way to enter text can reduce problems with repetitive stress.

If you use your mouse a lot and feel pain from repetitive stress, one suggestion I've found useful is to move the mouse and mouse pad to the other side of the keyboard so that you use it with your nondominant hand — the left hand in my case. It takes a little getting used to, but if you are starting to feel fatigued in your dominant hand, it's worth a try.

Chapter 15

Switching Your Business to Macs

Microsoft owns the enterprise desktop. Owns it. Most of Apple's small market share comes from home and educational users. Many large companies have strict Windows-only policies. Lots of business software is only available for Windows. So why even think about using Macs? Why did we kill a bunch of trees to bring you a chapter pushing Macs for businesses?

In this chapter, you find out how Macs can produce a good return on investment for a business, as well as services and products that help small and mid-size businesses stay nimble and competitive, with Macs working for them behind the scenes.

Why Use Macs in Your Business?

The cop-out answer is that Macs now run Windows too. That does at least answer the concern about the occasional Windows-only software you might need for your business. But by itself, it's not much of a reason. It doesn't make business sense to buy a Mac that may cost a few hundred dollars more, and then pay Microsoft for a Vista license, just to get a pretty computer that runs Windows. Sure, iMacs look spiffy in the front offices and MacBook Pros turn heads at meetings, but that won't convince the bean counters.

Total cost of ownership

Another common justification given for businesses switching to Macs is *total cost of ownership*. Macs may cost a bit more up front, but savings can be achieved down the road. Here's why:

✔ No need for antivirus software.

✔ Lower training costs because Macs are easier to use.

✔ Lower support costs because Macs have fewer software problems and users can often fix their own problems.

✔ Macs seem to have a longer service life than Windows machines, so they won't need to be replaced as often.

The total cost of ownership argument has some merit. One organization I work with pays over $1,000 per year in support for each Windows PC it owns. Cutting that down would go right to the bottom line.

But the counterargument usually given is that the organization has already made large investments in a Windows-oriented support organization. Firewalls and intrusion detectors are already in place. In the short run, adding Macs may increase cost because any additional support costs are a new expense. Who has time to worry about the long run?

Increased productivity

It's easy to count the initial purchase price of computers you buy. Support costs are more difficult to calculate, but a well-run organization has a handle on those as well. The impact of your choice of computer platform on individual worker productivity is much harder to measure. Most organizations do not have expense-tracking codes for "I'm purging viruses," "the network is down," "I can't get the printer to work," or "I'm waiting for tech support to call back." Pesky problems like that don't just eat up time; they sap energy, enthusiasm, and morale.

You get what you pay for

To succeed in the intense competition of a global economy, everything a business does has to stand out from the crowd. Mediocre tools ultimately lead to mediocre work. Your salesperson's PowerPoint presentation will look like every other salesperson's PowerPoint presentation. The huckster with a Mac and a Keynote show will stand out.

While it is hard to gauge productivity, it's not so hard to measure the effect of improvements. Suppose that working with a Mac increases productivity just 5 percent. Sum up the annual pay of each worker who uses a computer. Add in fringe benefits and direct overhead, stuff like the cost of office space and administrative support. Now multiply that by 0.05. That's how much using Windows costs you each year.

Plays well with Linux

In most organizations, some workers have little or no creative component in their computer work. Surely they don't need a Mac. They may not need Windows either. A number of Linux distributions can support workers whose main job is data entry or telephone support. Mac OS X and Linux share a UNIX heritage and generally work well together. Much Linux software has been ported to Macs, so tools can be used on both platforms. Best of all, you don't need to buy new computers to run Linux. It should run fine on the older PCs you are replacing with Macs or with Vista-capable PCs.

The only constant in business is change

The best reason to switch to Macs is because computer technology is chang-ing, and it's changing the world along with it. And Apple is leading the charge, not Microsoft. Microsoft is too busy making money off the way things were. Stay hitched to Microsoft, and you'll always be safely in the middle of the pack. Except the middle of the pack is where businesses wither and die.

What are some of these changes? Here's a partial list:

- ✔ **Electronic commerce:** The Internet now drives economic growth and levels the playing field between large and small companies. People who buy online shop online, and word-of-Web drives sales. First impressions of early customers are aggregated by blogs and RSS feeds and spread worldwide. Lapses in quality are magnified. You have to get it right the first time.

- ✔ **Web 2.0:** The World Wide Web is now a two-way medium. Consumers are spending more of their time viewing content produced by other consumers. A clever YouTube spoof can undo a multimillion-dollar marketing campaign. Speed is of the essence. It can't wait 'til the Monday morning staff meeting.

✔ **Globalization:** Your next competitor could emerge from a country you never heard of. And so could your next technology supplier. And so could your next market.

✔ **Service Oriented Architecture (SOA):** Legacy applications are being fitted with software adapters that allow them to be repurposed and reused. New applications are built to meet similar standards, so an organization's software investment can be more easily adapted to new needs. Business requirements now drive technology, not the other way around. IT is less platform-centric. For more on SOA, read *Service Oriented Architecture For Dummies,* by Judith Hurwitz, Robin Bloor, Carol Baroudi, and Marcia Kaufman (published by Wiley).

✔ **Open source business software:** The open source model — which has been so successful in the development of BSD UNIX, Linux, and Gnu — is being taken up by groups trying to create nonproprietary software systems. These groups are using open standards and open source code to create software that meets basic business needs. The wide adoption of XML as a standard for data interchange has spawned many efforts to create nonproprietary data exchange formats for specific business needs, such as `hr-xml.org` in human resources. As these efforts mature, they provide viable, platform-independent alternatives to expensive software packages.

✔ **Software as a Service (SaaS):** The other new approach to business software is for vendors to host the software on their own servers and sell the services over the Internet on a subscription basis, typically a per-user, per-month fee. This solution reduces the need for in-house hardware and support personnel and allows employees to access the service from remote locations. SaaS systems are accessed via standard Web browsers, reducing the importance of being on one operating system versus another.

✔ **Virtualization:** The relationship between computers and operating systems is no longer monogamous. One operating system can span several processor cores, and one processor can support several operating systems at once. The impetus for standardizing on the operating system you've always used makes less business sense. Pick the best tool for the job.

✔ **Computer crime:** In the good old days, malware, such as computer viruses and worms, was created by hobbyist hackers interested in the intellectual challenge. Now such activities are a big, if illicit, business and a significant distraction for legitimate businesses. There are direct costs in terms of data theft and denial of service and indirect costs of cleanup, damage remediation, and reporting. Finally, there is the hard-to-measure loss of customer trust and its impact on sales. Apple's malware-free track record has saved its users expense and can instill confidence with customers.

✓ **High-definition TV:** Some of us remember the transition from black-and-white to color television. At first, color sets were bulky and expensive. Programming was limited to a few shows that proclaimed "in living color" during their introductions. It took more than a decade, but eventually *everything* was in color. The same sort of transition is under way with high-definition TV (HDTV). Apple is following a strategy of "skating to where the puck is going to be" and incorporating HD throughout the Macintosh line. If your business needs to be HD ready, get Macs.

✓ **Mobile computing:** The chunk of our lives that resides on computers keeps increasing. Some of us feel naked without a live Internet connection at hand. The constant access to e-mail that BlackBerrys provide is so addicting that they are sometimes called "CrackBerrys." We carry our most important files in our pockets or purses on flash drives. Apple's iPhone points toward an integrated mobile computing future where we have all the tools we rely on with us wherever we go.

✓ **Internet content delivery:** Widespread high-speed Internet access has led to the Internet becoming a primary means of information content delivery. Traditional media is feeling the heat. College students with the right concept, like the students who created YouTube and Facebook, can become billionaires almost overnight.

✓ **Lean and mean organizations:** To stay competitive, businesses are streamlining, outsourcing grunt work, flattening organization charts, and increasing the span of control and the number of workers per manager. The emphasis is on lean-and-mean organizations where each employee has the ability to recognize opportunities and to respond to challenges, and is held accountable for performance. These workers need the best tools available.

If some of the changes described here are felt in your business, stop thinking of computers as a cost center, like lights and lavatories, and realize that they are competitive weapons if used properly. Realize that many of the most creative employees prefer Macs, and respecting their choice attracts them to and retains them for your firm. Realize that the quality of the tools you give your workers impacts your products and services in ways that are hard to measure, but are inescapable.

Macs in Small Businesses

The case for Macs is easiest to make in a small business. You are unlikely to have legacy software written in Cobol or a staff of information technology professionals wedded to doing things the Microsoft way. To run a small business and grow it into a bigger business, you must have a can-do attitude. Two of the most important software tools for small businesses, Microsoft Office and Quicken.com's QuickBooks, already run on Macs. Apple's FileMaker Pro is highly regarded as a database that can be easily customized by non-programmers. It's a cross-platform solution between Mac and Windows, with shared access via your in-house network. You can also find many specialized programs for Macs, such as computer-aided design and cash register operation. While the selection is smaller than what is available for Windows, the vendors are dedicated to the Mac market and generally enjoy the support of a strong user community.

Software as a Service applications, such as ConstantContact.com, Salesforce.com, and SugarCRM.com, are a natural for small businesses because these applications allow you to have world-class applications at very affordable prices without the need for IT support staff. And choosing Macs makes a statement to prospective staff and customers that you are forward thinking and open to new ideas.

Macs in Mid-Size Businesses

Mid-size businesses need an edge to survive against increasingly large corporate giants. Small businesses find niches too insignificant to attract the giants' attention. But when a mid-size firm finds a good market, some large company is soon sniffing around. The mid-size firm had better be more nimble and creative and in closer touch with its customer needs.

The World Wide Web makes reaching customers easier for mid-size firms. Internet advertising, such as Google's AdWords, targets customers who have already shown interest in your product categories. The networks of self-published writers known as the blogosphere can make or break your product. Having selected employees write blogs about your industry can be more effective than advertising in traditional ways, such as in trade magazines. OS X has tools that make blogging easy. Video iChat simplifies and speeds coordinating responses from different groups in different locales without expensive travel.

Apple's product lineup includes a number of tools that harness Mac OS X to provide industrial-strength solutions for your business:

✔ **It's a RAID:** Apple's server and Redundant Array of Independent Disks (RAID) products are ideal for mid-size businesses. They are priced competitively and do not require an IT staff to keep them working. Apple claims that its RAID multiterabyte storage solution offers the lowest cost per available gigabyte among major players. It works with Windows and Linux, too. Xserve has software management tools that are easy to use and don't require you to add server magicians to your staff. For more details about these products, flip to Chapter 2.

✔ **Supercomputing on the cheap:** Apple's Xgrid technology harnesses all the unused power in the Macs you purchased to create a supercomputing array that can tackle the most difficult computational problems. Drug research, structural engineering, animation, digital content rendering and format conversion, data mining — all these can consume large computing resources. Xgrid can make that available by splitting tasks and combining resources from all the desktops and laptops in your organization, even the one on the receptionist's desk.

✔ **Start Wine-ing:** If you do use custom in-house software written for Windows, consider testing it on the Windows API emulator Wine or its commercial version for Mac, CrossOver Mac, from www.codeweavers. com. In theory, it should just work. In practice, some debugging will be required. But the result frees you from buying expensive Windows licenses for all users of the software. For more about Wine, see Chapter 13.

✔ **X Serve your Windows:** Apple's Mac OS X server edition, which comes with Xserve but can be purchased for other Mac models, provides e-mail, open directory, WINS, NetBIOS, VPN, SMB/CIFS, and other services, with Mac-grade ease of management. OS X server also supports many open standards, allowing easy integration with UNIX and Linux. It's a viable alternative to Windows server products that charge expensive per-seat licensing fees.

Macs for the Enterprise

I'm under no illusion that this book will convince any large company to toss all its Windows boxes and switch everyone to Macs. I'd be happy if it lowered the barriers to using Macs in a few organizations. The IT staff in many companies promulgate strict Windows-only rules. The one common exception is the graphics department, which produces print and other media for outside consumption. My one suggestion is to give Macs a try in other places. Equipping a small department or field office with Macs is a low-risk experiment. The computers can be converted to Windows if need be. What do you have to lose?

For more on Mac applications in businesses, visit Apple's business site, www. apple.com/business. Also try www.macenterprise.org, a community of IT professionals sharing information and solutions to support Macs in an enterprise.

Chapter 16

Converting from OS 9 and Other Operating Systems

*M*ost of this book is aimed at Windows users. But other operating systems are out there whose users would consider Macs, but find conversion daunting. In this chapter, you find switching tips if you're looking to upgrade from Mac OS 9 (or even earlier versions) to OS X, and find out how to navigate the key differences in the interface and file structure and how to transfer files. You also find tips if you're moving from Linux to a Mac, or want to run Linux and your Mac together. Last but not least, this chapter offers pointers to game lovers who want to hold onto their favorite games while moving up to the latest Mac OS.

Switching from Mac OS 9 and Earlier

Millions of users of older Macs still run Mac OS 9 and even earlier versions. Apple's introduction of OS X in 2001 was potentially more traumatic to its loyal users than the switch from PowerPC to Intel. Apple made provisions for software developers to build OS 9 applications that would also work in OS X — the Carbon package. But some developers were not in a position to incur that expense, and other vendors were by then defunct. Nonetheless, some users relied on these programs.

Apple softened the blow by incorporating a facility to allow a version of the older operating system, Mac OS 9, that runs in OS X on PowerPC Macs. This feature, called Classic, allowed most, but not all, older Mac applications to run on the newer machines.

That safety net was removed for the Intel Macs. Classic does not run on the Intel versions of OS X. Apple did provide Rosetta to run PowerPC applications on the Intel platform. You might think that Rosetta could have run Classic, but Apple didn't take that route. Apple presumably assumed that most users have migrated to newer applications with OS X–compatible versions. Unlike the situation for Windows, no commercial solution lets OS 9 or earlier versions of Mac OS run on an Intel Mac. Open source emulators are available, and I talk about them later in this chapter, but they require some messy steps that limit their utility.

Differences between OS 9 and OS X

Moving from OS 9 to OS X is like moving to a new city from a town you really, really liked. You'll miss familiar places and faces, but you'll find new things you'll like and make new friends. Just keep an open mind and maintain a positive attitude.

The biggest difference between OS 9 and OS X is that OS X is based on a version of the UNIX operating system, FreeBSD. The presence of UNIX is not normally visible to OS X users — unless they go look for it, as I describe in Chapter 17. However, UNIX does influence many aspects of OS X indirectly.

User accounts

One concept that is foreign to pre–OS 9 users is individual user accounts. Prior to OS 9, only one user existed, and all files belonged to that user. OS X can also have multiple users, but the feature is organized the way UNIX does it. All users have their own home directory, and all their files are stored in that directory. All the home directories are found in a directory called User.

Users normally own their files. Each file in OS X has a set of permissions. These control who can read the file, write to the file, or execute the file as a program — another concept that comes from UNIX.

OS X knows which user you are by asking you to log on when you boot the machine. If you are the only user on the system, you don't have to log on, but from a security standpoint, it's best to require a logon. See Chapter 10.

File system structure

One big difference between OS 9 and OS X is how files are organized. In OS 9, your personal organizing touches start at your hard drive. In OS X, your playpen is your User directory. Outside of installing system-wide applications, you normally do not mess with files at the top level. Although you can see other user's folders, you normally can't poke around within them. Users get a certain amount of privacy in OS X, though if you have admin privileges, you can override most measures.

Figure 16-1 shows what you see when you double-click the icon for your main hard drive, the one that has OS X on it. As you can see, the top-level structure is quite simple.

Figure 16-1: The spartan top-level file structure of OS X.

I discuss the OS X file structure in greater detail at the beginning of the next chapter. I know it seems awfully restrictive compared to the total freedom you are used to in OS 9. Some of the structure is arbitrary and goes back to the early days of UNIX. But the UNIX file system structuring has logic, and the ability to have separate user accounts requires something along these lines.

Interface differences

Apple made some small but annoying changes to the classic Mac OS interface when it created OS X. I outline some of these here:

- ✔ The Apple menu (🍎) is still on the far left of the menu bar, but its contents are almost totally different.
- ✔ You can no longer easily add items to the Apple menu.

> ✔ The cute little mini-apps that used to live on the Apple menu have been moved to a more elaborate Dashboard (press F12).
>
> ✔ An application-specific menu now exists between the Apple menu and the File menu. It's where the Preferences, Hide, and Quit commands are located. I found this the hardest thing to get used to when switching to OS X. I've used every Mac OS since 4.1, and my muscle memory is deeply imprinted with where the File menu is *supposed* to be. And I still look for Quit on the File menu. T'aint there.
>
> ✔ The good news is that ⌘+Q still works, as do most of the command key shortcuts you're used to. One big exception is the shortcut that makes an alias for a selected file or folder, which is now ⌘+L. Also, ⌘+N now creates a new Finder window rather than a new folder. Finder windows are very handy in OS X, so this change makes some sense. Shift+⌘+N makes a new folder.

Other cute OS 9 features you've grown to love are missing in action, including the Window Shade feature and tab folders. They've been replaced by the less-handy Dock. Fortunately, the Dock stack feature replaces tab folders, and a shareware program called WindowShade X restores the Window Shade trick.

Some things OS 9 users won't miss include system extensions and rebuilding the desktop. Neither are needed in OS X.

Transferring files from older Macs

You can transfer your files from older Macs that have a FireWire port without much fuss. You need a FireWire cable.

When you start up OS X for the first time, you are asked "Do You Already Own a Mac?" If you say yes, OS X offers to "transfer your info from another Mac with a FireWire port." The transfer can copy files, network settings, and user accounts — including preferences and e-mail documents.

If you're way past the initial OS X startup, you can still transfer your files. Macs with FireWire start up in "FireWire disk mode" if you hold down the T key while rebooting. Then you can plug the FireWire cable into your new Mac, which should see the new machine as an external hard drive. Then run the Migration Assistant, found in the Utilities folder, and you get the transfer capabilities even later in the game. Or you can just copy everything over to your Documents folder and sort things out later.

Transferring files from geriatric Macs

If your Mac is so old that it does not have FireWire, you still have ways to transfer files. If you have Ethernet, you can try to use AppleShare. It doesn't work for all older versions of Mac OS, but it's worth a try. Running System 7.5.5 or later is recommended.

You can download disk images of older Mac operating systems from www.info.apple.com/support/oldersoftwarelist.html.

Transferring with Ethernet and AppleShare

The following steps explain how to transfer files with AppleShare:

1. **Connect the older Mac to your Ethernet router, or run an Ethernet crossover cable between the two Macs.**

2. **On your OS X Mac, select Sharing from System Preferences and turn on Personal File Sharing.**

3. **Select Network from System Preferences and click the tab that corresponds to how your new Mac is networked — that is, Ethernet or AirPort.**

4. **Make AppleTalk active by selecting the check box, and click the Apply button.**

5. **On the older Mac, select Control Panel from the Apple menu and select AppleTalk. Make sure that AppleTalk is set to connect via Ethernet.**

6. **Also on the older Mac, select Chooser from the Apple menu and click the AppleShare icon.**

   Hopefully, depending on the age of your older system software, you see the new Mac's icon in the old Mac's Chooser.

7. **Log on to the new Mac with your username and password.**

8. **After you're logged on, you should see an icon representing your new Mac on your old Mac's desktop. Double-click that icon to open it and navigate to a folder where you want to move your files. Then drag them to that folder.**

   See docs.info.apple.com/article.html?artnum=301183 for more info.

No Ethernet

If your Mac does not have Ethernet or the previous procedure does not work, your best option may be transferring data by writing to disk. Decide which files you care about and write them to disk. Your choices depend on what drives are usable on your older Mac:

 ✔ **If your older Mac has an optical drive that can write CDs,** it's your first choice. CDs can hold 650MB of data or more.

 ✔ **If your older Mac has a Zip drive,** look for a used USB Zip drive on eBay.com or Craigslist.com. You can use it with your new Mac to read Zip cartridges written on the older Mac. Zip cartridges hold 100MB or more, so you have fewer copy steps than would be required when using floppies. It's a good idea to check out the entire process first by copying a few files.

 ✔ **If your older Mac only has a floppy drive,** check whether it can write high-density (HD) floppies — these are the kind that are PC-compatible. The original Lisa, Mac 128, Mac 512, Mac Plus, some SEs, and Mac IIs cannot. Get a USB floppy drive for your new Mac and clear a few hours from your schedule for copying stuff from it. Again, it's worth trying the process all the way through on a disk's worth of files first.

If you have an ancient Mac that can only write single-sided or low-density double-sided disks, your best bet is to find a later-model used Mac that has a floppy drive. Apple Macintoshes with a built-in floppy drive can read the older disks. If possible, get a used Mac that has Ethernet and a drive that can write CDs.

For more information on older Macs and ways to keep them working, visit `lowendmac.com.`

Using modems to transfer files

If your older Mac has a modem and you purchased the Apple Modem for your new Mac, you may be able to transfer files by connecting the two modems with a telephone cable. The Kermit project at Columbia University distributes a tool for exchanging files over serial communications lines. The folks there have been at it for decades. The project is still around, and they even have a version of Kermit for OS X, as well as for older Macs (MacKermit), not to mention nearly every computer in existence. Visit their Web site: `www.columbia.edu/kermit.`

Converting older Mac files

Although current commercial applications, such as TextEdit and Microsoft Office, can read older Mac file formats, most applications cannot. Several solutions are worth considering:

✔ OpenOffice.org and GraphicConverter, both discussed in Chapter 7, can read a number of older Mac formats.

✔ Get a copy of MacLinkPlus Deluxe from DataViz.com. This software package runs on OS X and can translate files from a wide variety of older Mac and Windows formats. It's a little hard to find on the DataViz Web site. Try `www.dataviz.com/products/maclinkplus/mlp_xlators.html`.

✔ Open files on your older Mac and save them in a format that is more likely to be read by newer applications. For example, you can save word processing files as RTF files. TextEdit and any other word processor worth its salt can read RTF files. The content and most formatting is preserved. Other file formats that are still widely readable include SYLK files for spreadsheets and comma-separated value files (`.csv`) for spreadsheets and databases. Text files (`.txt`) are also universally readable, but you lose all formatting.

Check whether you have a later copy of pre–OS X Microsoft Word, particularly Word 5.1. It can read many older Mac formats, including MacWrite 4.5, and save them in RTF format. Also, Microsoft Office 2004 can read Word 5.1 files directly. I haven't had a chance to try Office 2008.

Purging your older Mac's hard drive

If you plan to dispose of your older Mac and you have files on the hard drive that you consider sensitive, it's always wise to securely erase them and wipe the drive clean.

If your older Mac has a FireWire port, you can try booting it in FireWire disk mode (hold down the T key) and connect it to your new Mac. After all the files are copied and backed up, you can delete your files from the old Mac and then use Disk Utility on the new Mac to erase free space.

If that approach doesn't work, you need another plan. Unfortunately, shareware programs for older Mac operating systems that erase files and wipe free space clean are increasingly hard to find. One commercial solution is ShredIt for Mac from Mireth.com. It can be downloaded for about $20; versions are available for older Mac operating systems as well as OS X.

Here's a quick-and-dirty solution that is not as secure as a proper file wipe utility, but provides some protection:

1. **After erasing your sensitive files, make a duplicate of a large folder, such as your Applications or System folder, by highlighting it and pressing ⌘+D.**

2. **Keep doing this until the hard drive is full.**

3. **Delete all the copies and repeat the procedure, preferably with a different starting folder.**

Another solution is to remove the hard drive from the old Mac before disposing of the rest of the machine and bury the hard drive in your basement.

Emulating older Macs on your Intel Mac

I'm not aware of any commercial products that enable you to run pre–OS X Macintosh operating systems on Intel Macs. But several open source efforts have developed emulators for older Macs, and these can run older operating systems and software with some caveats:

- The software has been developed by volunteers who offer no guarantee that it will work.

- You need to obtain a copy of the firmware that is built into older Macs. This is something called the system ROM (read-only memory). To do this properly, you need to own an older Mac. The sites that provide the emulators also provide a small software program that can copy the ROM to a file, which you must then transfer to your Intel Mac.

- After you have the emulator up and running, you still must install a version of Mac OS. You can download this from the Apple Web site at www.info.apple.com/support/oldersoftwarelist.html.

An alternative for older Mac upgraders

If you are a heavy user of an older Mac and are ready to upgrade to OS X, but have dreaded the prospect, you might want to consider buying a used PowerPC Mac instead of going directly to an Intel machine. A late-model PowerPC Mac (G4 or G5) can run the latest OS X 10.5 release while at the same time supporting OS 9 software in Classic mode. Most of the information in this book applies to PowerPC versions of OS X as well.

Unless you have a need to read old 800KB or, worse, 400KB floppy disks and want a Mac with an internal drive, I suggest buying a late-model PowerPC such as a flat-panel iMac and eMac or a PowerBook.

Buying a G4 or G5 PowerPC model could make it easier for you to make the transition to the newer generation of Macs, because much of your existing software may still run on the PowerPC. Although the PowerPC Macs are not as fast as the newer Intel Core Duo models, you should still see a significant speed improvement over the older Mac you've been using. When you feel comfortable with OS X and no longer depend on Classic applications, you can purchase a newer Intel Mac and move your computing environment to the new machine.

See the following emulator download sites for complete instructions:

- ✔ **Mini vMac:** Emulates older 68K Macs: `minivmac.sourceforge.net`
- ✔ **Basilisk II for Mac:** Emulates more recent models: `www.users.bigpond.com/pear_computers/BasiliskII.html`
- ✔ **SheepShaver:** Emulates PowerPC Macs: `gwenole.beauchesne.info/en/projects/sheepshaver`

Trying to get one of these emulators working takes some time and effort. When you do have everything working, make a backup of the disk image. That way, if your emulated software crashes and the emulated disk is damaged, you can simply replace it with a fresh copy.

Converting from Linux

I've dealt with switching from Windows and from older Macs. What's left? The other currently popular personal operating system is Linux. It might seem surprising that Linux users switch to Macs, but it makes sense if you think about it. OS X is based on the UNIX architecture — primarily BSD — so it's easy for Linux users to transition to it. Apple's hardware is elegant and reliable, and Mac customers are not forced to buy Windows and then uninstall it from their new computer to make way for Linux. And OS X is the only platform that supports Linux/UNIX applications and Microsoft Office.

Files can be transferred using standard UNIX command-line tools, such as ftp or ssh or a graphical shell. On the Mac side, command line is available through the Terminal application in the Utility folder. Terminal provides a bash shell and a complement of BSD tools, along with thousands of man pages.

Other packages from the Linux world are ported to OS X by the Fink project, `finkproject.com`. Fink uses Debian package-building tools and provides the infrastructure to install these packages on OS X. I have lots more to say about Terminal and the OS X UNIX layer in the next chapter.

Reclaiming Relics

Most of us never forget first loves, whether it's people or computers. A few of us have yet to give up our first computer. If you're stuck in the past, Macs bring hope for the future.

Older PC operating systems, such as MS-DOS, OS/2, and earlier versions of Windows, can be installed in virtual environments provided by Parallels and

VMware, as discussed in Chapter 13. DataViz, described earlier in this chapter, can read many of the older formats these programs used.

Reading old media (5¼-inch floppies, cassette tapes, ½-inch magnetic tape, DECTape, punched cards, and so on) is a different story. Your best bet is to buy an old machine that can read the media and transfer the data via a modem or serial port connection using Kermit. Because Macs don't have serial ports, your old PC may come in handy. Google can find you data-conversion firms that can transfer old formats to modern media, but the service is costly.

If you're into game nostalgia, www.emuscene.com, emulation.victoly. com, and MacMAME.org track a wide variety of computer and game console emulators for the Mac. You can even find Apple II, IBM System/370, and Digital Equipment Corporation PDP-8/e emulators. The SIMH project, simh. trailing-edge.com, has simulators for most minicomputers, including the IBM 1130, DEC VAX, and Data General Nova. Software kits, including many classic minicomputer and mainframe operating systems, are available under license at the site. Source code for the simulator is also available. You can find instructions for installing SIMH in OS X at simh.darwinports.com. You can have your cake and eat it too.

Chapter 17

Desktop to Dashcode: OS X Advanced

Apple's OS X is a very complex piece of software. It draws on rich heritages, including earlier versions of Mac OS; UNIX, particularly the Berkeley system Distribution; NeXTstep, developed by a company Steve Jobs founded when he left Apple; and the Mach kernel project at Carnegie Mellon University. In this chapter, I dive into some of OS X's inner workings. Feel free to skip this chapter if you're not interested in these details.

Peeking at the File System Structure

One of the most visible influences of UNIX on OS X is the way the file system is organized. A top-level directory contains the following folders:

✔ **Applications:** Holds the entire iLife suite and applications that come with OS X. It also contains a folder called Utilities, where programs like Disk Utility are found. Applications you install, like Microsoft Office, normally go here.

✔ **Library:** This contains other "under the hood" files that are needed system wide. A Library folder also exists within the System folder, and one Library folder is available for each user.

- ✔ **System:** Contains OS X itself. Nothing you'd want to work with directly dwells in this folder.

- ✔ **Users:** Each user has a home folder here. You can see other users' folders, but you can't look at files within them without permission, unless you are an administrative user.

You can add additional files and folders at this level, but it is generally not a good idea unless you have a good reason. This is one of the harder things for OS 9 users to get used to.

Exploring the User folder

Each User folder also has a standard set of subfolders. OS 9 users are used to setting up their folders any way they want and are often quite irritated by all this structure when they first encounter it. Swallow hard; it's worth getting used to.

The standard folders in a new User directory are as follows:

- ✔ **Desktop:** This folder has all the files on your desktop. Having them in a folder like any other is handy. If your desktop gets too cluttered to find things, you can see its contents in a Finder window instead and use the folder-sorting tools to arrange the files and folders on the desktop by name, date, size, and so on. The Desktop folder is also handy when making manual backups, because you can simply copy all the desktop contents to an external hard drive or optical disc.

- ✔ **Documents:** Apple wants you to put all your documents here. You don't have to, of course, but doing it Apple's way avoids hassles. You can, and should, add subfolders to whatever depth you want within the Documents folder. This is the place to go wild and make yourself at home.

  If you have all your files neatly organized on OS 9, copy them all here. Then move pictures, movies, and music to the appropriate folders below.

- ✔ **Library:** Programs store data that is unique for each user, such as preferences and caches.

- ✔ **Movies:** Your iMovie projects normally go here.

- ✔ **Music:** The iTunes library is stashed here.

- ✔ **Pictures:** The iPhoto shoebox goes here.

- ✔ **Public:** Each user has this special folder with permissions set so that any user on the Mac can access the folder. Within this folder is a folder called Drop Box in which other users can place files and folders, but they can't look inside. Only the user (and the computer administrator, of course) can see what's in the Drop Box folder.

✔ **Sites:** This folder contains Web page files you have created for OS X's Personal Web Sharing to publish on the Internet — or on your organization's intranet.

Understanding file permission basics

Permissions determine who can do what with a file. Traditionally, you find three levels of permission in a UNIX system:

✔ **Owner:** Each file in OS X is owned by someone, such as a user with an account, or something, such as the system.

✔ **Group:** A file is also assigned to one group. Groups consist of one or more users. You can belong to more than one group, and groups can include other groups.

✔ **Other (sometimes called World):** Other refers to anyone with authorized access to the computer.

Also in the UNIX tradition, you can do these three things with a file:

✔ Read it (r)

✔ Write to it (w)

✔ Execute it (x)

The execute permission takes a bit of explaining. For program files, including scripts, it means that you can run the program. For directories, it means that you can see what files are inside the directory. It doesn't mean that you can open those files, just see their names. The letters next to each action are abbreviations that are sometimes seen in directory listings.

With this structure, you have nine possibilities: Each level of ownership can have any combination of read, write, and execute access to a file.

This approach to organizing permissions may seem complex, but it is not complex enough for some situations. A file can only be assigned to one group. What if you want different groups to have different permissions? I hope your personal life is not that convoluted, but in large organizations, it can easily be.

A more complex set of permissions in OS X is called Access Control Lists, or ACLs. Each file and directory can have an ACL. They are ordered lists of rules. Each rule says so-and-so can do such-and-such. OS X ships with ACLs turned off, fortunately. The tools to administer them are included in OS X Server.

If you right-click a file and select Get Info from the shortcut menu (or just press ⌘+I), you see the Info window shown in Figure 17-1. It's somewhat analogous to the Properties window in Windows.

Figure 17-1:
The Info
window for
a file. I
clicked the
triangles
to show
details.

Permission information is toward the bottom. You may have to click the tiny triangles to view all the details. As you can see, OS X combines the write permission with read.

Permissions are so important to the underlying system software that OS X keeps track of what they are supposed to be for system software, and Disk Utility, in the Utilities folder, has an option to Repair Permissions, setting the ones for the system back to their pristine values.

Commanding UNIX

When I say that OS X is built on top of UNIX, you might imagine that I mean the way a house is built on top of a foundation. A door or hatch is at the ground level, and if you open it, you go down a creaky set of stairs to a place that's damp and kind of dark, with pipes and wires going every which way. It's good to know about if you blow a fuse or if the heat isn't working, but it's no place to hang out.

Uh-uh. That's not what I'm talking about. What I mean is more like a city built on top of another city. Tap on a magic mirror, and you're transported to an underground metropolis. The people dress funny and speak a different dialect, but it has lots of interesting places to visit and things to do.

You find a brief introduction to UNIX in the sections that follow. You can find more online at www.freebsd.org, or you can pick up a copy of *UNIX For Dummies,* 5th Edition, by John R. Levine and Margaret Levine Young (published by Wiley).

The magic mirror is Terminal

The magic application that takes you from the outer world of OS X to the inner world of UNIX is appropriately hidden and unpretentious. It's called Terminal, and it's in the Utilities folder inside the Applications folder. Double-click the Terminal icon, and you see a window like the one shown in Figure 17-2. The window is labeled Terminal — bash — 80x24. Here's a base run-down of what you see in the Terminal window:

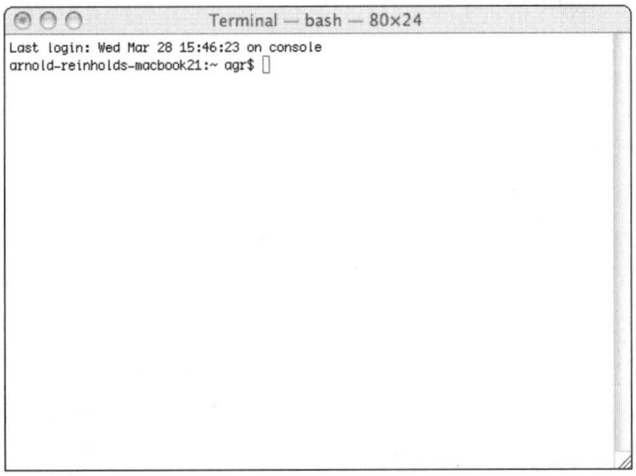

```
Terminal — bash — 80x24
Last login: Wed Mar 28 15:46:23 on console
arnold-reinholds-macbook21:~ agr$ 
```

Figure 17-2:
The
Terminal
window.

✔ The last number indicates that the window holds 24 lines, each 80 mono-spaced characters long.

✔ Drag the lower-right corner of the window and you can make it bigger or smaller, but the 80-character initial width has a long history. It's the number of characters in an IBM punch card (remember those?).

✔ The word `bash` in the window label is not requesting an aggressive act. It's the name of the UNIX program attending you, something that the UNIX world calls a *shell.* It's much like the Windows XP command interpreter, `cmd.exe`.

✔ The $ character in the Terminal window is the `bash` prompt — Windows uses a right-facing arrow (>) for its prompt. Type anything at the prompt. Press Return and the shell program — `bash` by default in OS X — tries to carry out your wishes.

✔ The letters `bash` stand for Bourne-again shell. It's an open source remake by the Gnu project of an earlier shell written by Stephen Bourne when he was at Bell Labs. Other popular Unix shells (`csh`, `zsh`, `ksh`, `tcsh`, and so on) are available as well, in case you grew up with one of them and prefer it.

Bash is more powerful than Window's `cmd.exe`, but Microsoft is offering a new Windows PowerShell that is comparable. (My technical editor says "Yeah, comparable in the way that a Geo compares to a Maserati.")

Bash ain't Windows

You find a number of differences as well as similarities between the Windows command line and UNIX. Many of these differences go back to the early days of DOS and were deliberately introduced to avoid legal problems from AT&T, the original developer of UNIX.

✔ **Pathnames:** A pathname specifies where a file is located, starting at the top-level or root directory. Windows separates names with a backslash (\), while UNIX, like the Internet, uses a forward slash (/). Versions of Mac OS 9 and earlier used a colon (:).

✔ **Hidden files:** Filenames that start with a period (.) are normally hidden and are often used to store the settings for various programs. Type **ls –a** to see them.

✔ **Home directory:** UNIX uses the tilde character (~) as an abbreviation for the home directory. You sometimes see this on the Internet as well.

> One URL for my home page is `http://theworld.com/~reinhold`. (`www.arnoldreinhold.com` redirects you there.)
>
> ✔ **Switches:** Like Windows commands, UNIX commands have switches that follow the command name to modify its action. In Windows, switches are indicated by a forward slash. In UNIX, switches are usually indicated by a hyphen (-).
>
> ✔ **More about commands:** Windows uses `help`. UNIX uses `man`, which stands for manual. In UNIX, type the following:
>
> ```
> man command-name
> ```

OS X comes with thousands of man pages mostly copied from BSD UNIX. UNIX aficionados love man pages because they don't waste verbiage on cute analogies and historical asides, and they tend to be authoritative. Beginners often find them maddeningly terse.

Working in the Terminal window

As in Windows, you can use an asterisk (*) as a wildcard in a filename in most commands. Also like Windows, `bash` can complete a partially typed command or filename, if it can figure it out, when you press Tab.

You can copy text from the Terminal window, but you can't cut or insert text. If you can paste text into the terminal window, it is appended to whatever you have already typed after the prompt.

If you drag an OS X file or folder icon to the Terminal window, the pathname of the file or folder is inserted where you are typing.

Introducing UNIX commands

Here you find an introduction to the most important UNIX commands: those that work with directories, those that work with files, and miscellaneous but commonly used commands.

Folders are called *directories* in UNIX. Commands that refer to filenames, as most do, assume that you are talking about files in the working directory. When you open the Terminal window, the working directory is set to your home directory, abbreviated ~. Bash shows you the current working directory and your username to the left of its prompt. Table 17-1 lists common directory-related commands.

Table 17-1	UNIX Directory Commands
Command	**What It Does**
`ls`	Lists the names of the files in the working directory. For more complete information, use `ls -alF` (see Figure 17-3).
`cd directoryname`	Changes the working directory to the one you named.
`cd ..`	Brings you up one directory level.
`cd`	Returns you to your home directory.
`pwd`	Displays the pathname of the current directory.
`mkdir newdirectoryname`	Makes a new directory.
`rmdir directoryname`	Removes (deletes) an empty directory.

Figure 17-3:
Listing files
with the
UNIX
`ls -alF`
command.
Characters
on the left
are file
permissions.

```
● ○ ○              Terminal — bash — 80×24
Last login: Wed Mar 28 15:46:23 on console
arnold-reinholds-macbook21:~ agr$ ls -alF
total 24
drwxr-xr-x  11 agr    agr      442 Mar 23 08:58 ./
drwxr-xr-x   5 root   admin    238 Mar 21 13:18 ../
-rw-r--r--   1 agr    agr        3 Feb  2 12:58 .CFUserTextEncoding
-rw-r--r--@  1 agr    agr     6148 Mar 23 08:58 .DS_Store
drwx------   3 agr    agr      204 Mar  8 17:06 .Trash/
drwx------   7 agr    agr      238 Mar 28 15:56 Desktop/
drwx------   4 agr    agr      238 Mar 23 07:44 Documents/
drwx------  33 agr    agr     1190 Mar 20 16:18 Library/
drwx------   2 agr    agr      102 Feb  2 12:58 Movies/
drwx------   3 agr    agr      136 Feb 13 14:20 Music/
drwx------   2 agr    agr      136 Feb  2 12:58 Pictures/
drwxr-xr-x   3 agr    agr      136 Feb  2 12:58 Public/
drwxr-xr-x   3 agr    agr      170 Feb  2 12:58 Sites/
arnold-reinholds-macbook21:~ agr$ []
```

TIP

As in Windows, you can redirect the output of a command to a text file. So if you want a record of the files in a folder, follow these steps:

1. **Type cd, followed by a space.**

2. **Drag the folder's icon to the Terminal window.**

   Its pathname should appear after the cd command.

3. **Press Return.**

4. **Type** ls > mydirectorylist.txt **and press Return.**

A file named `mydirectorylist.txt` will appear in the folder you chose.

You can open the file in TextEdit to see a list of the files in that directory.

Table 17-2 lists commands commonly used when working with files in the Terminal window; Table 17-3 explains other handy commands that anyone getting started in Terminal will likely want to know.

Table 17-2	Working with Files
Command	*What It Does*
cp *filename1 filename2*	Copies a file.
chmod	Changes permissions for access to a file. Study the man page before using this one.
diff	Compares two files line by line (assumes text).
more *filename*	Displays a text file one page at a time. Press the spacebar to see the next page; press Q to quit. The man command works through more.
mv *filename1 filename2*	Moves a file or changes its name.
rm *filename*	Removes (deletes) a file.

When you're working in Terminal, you don't have a Trash Can to which deleted files are moved pending ultimate disposal. Delete it and it's gone. In general, UNIX has no Undo function.

Table 17-3	Miscellaneous Commands
Command	*What It Does*
Control+C	Terminates most operations.
date	Displays the current date and time.
echo	Repeats whatever appears after the command (after expansion).

(continued)

Table 17-3 (continued)

Command	What It Does
help	Displays a partial list of bash commands.
history	Displays the last commands you typed. You can redo a command by typing an exclamation point (!) followed immediately (no space) by the number of that command in the history list. To repeat the last command, type !!. To repeat the last filename, type !*.
pico	A simple UNIX text editor.
ps	Displays a list of running processes.
sudo	Lets you carry out commands for which the account you are using lacks authority. You will be asked for an administrator's password.

Text files

Plain text files seem like the simplest, least complicated form of computer data. But there are differences in the ways Windows, UNIX, and Macs format these files. For the most part, if you use standard word processing applications, you needn't worry about these differences, but if you're mucking around with the innards of OS X or moving text files back and forth between different operating system, it helps to be aware of the issues.

UNIX text files terminate lines with an ASCII LF (line feed) character. Windows uses the pair of characters CR (carriage return) and LF. Mac OS 9 and earlier used just CR. Carriage return and line feed go back to the days of mechanical teletype machines, which had a printing element that went back and forth on a carriage across a roll of paper. Moving the paper up one line was a separate operation from returning the carriage to the left edge of the page.

OS X would rather forget about text files altogether. By default, TextEdit can read any of them, but doesn't save in text format, preferring the RTF format. (You can tell TextEdit to use text format in its Preferences.) Many third-party Mac text editors use the OS 9 convention, ending lines in CR, though they often give you a choice. The UNIX commands in OS X speak UNIX, however, and expect LF unless you specify otherwise with some switch.

Developing Software on a Mac

Many years ago, my parents asked what I wanted for my 16th birthday. "A computer," I replied. They asked what that was — few people had heard of them back then. Then they asked what one cost. "$500,000," I replied. It was a bad joke on my part — the first of many, you might be thinking. The smallest computer IBM made would take up most of our apartment, and back then, half a million dollars was a lot of money. We all had a good laugh and I ended up with a shortwave radio receiver.

The reason I wanted a computer was to run programs I would write. That's what one did with a computer for the first couple of decades. It was lots of fun. The MacBook I'm writing this on is a million times faster than the computer I lusted after as a 15-year-old. That's not hyperbole. It's probably closer to ten million times faster.

But the MacBook is harder to program. Sure, much better programming languages (too many of them, actually) are available, and compilers do their thing in seconds for all but the biggest programs. But everything is sooo much more complicated.

Introducing Xcode

Apple hasn't figured out how to make programming a Mac anywhere near as easy as using one. No one has. But Apple is trying its best, and a complete programming environment comes with your Mac. You only have to pop in the discs that come with it and install *Xcode*. That's what Apple calls its integrated development environment. Xcode supports a variety of compiled programming languages: Objective-C, C, C++, Java, and AppleScript. Objective-C is the native language for OS X, but the others can be used as well. Apple also supports scripting languages, including Perl, Python, and the currently hot Ruby on Rails. Xcode is built on top of many standard Gnu-UNIX tools, including the GCC compiler and GDB debugger. All the standard UNIX tools are there in their native form as well.

Xcode also has many Apple-specific tools, such as Interface Builder. The Xcode package includes most Apple developer documentation. You even find a Research Assistant to help you find application program interface (API) details and other arcane stuff you need to write programs these days.

Xcode supports both Intel and PowerPC Macintosh environments and produces universal binaries that run on both. It can produce programs that support either 32- or 64-bit addressing.

Sun's ZFS file system

Mac OS X has limited support for ZFS, a new file system developed by Sun Microsystems. File systems are the internal plumbing of an operating system that organizes and stores computer data files on mass storage devices. OS X supports several file systems, including HFS+, Apple's own file system, the UNIX file system, UFS, and a couple of Microsoft variants.

So why add another file system to the OS X repertoire? Because ZFS is an amazing technological achievement. Sun took decades of problems with file system design and synthesized a new approach that offers nearly unlimited capacity and built-in reliability. Apple's HFS+ file system achieves its high reliability by keeping side notes on what it's doing, so it can recover in case its operations are interrupted by a power failure or software crash — a process called *journaling*. ZFS eliminates the need for journaling by protecting the old version of data until creation of a new version is complete. So you have no need for disk recovery utilities and the like. ZFS has lots of other neat features, such as integrity checks on every file, the ability to add disk drives without creating separate volumes, and better techniques for using multiple disks to create a redundant array (RAID) that protects data even if a single disk drive dies. Some people think ZFS may become Apple's standard file system in the future.

Dash to the Dashboard with Dashcode

Apple provides a much simpler environment than Xcode for creating Dashboard widgets. It's called Dashcode, and it includes templates that let you quickly create an RSS feed, a podcast or Photocast viewer, a countdown timer, or a gauge. A blank widget template is also available if you wish to be more creative. You can find out more at `developer.apple.com/tools/dashcode/`.

When you're ready to release your spiffy widget, Dashcode collects all the little bits of stuff that must be present and packages them up for distribution as a professional-looking widget. Apple distributes selected widgets on its Web site, `www.apple.com`.

Part VI
The Part of Tens

The 5th Wave   By Rich Tennant

In this part . . .

The tense tenor of tens extends tenacious tendrils, testing our tentative tenets. This tract's top text tackles ten terrific techniques for troubleshooting OS X. Text two portends your PC's termination, tendering ten tenuous but tenable extensions to its tenure.

Chapter 18

Ten Terrific Troubleshooting Tips

*M*acs have a deserved reputation for reliability. But they're not perfect. Computer software is extremely complex, and stuff happens. In this chapter, I present some suggestions for dealing with problems that can arise and for preventing problems in the first place.

First Things First

Take two aspirins and call me in the morning. Every field has its basic nostrums. Here are the basic remedies every Mac user should know:

✔ **Back it up:** The first rule of computing. Apple's Time Machine automates the process if you attach a second hard drive and turn on Time Machine (see Chapter 5). In addition, I recommend a periodic manual backup of your most important files to DVD-R or an additional external hard drive.

✔ **Reboot:** Select Restart from the Apple menu. See the section "Rebooting a Hung Mac," later in this chapter, for more details.

✔ **Check the hard drive:** Run Disk Utility in the Utilities folder. Select your hard drive. Click the Repair Permissions button. Then click the Verify Disk button. If Verify Disk reports a problem, you can boot from the installation disc that came with your computer by inserting it and holding down the C key when you reboot. Running Disk Utility from that system will give you an option to Repair Disk. Do it.

If you can't find your installation disc, do a safe boot. Shut down your Mac. Press the power button. Right after the startup *boing,* hold down Shift. After safe boot is complete, restart your Mac. Safe boot repairs your file system as it starts up.

✔ **Fix preference file:** If an application is acting up, the file where it keeps your preference settings (called a plist file) might be messed up. One way to deal with this is to change some preference settings and quit the application. For Finder problems, also change the System Preferences Appearance settings.

Another approach is to quit the troublesome application, open the Library folder in your home directory, and then open the Preferences folder. Find the `.plist` file for the troublesome application, and change its name by tacking `.old` or something similar to the end of the filename. Then restart the application with its default preferences.

✔ **Zap PRAM:** Every Mac stores some basic info it needs in a small, separate memory called parameter RAM, or PRAM. To reset it, hold down the P and R keys while you reboot.

✔ **Replace the battery:** If you have a new Mac, you won't run into system battery problems for years. But if you have an older Mac that is behaving weirdly — a common symptom is the wrong date at startup — the small battery on the motherboard that keeps the clock and PRAM working might have run down. These batteries are easy to replace on older Mac desktop machines and not so easy on all-in-one units.

Replacing a battery is also a common solution to problems with wireless devices. If you use a wireless keyboard and mouse, and they don't seem to be working, replace their batteries.

✔ **Review Login items:** These are listed in System Preferences under the Accounts icon. Check to see whether something that doesn't belong has slipped in.

✔ **Figure out whether it's the hardware:** If your Mac is crashing frequently, it could be a hardware problem. For starters, disconnect all peripherals and see whether you still have problems. If they go away, reconnect devices one at a time to try and isolate which one is the evildoer. If the problems don't go away, try running the diagnostic disc that came with your Mac. It typically offers you a fast and more thorough mode. Try the fast mode first. Then do the slow test overnight. If the diagnostic program reports an error, write down exactly what it says, with all the error numbers, and bring that info along with the sick computer to your service tech or have it ready when you call AppleCare.

Spinning Beach Ball

Macs rarely crash, but applications sometimes hang. That means the application is no longer responding to inputs from the keyboard or mouse. A common indication is a spinning beach ball cursor that doesn't go away. The spinning beach ball is normal from time to time when an application is busy. It's the equivalent of the hourglass cursor in Windows. You can tell that a specific application is responsible if the spinning beach ball only shows when the cursor is over one of that application's windows.

Show a little patience. The application might be waiting on some Internet resource or reorganizing its sock drawer. Go have a cup of coffee. Safari, in particular, sometimes takes a while, but eventually responds.

If the beach ball is still spinning when you get back, try pressing ⌘+Tab to get to other applications you might have open, and save your work. Then close these apps (press ⌘+Q). If the Quit command doesn't work, you can try a more drastic measure called Force Quit. Follow these steps:

1. **Select Force Quit from the Apple menu or press ⌘+Option+Esc.**

   This brings up a small window showing all the applications that are active. If one of yours is hung, OS X will probably notice that and mark it as not responding in the Force Quit window.

2. **Select the hung application in the window, and click the Force Quit button.**

   If it's the Finder that's hung, pressing ⌘+Option+Esc may offer you the option to relaunch it. Otherwise, you must reboot.

Rebooting a Hung Mac

Hold down the power button while you count to ten. That's not to calm you down. A little power management processor in your Mac looks for the extended push and shuts down the main computer.

If that doesn't work, unplug the computer from its power source and, if it's a laptop, remove its main battery. To do the latter, follow these steps:

1. **Close the screen and gently turn the machine over — it's been bad but it doesn't need to be spanked.**

   You see a circle with a slot in it.

2. **Insert a coin in the slot and turn it to the unlocked position.**

3. **Remove the battery.**

4. **Count to ten again and put it back in.**

5. **Now press the power button briefly (count to one), and your computer should reboot.**

   This restart may take a little longer than usual because your Mac knows it wasn't shut down normally and is checking things out.

Reconnecting to the Internet

Your browser whines that you aren't connected to the Internet. Mail complains that it can't find the server. Debugging Internet connectivity problems can be frustrating. So many steps are involved in getting you online, and any of them can be the problem.

Safari offers you a Network Diagnostics button in the dialog that tells you you're not connected. Click it. You see a list of possible problems on the left, with colored lights that show green if okay and red if not.

If the Network Diagnostics feature doesn't help you resolve your problem, the following list offers other things to check:

- ✔ **Test for service:** Before you spend too much time tracking down possible problems, try these simple tests. If you're connected by a telephone line (dialup or DSL), check that you have a dial tone on your landline telephone. If you use a cable modem, check that you're getting TV reception. If not, the problem isn't with your computer equipment. Check with your phone or cable company.

- ✔ **Check the blinking lights:** If you have a modem and router or a WiFi/ AirPort access point, check that their lights are on and appear normal.

- ✔ **Can you hear me now?** If you are using WiFi/AirPort, check whether you have a strong enough signal — at least two solid arcs on the Signal Strength icon on the menu bar. If not, click the icon to turn it off and back on. Move your laptop. Moving closer to the router or access point is usually better, but any move can help. See Chapter 9 for more tips on getting a signal and solving interference problems.

- ✔ **Follow the wires:** If you are using a wired Ethernet connection, check that all the cables are connected properly. Disconnect and reconnect them at each end. You have to press a little tab to remove the cable, just like a telephone cable. You should hear a little click when it snaps into place as you reconnect. Follow the wire to make sure that the one going into your computer is the same one going into the router or modem and that it hasn't been damaged.

- ✔ **Cycle the power:** Shut down your computer and turn off all power. Count to 30. Then, one at a time, power up each unit, starting with the modem, then the router and access point, and then the computer.

- ✔ **Check network settings:** Select System Preferences from the Apple menu and click the Networks icon. Make sure that its settings match the instructions your ISP gave you. Also, check your router's settings. See Chapters 8 and 9.

Printing Problems

Most long-term Mac users have gotten a call from a friend that goes something like this: "I know you suggested I buy a Mac, but the salesman said the ZorchPC is just as good, and he saved me $300 on a package. I got it set up all by myself, but the printer doesn't work. Could you come over and help me?" Apple's Bonjour technology has made connecting a printer much simpler, even in the Windows world. But sometimes you click the Print button and nothing happens. The following steps can help you resolve your problem:

1. **Click the Print & Fax icon in System Preferences.**

2. **Make sure your printer is listed in the window that appears.**

   Your printer should be listed in the window.

3. **Look at the printer's lights and display for any error messages, such as out of paper or ink. Press its Resume or OK button.**

4. **Turn the printer off, wait until it shuts down completely, and then turn it back on.**

5. **Check that all cables are connected.**

   See the bullet for following the wires in the preceding section of this chapter.

6. **Download the latest drivers from your printer manufacturer's Web site.**

   Avoid using drivers on the disc that came with the printer. They're usually out of date.

If you've done all these things and still don't have a solution to your printing problem, check the printer's manual for other suggestions.

Resetting Passwords

Okay, everybody forgets a password sooner or later. That's why I advise most users to write passwords down and keep them in a safe place. See Chapter 10. Here's how to handle forgotten passwords:

   ✔ **If a user on your Mac forgot his password,** you can reset it to a new password by clicking the Accounts icon in System Preferences. You must click the Lock icon and then enter your administrator's password. If they forgot the user's Keychain password, use Keychain Access, which is located in the Utilities folder.

✔ **If you forgot your administrator's password,** you can reset it by inserting the installation disc that came with your computer and holding down the C key while you reboot. Select Reset Password from the menu that appears.

Ejecting CDs, DVDs, and Flash Drives

Most Macs come with slot-loading optical drives. That means you put a CD or DVD into the wide, thin slot on your Mac where it just fits. Never insert a mini-size CD or DVD into the slot. Only insert the full-size discs that are about 4⅝ inch in diameter (actually 120 mm). If you're having trouble ejecting a CD or DVD, here are some tips:

✔ The Eject button is on the keyboard, in the upper-right corner, and is marked ⏏.

✔ You can also right-click the disc's icon in the Finder and select Eject from the menu that appears.

✔ OS X won't eject a disc that some program thinks it is using. If your disc won't eject when you press the button, quit the application that was last using it, or quit all applications if you're not sure which one is using it.

✔ If all else fails, restart the computer while holding down the mouse button. That should eject the disc.

Flash drives and other removable hard drives have to be "ejected" as well. There is no mechanical response; you still have to unplug them yourself. But ejecting tells OS X to finish what it was doing and leave the file system on the removable device in a proper state. Right-click the drive icon and select Eject from the shortcut menu. Wait for the icon to disappear from the desktop and a few seconds more before unplugging.

If you did remove a flash drive prematurely, the file system may be damaged. Even if the drive is not readable on your Mac, it might be readable on some other computer, including your old PC. If you are able to read it, back it up by copying its contents to the hard drive of the machine that could read it. You can reformat a flash drive on your Mac using Disk Utility. Select the FAT file system format. You lose all the data on the drive.

Weird Noises

If your normally quiet new Mac starts making loud noises that sound a bit like a jet liner revving for take off, don't be alarmed. The Intel processors in your Mac use more power when they're thinking hard, as when rendering movies or 3-D images. They can sense their own temperature and call for the fans in your Mac to blast some air to cool things down. Sometimes an application will crash in a way that keeps the processors and the fans at full tilt. A reboot will usually quiet things. The Dashboard widget iStat Pro from www. islayer.com reports on system temperatures and fan speeds. CoreDuoTemp from macbricol.free.fr puts temp info on your menu bar.

Running Out of Disk Space

If you find that your Mac's hard drive is filling up for no reason, you can try several things. For starters, empty the Trash. The command is on the Finder menu.

Next, check for extraordinarily large files to delete or back up to a removable drive or disc:

1. **In Finder, open a new Finder window (press ⌘+N).**

2. **Open your home directory — it's normally the House icon in the sidebar.**

3. **Choose Finder⇨View⇨As List.**

4. **Choose Finder⇨View⇨Show View Options, and select the Calculate All Sizes check box.**

   When this check box is selected, OS X goes to the added effort of showing you how big each folder is, not just each file. The calculation takes a few minutes, typically.

5. **Look to see whether any of your folders seem unreasonably large. If so, look for unnecessary stuff to delete or move elsewhere.**

   Do the same procedure on subfolders as needed.

Another possible cause of disappearing disk space is overgrown log files. UNIX can generate lots of logs as applications do their thing. Mac OS X runs special maintenance programs periodically to clean these out. They run in the wee hours of the morning, so be sure to leave your Mac on overnight sometimes. A reboot can often help. You can also use shareware programs that clean out the logs. Yasu and Onyx are two popular programs.

A final possibility is to defragment the hard drive. OS X tries to keep individual files from fragmenting, but the disk structure as a whole can suffer from too many small, unused patches. Apple recommends against defragmentation for most users, as long as they are not doing disk-intensive work, like video editing, and their hard drive is not close to being full.

Of course, your hard drive might be filling up because you have lots of files you want to keep. In that case, consider getting a large external hard drive and moving less frequently used files and folders to it. It's generally a good idea to have at least 20 percent of the space on your main drive free.

Keeping Your Mac Safe and in Tip-Top Shape

Taking care of a Mac is mostly common sense. For the most part, no special tricks are required. You just need to pay attention to the software, hardware, and your habits every so often.

To maintain the software, keep the following points in mind:

- ✔ OS X checks Software Update once a week, unless you change its settings. I suggest leaving them as is.

- ✔ Dig out Disk Utility from the Utilities folder every few weeks and run Repair Permissions. If security is a concern, run Erase Free Space as well. It's best to do this overnight because it can take a while.

- ✔ Be judicious in the software that you download and install. While malware has not been a big problem on Macs to date, there's always a first time.

  The biggest risk in installing every software gizmo that catches your eye is that some are poorly written and can make OS X less stable.

- ✔ When your Internet connection is working properly, take a look at your router and modem — the box that connects your network to the telephone line, TV cable, or satellite dish. Note what the blinking lights look like when everything is okay so that you can recognize the difference when it isn't.

Following these tips can help you keep the hardware in good working order:

- ✔ The MagSafe connector is designed to keep an Apple laptop from falling if someone trips on its power cord. But avoid balancing yours precariously on top of books, papers, and other work-surface litter. And remember that MagSafe only protects the power cord. Someone tripping on an Ethernet, USB, FireWire, or audio cable can still send your laptop flying.

- ✔ Don't use cleaners that contain alcohol or ammonia or other strong solvents on your computer. And don't spray any liquids directly on your computer. Apple suggests a soft cloth and plain water for cleaning display screens. If that's not sufficient, a product called Klear Screen from `klearscreen.com` is recommended.

✔ Your Mac is designed to run in an ordinary home or office environment. Avoid running it in excessively hot locales or exposed to direct sunlight. If you put your laptop on a soft or cluttered surface, make sure that the fan exhaust, which is at the hinge, isn't blocked.

✔ Keep an eagle eye on your laptop in public places. Be especially vigilant going through airport security.

And last but not least, the following tips can keep you computing comfortably day in and day out:

✔ If you spend much time at your computer, you owe it to yourself to take ergonomic precautions. Repetitive motion injuries are best avoided altogether. Comfortable seating that puts your keyboard and mouse or trackpad at a level where your forearms are at right angles to your body tops the list. Apple has extensive suggestions at `apple.com/about/ergonomics`.

✔ Finally, you weren't put on the planet to be a computer peripheral. Practice the push-away exercise several times a day. Place both hands at the edge of your desk and slowly push your body away from the keyboard. Then get up and walk outside for a while.

Finding Help

I mention some common problems here and suggest how to fix them. But I can't foresee everything that can happen. You have a number of places to turn when problems arise that these tips don't fix.

Ask Google first

I always check the Internet first. Usually someone else has come up with an answer to the same problem, and Google (`www.google.com`) can find it if you come up with the right search request.

Be sure to include "OS X" or "Mac" in the search; otherwise, the answer will be lost in PC replies. Google seems to know that "OS X" is a single search term, even though a space is in it. But don't get too specific at first. You may have a MacBook, but the person who solved your problem may have seen the same problem on another model. Try searching different ways, such as once with the word "printer" and once with your printer's make and model number.

Also try your search at Google Groups. Click the More link at the top of the Google home page.

The online Mac community

The fabled loyalty of Mac users is reflected in a strong online community of Mac Web sites. Some are dedicated to rumors of new products; others strive to keep up with the latest problems and their fixes:

- MacInTouch.com is one of the most comprehensive sites, with a strong focus on reviews and issues with new products and freshly released software.

- VersionTracker.com can let you know if you have the latest software.

- MacOSXhints.com is filled with tips on solving problems and improving performance.

- Macnn.com and MacSlash.com have the latest Mac stories, along with user discussions.

- Lowendmac.com has resources you can use if you need to help someone with an older Mac.

Apple

It may seem surprising that I don't list Apple first when searching for help. But Google and the online communities can be checked in seconds and often pop up relevant links to Apple's Web site. So many problems are quickly resolved this way that it's worth a try before calling AppleCare or going down to the Apple store.

But Apple is the ultimate resource. New Macs typically come with 90-day free telephone support. You can extend this by purchasing AppleCare, which is generally a good idea if this is your first Mac.

If you are within driving distance of an Apple store, you can take advantage of its Genius Bar. See Chapter 3 for more on AppleCare and the service options at the Apple store.

User groups and consultants

Numerous Apple user groups are scattered about the planet. Apple will try to find one near you if you visit www.apple.com/usergroups. Getting to know the folks at your local user group can be valuable when you are stuck and in a hurry. Having a Mac-knowledgeable friend you can call can make all the difference. Your local user group can also recommend good Mac consultants in your area and give you some idea about what fees to expect.

Chapter 19

Ten Cool Mac Tricks

*T*here are so many ways you can use the added power of the software that comes with a Mac, you'll be glad you bought one. In this chapter, I describe just a few.

iChat AV: The Next Best Thing to Being There

Short-notice airfares have long been the bane of small business. If you live in Boston and want to visit Aunt Ellie in L.A. and can plan your trip two weeks in advance, it's often easy to find a nonstop round-trip flight online for under $300. But if you need to go tomorrow to solve a customer's problem or make that last-minute presentation to win a sale, you spend close to a thousand.

Using Apple's iChat AV to hold a video conference (instead of catching that last-minute flight) could save you enough to cover the cost of your Mac with just one trip avoided. The iSight camera built into your iMac or laptop is all you need. Plug-in cameras are available for Mac minis and Pros. You can even videoconference with Windows users via AOL Instant Messenger for Windows.

You always see yourself as well as the other people on the call. If you have visual materials to make your case, iChat Theater lets you share an iPhoto slideshow or a Keynote presentation while letting your audience see you as you talk them through it.

If you're working on a proposal or report with a remote colleague who also has a Mac, you can both edit the same document or search the Web together with iChat screen sharing, which lets one chatter control the other's desktop. If security is a concern, connecting through .Mac allows you to automatically encrypt your chat. Look for the Lock icon in the upper-left corner.

Podcasting with GarageBand

Podcasting is a new way to make yourself heard. Podcasts are usually audio files, but many come with slides or video. Podcasts are distributed using a publish and subscribe model, where people interested in a topic ask to be notified when new podcasts are available. Your Mac comes with all the tools you need to make podcasting easy:

- ✔ GarageBand, described in Chapter 11, has a built-in Radio Engineer feature that enhances sound quality automatically, even if you're using your Mac's built-in microphone. It also automatically "ducks" the background music you pick under your voice when you start talking.

- ✔ You can distribute your podcast through your .Mac account or another ISP.

Even if your expertise is in the narrowest of subjects, other people in the world are interested in what you have to say.

Building an HD Home Theater

High-definition television is changing the home entertainment experience. You can watch films and other media at a visual quality comparable to the big screen in movie theaters. If you are looking for another reason never to have to leave your living room, check out these options:

- ✔ A Mac mini makes a great control center for your home theater setup. It can drive an HD set directly and store hundreds of titles on a large, external FireWire drive.

- ✔ You can use an Apple TV to wirelessly connect your HD to a bigger Mac in the den or home office. (It's a good idea to get off the couch and dust your Mac every month or so.)

If you own a collection of movies on DVD, visit `handbrake.m0k.org` (that's a zero, not an *o* in m0k, by the way) or `www.mactheripper.org` for free software that can transfer the DVDs you own to your hard drive so that you can play the flicks you paid for without having to get up, find where you misfiled them, pop them in the DVD player, and get back to the couch. Handbrake also supports conversion to the MPEG-4 format that iPods and iPhones can play. Did I make it clear you should do this only with DVDs you actually purchased?

Automating Your Home

Years ago, home automation meant buying X10 lamp modules from Radio Shack and putting a controller on the night tables so that you could dim the lights from your bed. Home automation now means that you control every electrical device in your home, fine-tune your heating and air conditioning, and even patch in alternative forms of energy. You can also add video surveillance and intrusion detection systems, with security images shipped off-site where an intruder can't get at them. And you can control all this remotely and securely over the Internet.

Indigo is a software package from `Perceptiveautomation.com` that lets your Mac control both X10 and the newer Insteon family of home automation controls.

If you are using your Mac as a home controller, be sure to go to Energy Saver in System Preferences, click Options, and select the Restart Automatically after a Power Failure check box.

Putting a mini in Your Car or RV

A Mac mini in you car or recreational vehicle can serve many purposes. If you take children on long drives, the mini can store enough hours of diverting DVDs and sing-along CDs to make "Are we there yet?" a fond memory of trips past. If you're on the road for business, an onboard mini can be trip central, tracking mileage and expenses, snarfing e-mail from open WiFi hotspots, and backing up your laptop. If you'd like to podcast your vacation or try your hand at citizen journalism, a Mac-equipped van or RV can be a mobile broadcast studio. *Lights, camera, Mac action!*

For tips on installing a mini in a car, installing video displays, and integrating it with car electronics, see *Mac mini Hacks & Mods For Dummies,* by John Rizzo, with contributions from Arnold Reinhold (published by Wiley). It's filled with other clever ideas for using a Mac in ways Apple never intended.

Living the Paperless Portable Life

Okay, this is a pet fantasy of mine, but did you ever think about how much of our living situation is devoted to storing and managing papers? Imagine scanning every piece of paper that matters to you and storing it all on an external hard drive. Legal documents you need in original form can go in a rented safe-deposit box, along with jewelry and small mementos. If you have books and bigger tchotchkes you can't part with, rent a small storage room or a corner of a friend's basement. Imagine getting everything you need down to a laptop and portable hard drive. You're free! You can go anywhere, anytime.

Making a Photo Book

Although I like the idea of computers leading to less clutter, some folk, especially grandparents, still like to hold actual books in their hands. Apple's iPhoto lets your organize your photo collection into albums. Albums are basically a list of photographs in your iPhoto library; a photo can be in more than one album. You can do many things with these organized albums — make them into a slideshow or order prints, for example — but the one most likely to make someone very happy is to place the photos into a real album, the kind that sits on a coffee table. iPhoto makes this easy; just follow these steps:

1. **Click the plus (+) icon at the bottom left of the iPhoto window and select Album from the drop-down list.**

2. **Drag the photos you want to include to your new album.**

3. **Click the Book icon at the bottom of the screen.**

   You see a sheet come down that allows you to select a book format (hard/soft cover and size) and then pick a theme from those available for that format.

4. **Pick a theme, and iPhoto presents the photos in the selected album along the top of its screen.**

5. **You can drag individual photos to the image areas in the template or click the Autoflow button and iPhoto places the photos for you.**

6. **Double-click an image to zoom in or center it.**

7. **When you're done, click the Buy Book button.**

   For a modest fee, Apple sends your album off for professional printing and binding. It even ships the finished product directly to your recipient, if you like.

Producing a Movie for YouTube

One of the hardest aspects of the motion picture business used to be finding distribution for your work. Video upload sites such as YouTube.com make it possible for anyone to get his or her work seen. A couple of struggling film-makers with a Mac and a portable iSight camera garnered a huge audience producing a video blog on YouTube, purportedly of a teenage girl and her boyfriend in some mysterious trouble. Visit `www.lonelygirl15.com` to keep up with their series.

Curing Cancer

Your Mac is one powerful computer. How powerful? One Mac sent back in time to the 1940s or 50s could alter the balance of power in the world. Yet yours spends most of its time patiently waiting for commands. Can I find you a Web page? Can I? Can I maybe read you your e-mail? Pretty please?

Instead of consigning your Mac to total boredom, you can give it interesting work to do — work that helps cure cancer and other diseases. Living cells assemble proteins by linking different amino acids in a sequence specified by the cell's DNA. As the protein is completed, it folds itself up into a three-dimensional shape that determines how it functions in the cell. These days, biologists can determine a protein's sequence from the DNA, but figuring out how it folds up takes very demanding calculations. Stanford University's Folding@home project uses the idle cycles on your Mac to help carry out these computations. Visit `folding.stanford.edu` and download the OS X client. You have lots of options to choose from, but start with the Screensaver version, which only makes moderate demands on your computer and quickly gets out of the way when you wish to get your work done. After it's run long enough to get some results, the Folding@home screen saver displays the molecules it's working on so that you can see what's being accomplished.

Building a Supercomputer

Several universities and other research institutions have built supercomputers by purchasing a gaggle of Apple Xserves and mounting them in racks, along with high-speed switches to interconnect them. Virginia Tech's System X Terrascale Computing Facility uses 1,100 Xserves, each with InfiniBand high-speed communication cards, to create a world-class supercomputer at a fraction of what comparable systems cost. See www.tcf.vt.edu for more details and cool pictures.

If you have access to an office filled with Macs, you can make your own super-computer during off hours by harnessing them together with Apple's Xgrid.

Switching a Friend to a Mac

I hope you enjoy your new Mac. The one thing that has kept Apple alive through difficult years is the loyalty of its customers. If you like having a commercial alternative to Microsoft and Windows, consider helping a friend make the switch. If you found this book helpful, he or she might too.

Chapter 20

Ten Creative Uses for Your Old PC

In This Chapter

▶ Selling your PC to someone else

▶ Letting your kids discover something new from the PC

▶ Keeping the PC as a storage center

▶ Finding an artistic destiny for your PC

▶ Recycling the PC safely

As you wean yourself from Windows, you may wonder what to do with your old PC. Here are ten suggestions (with an extra thrown in), some more creative than others.

Before you send your computer away, be sure to clear its hard drive of all sensitive files. Dragging items to the Recycle Bin and then emptying the Bin does not erase your data. See Chapter 6 for instructions.

Sell It on Craigslist

If it's of fairly recent vintage, your PC may have some resale value. I suggest listing it on your local Craigslist.com. It's free to use, less complicated than eBay.com, and because it is local, you can ask the buyer to pick up the PC, avoiding shipping hassles. You can get an idea of what your computer is worth by checking what is currently on sale — but don't assume that the listed asking price is what people are getting.

Load Linux on It

I love OS X, but Linux, the free, open source operating system, is also becoming an important alternative to Windows. You can download and burn a CD to automatically boot up your PC in a version of Linux called Knoppix. (See Chapter 6 for detailed instructions.) By the way, this is the only way I recommend giving your old PC box to your kids. I'd rather see them have a Mac, but setting up and using Linux has real educational value — and fewer games are available. Get the kids a copy of *Linux For Dummies,* 8th Edition, by Dee-Ann LeBlanc (published by Wiley), and let them figure it out.

Give It to Charity

Donating your computer to a worthwhile organization is a great thing to do, and you may even get a tax deduction. However, most charitable organizations are not interested in computer donations from individuals — they've been inundated with them. Your best bet is to contact organizations you know. An offer to help set up the PC may be appreciated. But don't take offense if they say no. A posting on the free section of Craigslist.com often works — you can specify a preference for charities, but even a donation to an individual can be a good deed. Finally, you can find out about organizations that take PCs and refurbish them for donation at the U.S. Environmental Protection Agency's Web site, www.epa.gov/plugin. In any case, be sure to include all the software discs and documentation that came with the PC, if you still have them.

Use It as a Pedestal

Years ago, my employer sold all its computers to a leasing company and leased them back on a seven-year note. The equipment was obsolete after three years, so we kept the racks they were mounted in, which is where the leasing company's inventory tags were affixed, and used them for printer stands. The bean counters from the leasing company dutifully came around every six months and were satisfied to see the stuff that secured their loans (and our printers) was still there. A PC makes a great plant stand, but be sure to install the antitipping hardware that probably came with it. Two PCs of the same height with a wide board across them creates a nice work surface for young kids.

Have Your Kids Take It Apart

These days, kids don't get much opportunity to see how things are put together. Place the computer on an old bed sheet, give the kids a screwdriver set, and see how far they can get taking the computer apart. Hard drives are a bit tricky to open — you usually find screws under the "you'll void the warranty" labels — but they are full of fascinating parts.

Adult supervision is required. Some parts have sharp edges. This is not an activity that kids under four should be anywhere near, because small parts are a choking hazard. And *never* try to take apart a video monitor or any computer that includes a CRT display — they have high voltages inside, and the CRT tubes can implode violently.

Enjoy It as Art

If you've never looked closely at a computer's circuit board, you are missing a cultural experience. They are *objets d'art* — marvels of design, filled with colorful electronic components, including numerous integrated circuits in mysterious black slabs, and covered with thousands of tiny copper traces that carry all the signals. I think they are worthy of hanging on the wall.

Use It for Target Practice

I'm not seriously suggesting this one. It could be dangerous and may be contrary to laws in some locations, but years ago, when I had a gig at a local company that made spreadsheet software, someone brought in a 386 PC filled with .30 caliber bullet holes. Everyone appreciated the gesture.

Disconnect from the Internet

One way to continue to use a Windows machine safely is to disconnect it from the Internet. Unplug its Ethernet cable, and remove any wireless networking card. If it has built-in wireless, such as Intel Centrino, change the password on your wireless network hub and don't give the PC the new password. For extra credit, turn off wireless networking in the Network Connections section of the Control Panel, because the PC could still connect through a neighbor's open hub. When you need to move files between the PC and your Mac, use a USB flash drive.

Keep It for Old Media

If you have a PC old enough to have 5¼-inch floppy drives or Zip drives, wrap it in one of those big plastic bags you get from the dry cleaner and store it in the basement. Sooner or later, the world will no longer be able to read those old disks, and you'll be a hero for saving your machine. Or not.

Use It as a Picture Frame

An old laptop PC can be used as an electronic picture frame to show off your digital photos. If you can't afford to give your parents a nice iMac, I suppose giving them your old PC will still be appreciated. (See Chapter 14 for details.) Expect to do more work setting it up.

Recycle It Safely

Did you know that an old PC can contain four pounds of lead? It's best to keep computers out of the town dump. Several brand-name PC manufacturers have recycling programs. Check the home page of the folks who made yours. Also check with your municipal trash collection department to see what programs it offers for old PCs and monitors. The EPA Web site www.epa.gov/plugin also has recycling information.

Mac Speak versus Windows Speak: A Translation Glossary

~ : The tilde character, used in Mac OS X and other UNIX operating systems, is an abbreviation for "the home directory of." Sometimes called twiddle.

.Net: Also known as "dot net," this is Microsoft's software framework for Web services. See also Mono, a compatible system that runs on other platforms, including Mac OS X.

.ps: A PostScript file.

.sit file: A StuffIt compressed Mac file. (A version for Windows exists, too.)

10BaseT, 100BaseT, 1000BaseT: Ethernet signaling standards at 10, 100, and 1,000 megabits per second. The last is also called Gigabit Ethernet.

16-bit, 32-bit, 64-bit: When referring to a program or operating system, the maximum size of program addresses used. More bits allow more memory to be addressed, the amount doubling for each added bit.

68K: Motorola 68000 series microprocessors used in the original Macintosh. Superseded by the PowerPC and then the Intel Core line.

accessibility: Ability of software and hardware to be used by people with disabilities.

ACID: A set of criteria for database systems intended to ensure that all transactions are handled properly — either going through completely or not going through at all — even if a system failure occurs during processing. The letters stand for atomicity, consistency, isolation, and durability.

Acid2 test: A series of documents used to test browser compliance with the industry standards.

Acrobat reader: A free program from Adobe.com used to read PDF files. OS X's Preview performs many of the same functions.

ADA: The Americans with Disability Act. A U.S. law requiring reasonable accommodations for workers and customers with disabilities. Also a computer programming language developed under the auspices of the U.S. Department of Defense.

ADB: Apple Desktop Bus. A technology used in older, pre-USB Macs to connect keyboards and mice.

adware: Software that is provided free but which displays advertising.

AES: Advanced Encryption Standard. A strong encryption cipher developed in Belgium and adopted by the U.S. government. See Chapter 10.

AFP: Apple File Protocol. Used in AppleShare.

AIFF: Audio Interchange File Format. An Apple-developed format for sound files. Lossless, but tends to be large compared to compressed formats like MP3. Same idea as Microsoft's WAV format.

AIM: AOL Instant Messenger, an instant messaging (IM) system supported by AOL and iChat.

AirPort: Apple's brand name for WiFi wireless networking. Also called IEEE 802.11.

alias: A small file that points to another file.

Apache: A popular program supplied with OS X for serving Web pages over the Internet. Visit www.apache.org.

Aperture: Apple's high-end program for still photographers. Not included in OS X.

API: Application program interface. A set of services that one program, such as an operating system, provides to another.

Apple I and II: Apple's original computers, based on an 8-bit microprocessor, the 6502.

Apple key: The key with the Apple logo () and the command symbol ⌘. It's next to the spacebar on Apple keyboards. Also called the Command key or fan key.

Apple lossless: An audio file format that features lossless compression. Can be played on most iPods.

Apple remote control: A small infrared remote that can command Macs and Apple TV.

Apple store: Apple's retail outlets, including a Web site, store.apple.com, and brick-and-mortar (more often glass-and-silicone) stores that you can walk into. These are located in many major cities and shopping centers.

AppleScript: A programming language designed to allow repetitive tasks on a Mac to be automated. Many Mac apps can respond to AppleScript commands and are said to be Apple scriptable.

AppleShare: Apple's file-sharing technology for local networks.

applet: A small program in the Java language that can be automatically downloaded and executed by your browser.

AppleTalk: An older Apple networking technology that has been largely replaced by industry-standard technologies such as Ethernet, AirPort, and TCP/IP.

AppleWorks: A suite of office applications sold by Apple that runs only on older PowerPC machines. Some users find it works okay in Rosetta emulation on Intel Macs, but Apple doesn't support this. Previously called ClarisWorks.

Aqua: Apple's semitranslucent styling for the OS X graphical interface.

ASCII: American Standard Code for Information Interchange. A way of encoding characters in 8-bit bytes that is widely used in modern computers, though increasingly being replaced by Unicode and UTF-8.

ATA: Advanced Technology Attachment. A widely used standard for connecting hard drives and optical drives to computers. A newer version, SATA, or serial ATA, is used in Macs. (Advanced Technology refers to the PC-AT, which is hardly considered advanced anymore.)

Automator: A facility in OS X that simplifies creation of scripts to perform repetitive tasks.

bash: Bourne-again shell. A UNIX shell developed by the Gnu project that is used in OS X. See Chapter 17.

baud: A measure of modem speed that means one symbol per second. Bits per second is more commonly used these days.

BinHex: An older Mac format for sending binary data encoded as an ASCII text file.

BIOS: Basic Input/Output System. Firmware in a PC that determines what happens when you turn on power. Intel Macs and some newer PCs use EFI instead.

bit: The basic unit of information, with only two possibilities, represented by 0 and 1, or on and off.

BitLocker: A disk-encryption scheme in the Pro versions of Windows Vista. See FileVault and Chapter 10.

BitTorrent: A popular system for sharing files on the Internet, capable of handling very large files.

Blue Box: An early code name for what became the Classic environment in OS X for PowerPC. See also Red Box, Yellow Box.

Bluetooth: A wireless networking standard for short range uses such as connecting computers, keyboards, mice, and cell phones.

Blu-ray: An optical disc the same size as a DVD, but capable of storing ten times as much data. One of two contenders to replace DVD; the other is HD DVD.

BMP: A graphics file format used in Windows.

BNC: A coaxial connector type used in high-end video equipment.

Bonjour: An Apple-sponsored technology to allow devices such as printers to announce their presence over local computer networks.

boot from CD: Starting your computer from a compact disc or DVD. Hold down the C key on a Mac while restarting.

bootstrap: Short for pulling yourself up by your bootstraps. Refers to the complex process by which computers start up when power is first applied. Usually shortened to just *boot*.

broadband: A high-speed transmission technology used with cable modems that allows multiple streams of information on a single coaxial cable.

browser: A program that finds and displays information on the World Wide Web. Macs come with the Safari browser.

BSD: Berkeley System Distribution. A variant of the UNIX operating system developed at the University of California, Berkeley. It is the basis for Mac OS X.

byte: A block of information, usually 8 bits.

cable modem: A small box that connects your computer or router to the cable TV system.

Carbon: A set of application program interfaces provided by Apple to make it easier to convert older Mac programs to OS X.

CardBus: See PCMCIA or PC card.

CD-R, CD-R/W: A compact disc that can be written on by a computer, for example, a Mac. CD-Rs can only be written once. CD-R/Ws can be erased and rewritten multiple times.

CD-ROM: Compact Disc Read-Only Memory. A compact disc that contains data that cannot be modified.

CERT: Computer Emergency Readiness Team. A U.S. group that responds to viruses and other computer and Internet attacks.

Claris: A no-longer-existent software division of Apple.

ClarisWorks: See AppleWorks.

Classic: A feature of OS X that allows Mac OS 9 programs to run. Classic is not supported on the newer Intel Macs.

client: A computer that uses the services of another computer. Also someone who helps pay the bills.

Cocoa: A set of application program interfaces provided by Apple for building native OS X applications. See Carbon.

codec: Coder-decoder. A piece of software necessary to compress a media file or to process a compressed media file.

Command key: Keyboard key with the ⌘ symbol. See Apple key.

composite video: An analog video signal standard where all picture information is carried on a single wire (usually yellow).

console: A text stream on which UNIX-based operating systems send out messages about their operation. One is running in OS X, but you must launch a special window to see it.

cookie: A small blob of data that Web sites try to store on your hard drive so that they can be reminded of certain information the next time you visit. You can turn cookies off in Safari.

Core 2 duo: Intel *x*86 microprocessors featuring two processors on a chip, used in many Macs.

CRM: Customer Relationship Management software. Helps sales and marketing organizations track leads and customers.

cron file: A file in a UNIX-based operating system that lists actions to be taken at specific times in the future.

cryptovariable: Another name for a cryptographic key.

Darwin: The UNIX operating system underlying Mac OS X.

Dashboard: A feature of Mac OS X that pops up small, useful programs, called Widgets, whenever you press F12. Widgets can be downloaded from Apple.com.

data remanence: The often-recoverable traces of information left behind when you think you have deleted your files. Secure Empty Trash reduces the problem, as does Disk Utility's Erase Free Space.

desk accessory: An older version of Dashboard widgets used in Mac OS 9 and earlier.

dialup: A form of Internet connection where you dial a phone number that connects you to an ISP. Limited in speed to about 56 kilobits per second.

Diceware: A technique for generating strong passwords using ordinary dice. Visit Diceware.com.

Direct3D: One of two popular ways for programs, particularly 3-D games, to communicate with graphics cards. Microsoft uses this one. Apple uses the other, OpenGL.

directory: Another name for a folder, a named collection of files and other directories.

disk encryption: A method of securing data that scrambles an entire disk, rather than individual files or folders.

DMCA: Digital Millennium Copyright Act. A U.S. law that restricts circumvention of digital copy protections, such as DRM.

doc: Files saved by versions of Microsoft Word before Word 2007 have a `.doc` extension. Word 2007 and Word 2008 use `.docx`.

Dock: In OS X, a place where icons of frequently used applications and folders can be kept. Currently running applications are always shown. By default, the Dock is at the bottom of the screen. Roughly the equivalent of the Windows taskbar.

dongle: A small device that plugs into a computer and contains special codes that allow a purchased program to run. Dongles restrict users of expensive software to using only the number of copies they purchased.

DRAM: Dynamic random-access memory. A type of high-speed main memory used in computers. It must have its contents refreshed regularly, but it uses the minimum number of transistors per bit of any solid-state memory.

DRM: Digital rights management. Technologies designed to limit the copies you can make of media you own. Apple uses a form of DRM in its iPod.

DSL: Digital subscriber line. A form of high-speed Internet access brought to you by your phone company.

DVD: Digital versatile disc or digital video disc. Plastic discs, the same dimensions as CDs (120-mm diameter) that can store an entire movie in pre-HD resolution. Also see Blu-ray and HD DVD.

DVI: Digital Visual Interface. A digital video interface standard used in several Mac models and many PCs.

Earthlink: An Internet service provider.

ECC: Error Correcting Code. Used on hard drives and sometimes on RAM to catch and fix errors.

EFI: Extensible Firmware Interface. A technology used by Intel Macs to start up the computer. Replaces the BIOS in PCs.

EmPower: A connector for supplying low-voltage direct current power to airplane seats for use in powering laptops and so on. Defined by the ARINC 628 specification. An earlier version, now called EmPower Classic, used an automobile cigarette lighter connector.

emulation: One computer pretending to be another with a different instruction set by running a program that knows what to do with each instruction of the foreign computer.

encrypting file system: See disk encryption.

encryption: Scrambling data in a way that is difficult or impossible to undo without knowledge of a secret key.

Entourage: Microsoft's mail client and personal information manager for the Mac. Part of Microsoft Office.

entropy: A measure of randomness. The logarithm of the number of possible states a system can be in.

Ethernet: A method for computer-to-computer communication that requires one computer to be in charge, that is, it supports peer-to-peer communication.

Eudora: An alternative e-mail program for OS X and Windows from Qualcomm.com.

ExpressCard: A new standard for small plug-in expansion cards. The MacBook Pro has an ExpressCard/34 slot. Replaces the PCMCIA PC card standard.

F connector: A video coaxial connector with a threaded sleeve widely used in consumer electronics.

FairPlay: Apple's digital rights management system for music.

fan key: Keyboard key with the ⌘ symbol. Also called the Command key, Apple key.

FAT: File allocation table. A file system used on older PCs. Macs can read and write devices formatted in the FAT format, such as flash drives.

file extension: A string of letters added to a filename after a dot that indicate the program that can open that file. OS X also stores a file type that serves a similar purpose.

file path: The sequence of folders or directories leading from the root directory or home directory to the file. For example: `~/Documents/Projects/Wiley/S2M4D/Glossary.doc`.

file permission: Codes associated with each file that indicate who can read, modify, or execute the file.

file type: Metadata in Apple's file system that indicates what application should open the file. See also file extension.

FileMaker: A database management program for Mac OS X and Windows sold by Apple.

Final Cut: Apple's high-end movie-making software. Not free.

Fink: A group dedicated to porting UNIX and Linux applications to the Mac. Visit `www.finkproject.org`.

Firefox: An alternative browser popular on Macs and PCs.

FireWire: A high-speed data bus for connecting computers, hard drives, video cameras, and so on. Also called i.Link and IEEE 1394.

firmware: Computer programs associated with a computer or other device stored in read-only or flash memory that are not normally changed. "Ware" that is between hard and soft.

Flash: A proprietary format for multimedia data on the World Wide Web. Originally developed by Macromedia, and now owned by Adobe.

flash drive: A thumb-sized device that plugs into a USB port and looks like a hard drive to the operating system. Uses flash memory, hence the name. See also sneaker-net.

flash memory: A solid-state memory technology that retains data even when it is not connected to electrical power, but can be rewritten. Used in flash drives, iPods, iPhones, and digital cameras.

folder: See directory.

FOSS: Free Open Source Software.

FreeBSD: An open source distribution of the BSD UNIX operating system. OS X is built on FreeBSD. Other BSD distros exist, for example, OpenBSD and NetBSD.

Freescale: A semiconductor company formerly owned by Motorola, and a manufacturer of the PowerPC.

Front row: Apple's technology for remotely controlling Macs and other devices. Run your Mac from your couch.

FTP: File Transfer Protocol. An early Internet technology for moving data files. Anonymous FTP sites let you get data with "anonymous" as the user-name and your e-mail address as the password. I like the Fetch ftp client for OS X; visit www.fetchsoftworks.com.

GIF: Graphics interchange format. An image file format developed by CompuServe that is popular on the Web. Has limited color capability but can do simple animations.

Gigabit Ethernet: Ethernet operating at a billion bits per second. Also called 1000BaseT.

gigabyte: One billion bytes. Sometimes 2^{30} bytes or 1,073,741,824 bytes. Some call the latter number a gibibyte.

GIMP: An open source image-editing program that is available for Macs. Runs in X11.

Gnu: Gnu is not UNIX. A project started by Richard Stallman to develop an open source version of UNIX. Gnu developed much of utility software shipped with Linux, and many Gnu utilities are in OS X.

GPG: Gnu Privacy Guard. A free open source encryption program compatible with PGP. Available for the Mac.

GPL: Gnu Public License. A commonly used legal agreement attached to open source software that requires an improved version to carry the same license. See gnu.org/licenses/gpl.html.

GUI: Graphical user interface. A way for humans to interact with a computer by manipulating objects and icons on a display screen using a pointing device, such as a mouse.

H.264: A video data compression standard used in iChat and other Mac software.

hard drive: The main, permanent data store in most computers. Uses rotating magnetic disks and a read/write head on a movable arm.

hash: A cryptographic tool that mushes data into a small block in a nonreversible way. The hash serves as a signature for the file. It is hard to make two files with the same hash. Some common hash algorithms include MD5, SHA-1, SHA-256, and SHA-512.

HD DVD: A higher-capacity replacement for DVDs. See Blu-ray.

HDMI: High-Definition Multimedia Interface. A standard for high-definition TV cable connectors that includes digital video, similar to DVI and digital audio. Includes provisions for digital rights management.

HDTV: High-definition television. What every couch potato craves.

HFS+: The file system used in Mac OS X.

hibernate: See sleep.

Home directory: The folder that contains all the data associated with your user account. Abbreviated ~ at the command line.

HyperCard: A programming environment on early Macs that anticipated many hypermedia features of the Web, a predecessor of AppleScript.

hypertext: A system of writing and displaying text that enables text to be linked in multiple ways, be available at several levels of detail, and contain links to related documents.

ICANN: Internet Corporation for Numbers and Names. A controversial nonprofit corporation format that administers Internet addresses.

iChat: Apple's instant messaging, voice communication, and videoconferencing software included in OS X.

ICQ: An instant messaging service, now owned by AOL. Users are identified by a number.

IEC standards (power cord, button icons): International Electrotechnical Commission. A standards organization dealing with electrical and electronic technologies.

IEEE: Institute of Electrical and Electronics Engineers. A professional organization that also sets standards.

IEEE 1394: The FireWire standard. Also called i.Link by Sony.

IEEE 802.11: The family of wireless networking standards known as WiFi or by the Apple brand name, AirPort. See Chapter 9.

IETF: Internet Engineering Task Force. A group that sets standards for the Internet.

iGo adapter: A line of third-party power sources for small electronics such as cell phones that have interchangeable adapters for different devices.

iLife: A family of media-editing and production software included with each Mac: iTunes, iPhoto, iMovie, iDVD, GarageBand, and iWeb. See Chapter 11.

IM: Instant message. An electronic text communication system where both parties of a conversation are at their computers at the same time and send messages back and forth.

IMAP: Internet Message Access Protocol. One of the two popular ways e-mail is handled on the Internet. With IMAP, e-mail can be kept on a server and accessed over the Net. The other method is POP.

infrared: A form of invisible light in the electromagnetic spectrum with wavelengths just longer than red and shorter than 1 mm.

Intel: The company that invented microprocessors, has long made the microprocessors for most Windows PCs, and now makes them for Macs.

internationalization: The process of adapting computer software to work in different languages and cultures.

Internet: All the computers in the world talking to each other.

iPod: Apple's line of portable music players.

IRC: Internet Relay Chat. An early form of instant messaging still used on the Internet.

ISA bus: A type of plug-in card used in early PCs. Replaced by PCI.

iSight: Apple's line of FireWire cameras, now built into many Macs.

iTV: An early internal code name for Apple TV. Not to be confused with EyeTV.

iWork: Apple's office productivity suite that includes Pages word processing and Keynote presentation software.

journaling file system: A file system that separately keeps track of recent changes. In the event of a system crash, the journaled changes can be used to reconstruct a damaged file system, significantly improving overall data reliability.

JPEG: Joint Photographic Experts Group. A body that developed a widely used standard format for photographs (.jpg).

kernel: The innermost part of an operating system, the stuff that talks to all the hardware. OS X uses the Mach kernel.

key: As used in cryptography, a block of information needed to encode or decode a message.

keyboard shortcut: Pressing two or more keys to initiate a command without selecting an item from a menu.

Keynote: Apple's presentation software that one-ups Microsoft's ubiquitous PowerPoint.

kilo: The standard prefix meaning 1,000. In computing, it sometime means 1,024, which is 2^{10}. Another prefix for the latter number is kibi.

KVM switch: A box that lets you use a single keyboard, video display, and mouse to operate more than one computer.

LDAP: Lightweight Directory Access Protocol. A system for finding people and resources on computer networks.

Leopard: Apple's code name for Mac OS X 10.5.

line in: An analog audio signal amplified to a certain nominal level for connection to other audio equipment.

Linux: A open source computer operating system inspired by UNIX. See also Gnu.

Lisa: A short-lived Apple computer that was a predecessor to the Macintosh and, toward the end of its product life cycle, was called the Macintosh XL.

LocalTalk: An early Apple wiring standard for AppleTalk networking that used telephone wires. It has since been replaced by Ethernet.

location: In Apple networking, a way to group settings so that they can be easily changed when moving to a different locale, such as home to work.

Lock icon: A small image of a padlock that is shown in Web browsers to indicate whether the current connection is securely encrypted, in which case the lock is closed, or is not securely encrypted, in which case the lock is open. Worth checking before entering personal information on a Web form.

Mac OS X: An operating system developed by Apple, using technology from NeXT, BSD UNIX, Mach, and earlier versions of Mac OS. Currently only available for Apple Macintosh computers. A server edition also comes with Xserve.

MacBinary: An older Mac format for sending binary data over the Internet.

Mach: An operating system kernel developed at Carnegie Mellon University and used in OS X.

macintouch.com: A popular Macintosh support Web site.

MacPaint: A classic drawing program included with the earliest Macs.

MacWrite: Apple's earliest word processor for the Mac.

MagSafe: The power connector used on Mac Intel laptops. The connection is magnetic and is designed to safely pop off if someone trips on the cord.

malware: A computer program that is up to no good, such as viruses, worms, and spyware.

McIntosh: A type of edible apple popular in New England. Also a brand of audio equipment. Not to be confused with Macintosh, an Apple Inc. brand name.

mega: The standard prefix meaning one million. In computing, it sometimes means 1,048,576, which is 2^{20}. Another prefix for the later number is mebi.

metadata: Information about data, such as what it means and where it comes from.

MIDI: Musical Instrument Digital Interface. A way to communicate music as named notes rather than digitized sounds. Used to connect digital instruments to computers.

MightyMouse: Apple's concession to mouse multibuttonness. For decades prior, the single-button mouse was Mac dogma.

MIME: Multipurpose Internet Mail Extension. A standard that allows Internet e-mail to carry information in a variety of formats besides plain ASCII text.

mini-DVI: A smaller version of the DVI connector. Used in some Mac models.

modem: Modulator/demodulator. A device used to send digital signals over analog circuits, such as a phone line or television cable.

Mono: An open source effort to develop Web service tools compatible with Microsoft's .Net that can run on non-Windows platforms, such as OS X. Visit `mono-project.com`.

MP3: A popular compressed audio format. Stands for MPEG-1, Audio Layer 3.

MPEG: Motion Picture Experts Group. A body that sets standards for video compression.

mpkg: File format used to distribute OS X software.

MSN: Microsoft Network.

MySQL: A widely used open source database system. SQL stands for Structured Query Language. MySQL runs in OS X. A commercially supported version is also available. Visit `www.mysql.com`.

Newton: A short-lived Apple product that created the personal digital assistant market.

NextStep: An operating system developed by NeXT that Apple evolved into OS X.

NTFS: NT File System. The file system used in Windows NT, XP, and Vista. Macs can read NTFS files.

NTSC: A standard for television signals used in North America, Japan, and parts of South America. See also PAL video.

NuBus: A standard for plug-in cards used on older Macs.

object file: The output of a compiler. A version of a program that is ready to be run by the computer.

Objective C: A variant of the C programming language that is widely used in OS X and its application programs. It takes a different approach to object orientation than C++.

Office Open XML: A controversial standard for electronic documents proposed by Microsoft and based on its Office suite's internal format. Also called OOXML. Competes with OpenDocument.

Ogg: A nonproprietary multimedia file format. See `www.xiph.org/ogg`.

open source: An approach to software development where the original human-generated instructions and comments are publicly available. Visit Opensource.org for the official definition.

open source license: One of several copyright licenses under which open source software and documentation are distributed. They typically allow wide use but require the same copyright notice be included on redistributed versions. Over 59 different licenses are listed at `www.opensource.org/licenses/alphabetical`, and they are often incompatible with each other.

OpenDocument: A nonproprietary file format for electronic documents. Also called ODF and the OASIS Open Document Format for Office Applications. Competes with Office Open XML.

OpenGL: A nonproprietary way for programs, especially 3-D games, to talk to graphics cards. OS X supports OpenGL. Competes with Microsoft's DirectX.

OpenOffice.org: An open source suite of productivity applications — word processing, spreadsheet, and so on. Runs in OS X, but with X-window interface.

optical digital audio: A replacement for analog sound wiring in home electronics that uses fiber-optics instead of shielded copper wire. No more annoying hum loop.

OS 9: Short for Mac OS 9. An earlier Mac operating system. OS 4, 5, 6, 7, and 8 were also released. There is an unrelated real-time operating system by RadiSys called OS-9.

Outlook: Microsoft's e-mail client for Windows. See Entourage.

package: Apple's way of distributing applications for OS X that combines numerous files and folders associated with a program into what looks like a single file. Sometimes called a bundle.

PAL video: Broadcast video signal standard used in Europe and much of the world. See also NTSC.

pane: A simple window in a graphical computer interface.

Panther: Code name for Mac OS X 10.3.

parallel port: A printer interface once common on PCs but never used on Macs. Also known as a Centronics port or IEEE 1284 port.

Parallels: A virtualization package that lets Windows and other operating systems, such as Linux, run at the same time as OS X. See Chapter 13.

partition: To divide a hard drive into two or more smaller disk volumes, sometimes done with a hacksaw or axe, but Disk Utility is the preferred method.

passphrase: A longer form of a password, often made up of several words. See also Diceware.

password: A string of characters that you type into your computer to let it know for sure that the person typing is you. See Chapter 10.

PCIe: Peripheral Component Interconnect Express. A third-generation interface standard for computer expansion cards, used in the Mac Pro. Replaces PCI and PCI-X.

PCMCIA or PC card: A standard for small, credit-card-sized cards that plug into laptops to add capabilities. MacBook Pro uses a newer standard, ExpressCard/34.

PDF: Portable Document Format. An Adobe standard for digital documents that can be read on most computers using a free Adobe reader program. Mac OS X uses PDF as its document format, and the included Preview application can read .pdf files.

perpendicular recording: A method of increasing the amount of information that can be stored on a hard drive.

PGP: Pretty Good Privacy. A popular public key encryption package available for the Mac, Windows, and Linux.

phone plug: A type of audio connector that consists of a long, cylindrical sleeve with one or two insulated contacts at the tip. Comes in ¼-inch, 3.5-mm, and 2.5-mm diameters. Not to be confused with the cube-shaped RJ series telephone plugs.

phono plug: See RCA plug.

PhotoBooth: A small but fun application that comes with OS X and takes pictures using the iSight camera. Operates much like the old four-for-a-dollar photo booths found in amusement parks and arcades.

Photoshop: Adobe's powerful image-editing software. Photoshop Elements, a much lower-cost, less-capable version, is also available.

PHP: A scripting programming language often used with database programs such as MySQL to create Web applications.

PICT: A graphics file format used on older Macs.

PKI: Public Key Infrastructure. A way to distribute keys in public key cryptography.

PlaysForSure: A DRM-protected music format promoted by Microsoft, but not supported on its Zune player.

plug-in: A piece of software that can be easily incorporated into an application to increase functionality.

PNG: Portable Network Graphics. A nonproprietary format for exchanging images.

POP: Post Office Protocol. The most common way e-mail is handled on the Internet. See also IMAP.

pop-up: An additional window that appears when accessing a Web site. Sometimes used to add functionality to a Web page, but more often for advertising. Also pop-under, a window that is added behind the window in use so that it only appears when that window is closed or moved, sometimes known as a leave-behind.

POSIX: Portable Operating System Interface for UNIX. A standard application program interface (API) promoted by the U.S. government to enable programs to be easily ported to different operating systems. OS X supports POSIX.

PostScript: A printing file format developed by Adobe.

PowerBook: An earlier brand of Apple laptop.

PowerPC: A microprocessor architecture developed by a consortium of Motorola, IBM, and Apple and used in Macs until the switch to Intel microprocessors.

PPP: Point-to-Point Protocol. Connects two computers; most often used in dialup Internet access. Also PPPoE — PPP over Ethernet.

PRAM: Parameter RAM. A small block of storage used to save information needed during startup. Resetting PRAM is a common Mac nostrum. See Chapter 18.

preferences: Application settings in Mac OS. Deleting an application's preferences file sometimes solves problems if it has become corrupted.

propeller key: See fan key.

protocol: An agreed-upon way that computers use to talk to each other.

PS2: A second-generation IBM PC. The electrical connections it used for hooking up a mouse and keyboard are still used on some PCs. Macs use USB instead.

public-key cryptography: A method of sending secret messages and electronically signing documents that uses two keys, one that can freely be made public and a second that is kept secret by the person who receives the coded message or signs the document.

quad core: Having four separate CPUs.

Quartz: Apple's name for the display-rendering technology in OS X.

QuickTime: Apple's format for multimedia content. Competes with Windows Media and Real.

RAID: Redundant Array of Inexpensive Disks. A way to build large, reliable storage systems out of PC-grade disk drives.

RAM: Random-access memory. The main fast memory in a computer.

RAW file: Image data from a digital camera in its original form, without any compression or other processing that can lose information. iPhoto has some support for RAW images; Aperture has much more.

RCA plug: A push-on coaxial connector invented in the 1930s by the Radio Corporation of America to allow phonographs to be played through table radios. Also called phono plug and jack.

reality distortion field: A humorous reference to Steve Jobs' ability to sell ideas convincingly.

reboot: Shutdown and restart. See bootstrap.

Red Box: A code name for a long-rumored project that was supposed to allow Windows apps to run in OS X, somewhat like Wine. See also Blue Box, Yellow Box.

regular expression: A UNIX term for a cryptic but very powerful way to specify search criteria as a string of characters. Also regexp. Popularized by the UNIX program grep.

RGB video: A way of transmitting video signals as three separate analog channels for red, green, and blue.

RJ-45: A cube-shaped electrical connector used on twisted-pair Ethernet cables. Not to be confused with the similar, but smaller, RJ-11 connector used with telephones.

root: Top-level directory in a file structure. Highest level of access privilege in a UNIX system.

router: A box that helps direct information packets among connected computers to create a network.

RS-232: A standard for serial ports used on PCs. Increasingly replaced by USB.

RSA: Rivest, Shamir, and Adleman. An algorithm for public-key cryptography based on the difficulty of factoring numbers.

RSS: A set of standards for delivering Web content that is updated regularly. Users subscribe to different feeds that are aggregated and displayed by software in their computer.

RTF: Rich Text Format. An older Microsoft word processing format used by TextEdit and other OS X programs.

RTFM: A suggestion that people read the manual before asking for assistance.

rumors community: A group of Internet sites that speculate about Apple Inc. and its products and sometimes publish what they claim to be inside information.

SATA: Serial ATA. A high-performance connection standard for mass storage devices, such as hard drives, used in many new computers, including Macs.

SCSI: Small Computer System Interface. A connection standard for mass storage devices used in older Macs.

SDRAM: Synchronous dynamic random-access memory. A variant of DRAM that offers higher performance by tying its operation to the CPU's clock pulses. Think of the galley scene in Ben-Hur where the slaves pull their oars to the beat of a drum.

serial port: A computer connection that sends data sequentially, bit by bit, over a communication line. See also RS-232, parallel port.

shareware: Software programs that are freely distributed over the Internet, but with the expectation that people who decide to use them will voluntarily pay a fee to the author.

shell: An operating system program that listens to commands typed by the user. The Windows Command Line Interpreter is a shell. OS X uses the bash shell by default, though others, such as the Korn shell, are available. Before GUIs, the shell was the outermost, visible part of an operating system. The innermost part was and is called the kernel.

shut down: Turning off the computer.

sleep: Temporarily suspending the operation of a computer, usually to save energy, particularly battery power on a laptop. Also called hibernate in Windows, which has several sleep modes.

SMTP: Simple Mail Transfer Program. The basis for electronic mail on the Internet.

snd file: An early Mac audio format.

sneaker-net: Transferring information between computers by having some-one carry the data on removable media, originally floppy disks, but now flash drives and CD/DVD optical discs.

socket: A software port that one program uses to connect to another pro-gram running on a different computer.

Software Update: Apple's facility for distributing revisions to OS X and its application programs. It automatically notifies users when new stuff is avail-able, by default once a week.

Spaces: A feature in OS X Leopard that supports multiple workspaces for a single user. See Chapter 12.

spam: Unsolicited commercial e-mail.

Spotlight: The OS X search tool.

spring-loaded: An icon that pops open or takes some other action when the cursor hovers over it for some time.

spyware: Software that covertly gathers personal information about a user, such as Web-surfing habits, without the user's consent, and conveys it to a third party.

SSH: A program and a set of standards for establishing a secure connection between two computers. Relies on public-key cryptography. OS X has SSH support.

SSL/TLS: Secure Socket Layer/Transport Layer Security. Two names used to describe the most commonly used method for securing Internet connections.

startup disk: The disk drive that contains the operating system that will be used to start the computer the next time it's turned on or rebooted. Set by a pane in System Preferences.

Steve Jobs: Chief executive officer of Apple Inc. and one of its founders. Also founded NeXT, later acquired by Apple, and Pixar Animation Studios, later acquired by Disney. Currently the largest shareholder in Disney.

Steve Wozniak: One of the founders of Apple Computer and designer of the Apple I. Visit www.woz.org.

StuffIt Expander: A free program that unpacks a number of compressed file formats, including .sit files.

sudo: A UNIX command that prefixes other commands, causing them to execute with super user privileges. Requires an admin password in OS X.

S-Video: An analog video signal standard that has separate wires for color and brightness. See also composite video.

SYLK: Symbolic Link. An older Microsoft spreadsheet file format that is still used at times to exchange data with other programs.

tar file: A compressed archive format used in UNIX systems.

taskbar: A Windows feature, located along the bottom of the screen, that is somewhat similar to the OS X Dock.

TCP/IP: Transmission Control Protocol/Internet Protocol. The way computers communicate with each other on the Internet.

telnet: A program that lets you log on to other computers on the network.

tera: Standard prefix for one trillion. Terabyte hard drives (1TB) are now available for under $400.

Terminal: A program in OS X that gives you access to the underlying UNIX operating system through a command-line interface.

terminal emulator: A program that communicates with legacy systems by pretending to be a dumb computer terminal, such as a VT-100 or IBM 3270.

text file: A computer file that only contains characters, usually encoded in ASCII. Uses the `.txt` extension.

thumb drive: A finger-sized device that contains flash memory that plugs into a USB port and looks like a hard drive to the computer. Also called flash drive.

Tiger: Code name for Mac OS X 10.4.

Time Machine: Apple's automated backup system for OS X Leopard.

Treo: A popular smart cell phone from Palm. Competes with iPhone.

trusted platform chip: A tamper-resistant microprocessor chip on Macs and newer PCs designed to hold cryptographic keys and certificates. The rub is, trusted by whom??

unicode: A computer character code that attempts to include all the written languages in use in the world.

universal binary: A way of distributing computer programs so that they can install and work on both PowerPC and Intel Macs.

UNIX: A computer operating system developed in the 1960s at AT&T Bell Labs. Mac OS X is based on UNIX.

USB: Universal Serial Bus. A means for connecting peripheral devices to computers, used in Macs and PCs. USB 2.0 is considerably faster than, but backward compatible with, USB 1.

V.92: An ITU standard for dialup modems operating at speeds up to 56 Kbps. Used in the Apple Modem.

VGA connector: A widely used analog video cable connector with a D-shell and 15 pins in three rows. Most Macs come with a VGA adapter cable.

virtual memory: A technique that allows an operating system to assign more random-access memory than the computer physically has by writing sections of memory that have not been used recently to disk storage.

Virtualization: A way of splitting the resources of a computer among more than one operating system so that each thinks it has a separate computer all to itself.

virus: A program that attaches itself to another program or document and then transmits copies of itself to infect other computers.

Vista: The latest version of Microsoft's Windows operating system.

VNC: Virtual Network Computing. A standard for remote control of a computer desktop from another computer. Used in Apple Remote Desktop.

watermark: Bits hidden in a media file that allow digital rights management software to detect copyrighted works.

WAV: A Windows audio file format.

white list: To specify addresses from whom you welcome messages. Opposite of black list.

widget: A small program run on the Dashboard layer of OS X.

WiFi: Brand name applied to devices that meet interoperability criteria for wireless networking based on the IEEE 802.11 standards. Apple uses the brand name AirPort.

Window Shade: A feature in OS 9 that lets users collapse a window to just its title bar.

Windows CE: A Microsoft operating system for small devices, such as PDAs and smart cell phones.

Windows Genuine Advantage: Microsoft's program to discourage people from using unlicensed copies of Windows. Considered too heavy-handed by some.

Windows Media Player: A Microsoft program and file format for handling multimedia content, usually with the .wmp extension.

Windows XP: The version of Microsoft's Windows operating system that shipped with most PCs from October 2001 until Windows Vista was introduced.

wireless access point: A base station in a wireless network.

WMP: See Windows Media Player.

worm: A self-replicating computer program, usually malicious. Differs from a virus, which attaches itself to another program.

WWAN: Wireless wide-area network. A way for mobile computers to connect to the Internet using the cellular telephone network.

X11: A windowing standard developed at MIT that is used in Linux and UNIX systems and can optionally be installed as part of OS X so that it can run programs created for those systems.

XLR connector: An industrial-strength audio connector, typically with three pins.

yarrow: A high-grade random number generator used in OS X. High-grade random numbers are essential for computer security programs.

Yellow Box: An early code name for what became the Cocoa environment in OS X. See also Red Box, Blue Box.

zero configuration: See Bonjour.

zero-day exploit: A computer security attack that appears at the same time a vulnerability is announced.

ZFS: Sun's new high performance, ultra-reliable file system. It has limited support in OS X — for now.

Zip archive: A file that is a collection of other files compressed with the Zip algorithm. Look in the Finder File menu.

Zip drive: A computer mass storage system that used removable cartridges and could store 100MB or more on each cartridge. Used on some older Macs; USB versions are still supported by OS X.

Zune: Microsoft's personal music player, intended to compete with Apple's iPod. Brown, 'nuff said.

Zune Marketplace: Microsoft's equivalent to Apple's iTunes Store.

Index